10/-   5

39-46 stained

The Viceroy at Bay

The Viceroy with his granddaughter

List of Illustrations

Acknowledgments

I would like to acknowledge my gratitude to Sir Gilbert Laithwaite and to those other colleagues of my father's years in India who have helped me with corroborative detail of some of the events of the viceroyalty: to the family of the late Sir Tej Bahadur Sapru for access to correspondence: to Mr H. V. Hodson for permission to quote from his book *The Great Divide* (Hutchinson 1969): to Mr K. Shankar Pillai for permission to reprint his cartoons from *The Hindustan Times*: to Lady Joan Gore-Langton and Sir Allan Noble for the use of photographs from their collections. Finally, I owe a special word of thanks to Mrs Pamela Nightingale, whose tireless help with my father's papers added much to the pleasure of my task, and to Mr Handasyde Buchanan for reading through the manuscript and helping very much with his constructive suggestions.

He took great burdens and he bore them well,
Believed in God, but did not preach too much,
Believed and followed duty first and last
With marvellous consistency and force,
Was a great victor, in defeat as great
No more, no less, always himself in both.

Stephen Vincent Benét

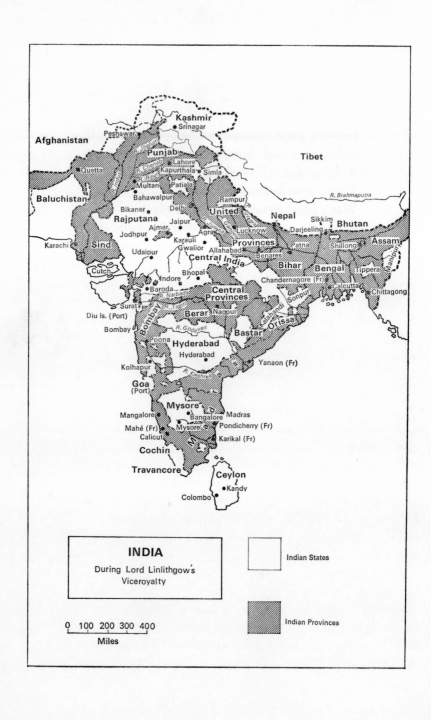

INDIA

During Lord Linlithgow's
Viceroyalty

☐ Indian States

▨ Indian Provinces

0 100 200 300 400
Miles

Introduction

This book is not the life story of my father, the second Marquess of Linlithgow. It is the story of his long viceroyalty of India (1936–43) and of his courage through years of strain such as few men have had to bear. The personal influence of the Viceroy, however, upon events in India was decisive and no account of a viceroyalty can be complete without a description of the man himself and his background.

Linlithgow came from the Scots family of Hope. The earliest ancestor who can be traced with certainty was John de Hope, who came to Scotland in the train of Magdalene, Queen of James V, in 1537. He was probably of Norman stock. His great grandson, Sir Thomas Hope, was famous in Scottish history as Lord Advocate under Charles I. Although in the royal service, Sir Thomas stood up to his master over the rights of the Scots. With Johnston of Warriston he drew up the National Covenant, which his countrymen greeted with great enthusiasm and, much to the King's displeasure, helped the persecuted supporters of the later Solemn League and Covenant. From then onwards the Hopes were staunch supporters of the Church of Scotland.

Sir Thomas's great-grandson Charles was created first Earl of Hopetoun and was a champion of the Union of 1708. It was he who began the building of Hopetoun House on the shores of the Firth of Forth, where the family has lived ever since. Charles's descendants played their part in Scottish affairs until General Sir John Hope made his name as a soldier, commanding one of Wellington's divisions in the Peninsular War and receiving the Duke's praise as one of the ablest of his commanders. There is a statue of him in Edinburgh, the inscription upon which lists his Roman qualities as those of 'a man worthy to serve with Abercrombie, Moore and Wellington.' Sir John, who became fourth

Earl of Hopetoun on the death of his half-brother, was the great-
great-grandfather of the subject of this book.

The next two generations passed uneventfully across the stage,
the sixth Earl dying of typhoid after a brief life devoted to Paris
and the Pytchley Hunt. Linlithgow's father, however, was of very
different calibre. He, too, died young – of pernicious anaemia at
the age of forty-eight – but by that time he had been Governor
of Victoria (at 29), Lord Chamberlain, the first Governor-General
of Australia and Secretary for Scotland. He was created Marquess
of Linlithgow. A man of integrity and charm, he had also been
an extravagant spender and left his son, who adored him, a good
many financial problems.

Not quite 21 when his father died, the second Linlithgow was
thus faced with responsibilities at an early age. This had a crucial
effect upon his development. He had had the orthodox education
of his kind, a preparatory school and Eton. His schooldays were
undistinguished but they were happy until he was sixteen. In that
year he was stricken by polio. He recovered well but the attack
left a physical legacy which was first noticed by his Irish mother[1]
while she was having tea with him as he was convalescing. She
saw that he had to support his chin with his left hand to drink his
tea. In fact the muscles of his neck were permanently weakened
so that he was never able to turn his head without turning his
shoulders as well. In later life this was to make him appear
rather formidable to a stranger sitting next to him.

Linlithgow seldom referred to this early affliction but as a
result of it he was always careful of his health in a sensible way
and he acquired a deep knowledge of medicine. During his
viceroyalty of India he was to remark upon the coincidence of his
case with that of his contemporary, President Roosevelt – each
had had polio and each was responsible for more millions of
people than any other man.

In 1911 he married a Yorkshirewoman, Doreen Milner. She
was beautiful, artistic, gay and delightful. They met and became
engaged when staying with the Portlands at Welbeck, where they

[1] She was the Hon. Hersey de Moleyns.

and their family were to spend many happy days as the years went by. They were an imposing pair, he being six feet five tall and she only just under six feet.

So began the married life of Hopie and Doreen, as their friends always knew them.

A honeymoon abroad included a visit to Australia. Linlithgow was there to attend the unveiling of an equestrian statue of his father in Melbourne. A few days after the ceremony he was entertained at dinner by the Caledonian Society. He made a speech which attracted the attention of the Press by its modesty and wisdom. The *Herald* indeed thought the modesty overdone and published a leading article on the theme. Linlithgow had said, referring to his father's Australian career, 'He came out here with perhaps the greatest gift a man can have – and that is the belief that he is no better than his neighbour.' The *Herald* did not think such a sentiment realistic, however democratic it might be. With impeccable logic it suggested that if the popular Governor-General had been no better than others he would not have had a statue erected to his memory: great men had put their faith in the ancient precept 'Know thyself': the late Marquess knew himself and was great enough not to give himself the airs of a superior person: a man of his quality and character could dispense with the trouble of putting himself on the same plane as his neighbour.

In April, 1912, Lady Linlithgow gave birth to twin sons, Charlie and John.[1] Two years later their eldest daughter, Anne, was born, followed by Joan a year later. The youngest daughter, Doreen, was born in 1921.

When war broke out in 1914 Linlithgow was serving in his local yeomanry, the Lothians and Border Horse. With them he saw active service in France early in the campaign but his health did not hold up and he was invalided home. He recovered sufficiently to be appointed to the command of a battalion of the Royal Scots. In this capacity he commanded a brigade in Ireland. The brigade was sent at short notice in April, 1918, to Claremorris

[1] The author.

in County Mayo to forestall a possible German landing with arms and ammunition on the undefended coast of Western Ireland. He was billeted at this time with the family of Katharine Tynan (Mrs Hinkson), the Irish poetess.

*

Linlithgow had always been interested in politics. He was a conservative but was never extreme in his views; he was too calm and thoughtful for that. As he came to know men in public life so his qualities impressed them. Arthur Balfour said of him that he had a better brain than his father and if he had half his father's character he would go far.

He was never an orator but he spoke sensibly, although sometimes the sentences of his prepared speeches were too long. On the hustings he gave as good as he got.

In the Conservative Government of 1922–4 he was appointed to office as Civil Lord of the Admiralty. The post interested him greatly and he was President of the Navy League from 1924 to 1931. In 1924 he was offered the governorship of Madras. He declined the offer, partly at least for family reasons: his sons were twelve and he would see little of them at an impressionable age if he went to India. But mainly he was influenced by his financial situation. He had already shut Hopetoun for some months in 1922 as an economy (he was to do so again a few years later) and was anxious to enter the business world with a view to earning money. He joined several company boards.

From 1924 to 1926 he was deputy-chairman of the Conservative Party. He was chairman of the Committee on the Distribution and Prices of Agricultural Produce in 1923 and his work on this body was a main factor in his selection for his first major appointment as chairman of the Royal Commission on Agriculture in India from 1926 to 1928. This Commission toured British India and produced a masterly report which enhanced Linlithgow's growing reputation; he was made a Knight of the Thistle in 1928.[1]

[1] He was to become a Knight of the Garter for his services in India and was

The variety of his interests (he was also to be Chairman of the Medical Research Council and of the governing body of the Imperial College of Science and Technology from 1934 to 1936) illustrates well the questing and inquisitive side of his mind and the breadth of the base from which he was to embark upon the most difficult of all proconsular appointments. It may be set against a background of family life at its happiest. To his children he was not only a wise and beloved father but an enchanting companion as well. Whether playing childhood games with them in their early years or taking them bird-watching later on – wading down a burn in search of the grey wagtail's nest was a favourite expedition – he taught them how much life had to offer at its simplest.

He taught them also to take nothing for granted. When his sons came of age in 1933 he spoke at a lunch given to the Hopetoun tenants. Saying that he hoped the association of landlord and tenant, pleasant and precious as it was, could be continued for at least one more generation, he added: 'It is possible to exaggerate these things in life. I have tried to teach my sons that the world is their home and that whatever may come to them . . . there is always room for a stout heart joined to a good character.'

His literary taste was for biography and essays rather than for novels. Musically it was the other way round; he preferred the light to the serious. He enjoyed singing with his family and would howl like a dog when a wrong note was sung. Pictures he loved, and he knew all about the fine collection of old masters with which his ancestors had endowed Hopetoun. He greatly valued his appointment as Chairman of Trustees for the National Galleries of Scotland in 1945.

Of all his qualities it was his wisdom which chiefly struck those with whom he came into contact. Duff Cooper, who visited India on ministerial duty during the second world war, described how much it had impressed him, defining wisdom as 'a quality

thus one of the very few outside the Royal Family to hold the double distinction.

rarer and more precious than cleverness.'[1] The phrase was particularly apt as Linlithgow was certainly wise rather than clever.

With his wisdom there went a great sense of humour which was quite capable of a Rabelaisian turn: Bud Flanagan and 'Monsewer' Eddie Gray were his favourite comedians. But he was shy with strangers, to whom he sometimes gave a misleading impression of brusqueness. His shyness also contributed to an intense dislike of ostentation and this in its turn caused him to underrate the value of publicity.

Finally, he believed in God. He loved the Church of Scotland, of which he was an elder, but he was never dogmatic and he was never smug. He was ready to be amused as well as moved by the *extempore* prayers of the kirk and he remembered with delight the minister who began a prayer with the words: 'O Lord, thou who paintest purple the petals of the polyanthus . . .'

He was a well rounded man.

[1] Duff Cooper, *Old Men Forget* (Hart-Davis, 1953).

1

When Linlithgow was appointed to India the total population of British India was, in round figures, 390 millions. Of these nearly 300 millions were Hindus and the Muslims numbered a little over 90 millions. In addition there were 660 Princely States with a population of about 91 millions. They varied in size from Hyderabad, which was half the size of France, to little territories of a few square miles. Scattered throughout British India they were not constitutionally part of it but they acknowledged the paramountcy of the Crown.

Linlithgow inherited a constitution which had been established by the British Parliament in 1919. There was a central Government with a Legislature at Delhi and there were provincial Governments and Legislatures in the Provinces.

The central Government consisted of the Governor-General and his Executive Council. He was in fact the same man as the Viceroy. The latter term referred, strictly speaking, to his representation of the Sovereign as Head of State. As chief executive he was Governor-General, or Governor-General in Council. He therefore combined two functions in one and he was in fact always spoken of as the Viceroy.

The Governor-General was required by the constitution to obey the orders he received from the Secretary of State for India (in the name, of course, of the Cabinet) although he was given wide discretion as the man on the spot. His Executive Council normally consisted of seven members appointed by the Crown. Three at least had to have served for a minimum of ten years in India and three by convention were Indians.

The main responsibilities of the Governor-General and his Council were for defence, external affairs, communications, commerce, currency, banking, the law, relations with the States

and the Indian Civil Service (I.C.S.). Each member of Council
was responsible, with a department under him, for one or more
of these subjects except for the foreign and political departments.
For these two the Governor-General himself held the portfolios
so that he was directly in charge of relations with foreign powers
and with the princely States.

If there was a division of opinion on policy in Council the
Governor-General was, with one vital exception, bound by the
decision of the majority present, with a casting vote in the event of
a tie. The exception was that if the Governor-General considered
that the 'safety, tranquillity or interests of British India' were
'essentially affected' he could overrule his Council. Even here
there was a safeguard, for any two members of Council could
require that the matter be reported to the Secretary of State.

The central Legislature at New Delhi was composed of two
chambers, the Legislative Assembly and the Council of State.
Each contained a majority of elected members and included
certain nominated members, both official and non-official. In
each chamber election was by property qualification. In the
upper chamber (Council of State) certain seats were reserved for
Muslims and other minorities.

The powers of this central Legislature were limited. Without
the Viceroy's assent no Bill could be introduced which affected
the revenues of India, religion, the armed forces, customs,
currency, the rights of European subjects, or foreign relations.
Even when a bill had been passed by both chambers the Governor-
General could return it to the Legislature for reconsideration or
he could disallow it by certifying that it affected the safety or
tranquillity of the country. The Governor-General could also
'certify' that the passing of a bill was essential for the 'safety,
tranquillity or interests of British India'. In that event it became
law either by passage through one chamber or, failing that, with
the assent of Parliament.

The power of certification was used ten times between 1921
and 1937.

The Legislative Assembly was elected for three years and the

Council of State for five, but the Governor-General had the right to dissolve both chambers or to extend their terms.

*

The Provinces each had a Governor and Executive Council and elected ministries. Certain subjects, including defence, were reserved to the central government, all other subjects were in provincial control.

The Governor's Executive Council, of which half were Indians, was appointed by the Crown. The Governor had the same power to overrule his Council as had the Governor-General with his, if he thought that the safety and tranquillity and interests of the Province required it.

The provincial electorate was decided by property qualification and again there were separate seats in the Legislatures for Muslims and other minorities. The Governor had the same power of certification as had the Governor-General. The constitution had provided for a division of the provincial subjects into two classes, the 'reserved' and the 'transferred', a system which was known as diarchy. The reserved subjects, including law and order, land revenues, and famine relief, were administered by the Governor and his Executive Council who were responsible to the Governor-General and therefore to the Secretary of State. The transferred subjects, local self-government, education, public health, public works, agriculture and co-operative societies, were handed over to ministers who were appointed by the Governor. The Governor had to be guided by their advice unless he saw serious reason to differ, in which case he could reject the advice. If there were no ministers the Governor-General could, with the sanction of the Secretary of State, cause the transferred subjects to relapse temporarily into the reserved group.

The Governor-General could intervene in the administration of the transferred subjects only if control of central subjects was threatened or there was need to safeguard imperial interests or the rights of civil servants appointed by the Secretary of State. He could also – again with the Secretary of State's approval –

declare any part of British India a backward area and place it under his own control.

A word must now be said about relations between the Crown and the Princely States. These relations had in the past been construed differently by different Viceroys. The powers of the Viceroy over the Princes had never been defined, but the constitutional relationship rested basically upon the treaties which had been negotiated separately with each State at different times. The British claimed and exercised paramountcy over their foreign relations and the external and internal security of the States. In fact if a ruler misbehaved badly enough he was removed. But the Princes could not be forced into a particular constitutional mould. They could only be persuaded. It will be seen later what a serious effect this had on Linlithgow's efforts to federate India.

The Chamber of Princes had been set up in 1921 in the hope that it would encourage the Princes to move towards Federation. It met at regular intervals. The Viceroy presided over the meetings of the Chamber but most of the more important Princes seldom attended because they did not wish to get involved in political discussions. They wanted to be left alone.

If the Princes were satisfied with the existing position, it was certain that British India could not be left to wait upon events. Ever since the Crown took charge of India from the East India Company in Queen Victoria's reign there had been a series of reforms designed to set the stage for self-government within the Empire.

We have mentioned the 1919 development. This had been followed by the Simon Commission in 1928 and by two round-table conferences in 1930/31 and 1932. Then in 1931 a Joint Select Committee of both Houses of Parliament was set up to pave the way for the India Act of 1935. Linlithgow was appointed its chairman and was thus an obvious candidate for the vice-royalty in succession to Lord Willingdon, whose five years (the normal period) would be completed in 1936.

By 1930 the British Government had specifically pledged

itself to work for the achievement of Dominion Status for India. The right wing of the Conservative Party never willingly accepted this commitment but the majority of the Party did so. The objective had thus been defined and accepted before the 1935 Bill was drafted and therefore before Linlithgow became Viceroy. It is important, in what is to follow, that this should be understood.

The chief provisions of the India Act were as follows. First, the Provinces were to have responsible government of the parliamentary type, but their Governors would be armed with special powers for the protection of minorities and also to take over the administration in the case of a breakdown. These were sometimes called 'Section 93' powers from the number of the relevant section of the Act.

Secondly, the franchise was extended to 30 million voters and there would be separate electorates for Hindus and Muslims under what was known as the Communal Award.

Thirdly, at the Centre a Federal Government was to be set up consisting of representatives both of British India and of the princely States, the latter to be nominated by their rulers. The Legislature would consist of two houses, a Legislative Assembly and a Council of State.

Fourthly, diarchy was to be abolished in the Provinces and introduced at the Centre. The Governor-General in Council was to be responsible for the portfolios of Defence and External Affairs, all the remaining posts being held by Ministers responsible to the Legislature. The Governor-General was armed with emergency powers similar to those of the Governors.

Fifthly, the Federation could not be brought into force until half the number of princely States entitled to sit in the Council of State acceded, provided that this half also represented half the total population of all the States.

In Parliament the federal part of the Bill was bitterly opposed through all its stages by the right wing of the Conservative Party led by Winston Churchill in the Commons and the Marquess of Salisbury in the Lords. Churchill lashed into it with all

the invective at his command. In a debate in June, 1935, he called
the Bill 'a gigantic quilt of jumbled crochet work, a monstrous
monument of shame built by pygmies'. Others thought it a
brave attempt by the most experienced minds in Britain and
India to chart a course that could lead India to independence as a
united country within the British Empire and Commonwealth.
Among these was L. S. Amery. Speaking in the same debate, he
declared that Churchill's speech, like all his speeches on the
subject, had been utterly negative and devoid of constructive
thought.

This was not Churchill's first attack on Federation. In a debate
on 12th March, 1935, he had said that he would continue to warn
the Princes against it and added: 'I should be ready to take on my
own shoulders the responsibility of persuading them to stand out
of it.' He was as good as his word. He and his friends must share
much of the responsibility for the failure of the Princes to agree
to Federation while there was still time to organise themselves
effectively for the challenge of independence.

In India the provincial part of the Act was generally approved,
although the Congress Party condemned the whole Act as 'a
charter of slavery.' This was because they refused to consider any
constitution that was not drawn up by a constituent assembly of
the Indian people. The Muslims for their part were fearful of
being subjected to a Hindu raj of nearly 400 millions. They did
not, however, reject Federation outright, relying on the safeguards as well as on a reasonable number of years before the
British left India. During the interval they hoped there would be
signs of helpful co-operation by the Hindu majority under the
influence of responsibility.

The moment arrived for a new Viceroy to be chosen to succeed
Lord Willingdon. There were no illusions as to the weight of the
burden he would have to bear. Sir Robert Horne, one of the
ablest men in the Conservative hierarchy, had defined the
position with accuracy in the Commons when he said that the
Viceroy would be the keystone of all that mighty fabric: if he
failed nothing could save the system which had been set up: the

duty to be laid upon him was the most exacting laid upon any one man in the history of our legislature.

The Prime Minister (Baldwin) confined the issue to two men – Linlithgow and the Marquess of Zetland, who had been Governor of Bengal. He proposed to give the choice to Linlithgow first, telling him that he could be either Viceroy of India or Secretary of State for India. Baldwin hoped that he would choose the India Office as he would be of more general help in the Cabinet than Zetland, but Linlithgow accepted the greater challenge of the two and Zetland was appointed as Secretary of State and therefore, constitutionally, his master.

The new Viceroy left London for Bombay on 2nd April, 1936, with his wife and daughters. Among the staff which accompanied them was Gilbert Laithwaite,[1] who was to occupy the key position of Private Secretary to the Viceroy. A former scholar of Trinity College, Oxford, Laithwaite had had much experience in the India Office, part of it in India, and he served the Viceroy with devotion and absolute reliability throughout his term of office. As they sailed through the Indian Ocean Linlithgow told him that from now on he would let him completely into his mind at all times and would expect the same treatment for himself.

Before the party landed in India the grass edges of the path to the family mausoleum at Hopetoun had been trimmed and tidied. John Fergusson, the factor left in charge of the estate, was taking no chances. He said you never knew what might happen.

[1] Sir Gilbert Laithwaite, G.C.M.G., K.C.B., K.C.I.E., C.S.I., Ambassador to the Republic of Ireland 1949–51, High Commissioner to Pakistan 1951–4, Permanent Under Secretary of State for Commonwealth Relations 1955–59.

2

Linlithgow had known that he would arrive in India against a background of widespread mistrust of Britain's good faith over India's political future. He was determined to dispel these suspicions if he could. 'You must get to their hearts,' he had said, 'and this is what I mean to do.' He therefore took the first opportunity of showing India what sort of man he was.

By nature he was strong, but he was also sensitive and this combination of qualities showed clearly in his first broadcast to India. He made it immediately after taking the oaths of Allegiance and Office on 18th April, 1936 – he was the first Viceroy to do so.

'Now speaking to you in your homes,' he began, 'with those you love about you, I wish you to know that as I promised my true allegiance to His Majesty and dedicated myself to the service of India, I was conscious that I spoke not only for myself but also for you all . . . I am confident that every one of you will wish, on this solemn occasion, with me to pledge yourselves anew to the service of your motherland and of your fellow men.'

The new Viceroy made it unmistakably clear at the outset that there could be no progress without law and order. 'Amongst the manifold duties of the Viceroy, none is more vital than that of the maintenance of peace and good order throughout India. Believe me, my friends, that I can do you no greater service than by the vigilant and effective discharge of this duty. The long story of progress and political evolution throughout the world proves beyond all question that of all the factors that may make for retrogression and reaction, none is more powerful than civil disorder to inflict irreparable hurt upon the body-politic. This and all other duties and responsibilities laid upon me by law and by the Instrument of Instructions which the King-Emperor has been graciously pleased to bestow upon me I will discharge without fear or favour, affection or ill-will, including that to do right to all manner of people after the Laws and Usages of India.'

He reminded his audience that he was no stranger to this lovely land and to its kindly peoples. But in his journeyings with the Agricultural Commission he had had to confine his activities to British India. Of Princely India he now hoped to see something as soon as he could. He had ever in mind the constant and devoted loyalty to His Majesty the King-Emperor of the Princes and Peoples of the Indian States and affirmed his admiration of their services in peace and war.

After tributes to the armed forces of the Crown and to the Indian Civil Service, Linlithgow had a word for the children of India. 'Children! I speak to you as your King-Emperor's Viceroy and as your friend. Remember that when you grow up it will be with you that the honour of your country will rest. Remember that no man or woman can be a good citizen and a true patriot who does not first of all learn to govern and subdue his own nature. That is never easy . . .' This was the man speaking very much from his strong belief in self-discipline.

He now came to a part of his address which made a very deep impression upon those who heard it. It was to be the key to much of his Viceroyalty:

'I turn now to a matter of the highest importance. I would have you know that I am incapable of preferring any one community before another. Let me bring home to you my inflexible resolution in this matter by a homely illustration. God has indeed been good to me for he has given me five children. They came into the world each one with a nature and with characteristics different from their brothers and sisters. I have tried my utmost to understand those differences and to deal with each one of my children in a fashion appropriate to his or her nature; to give support where support has seemed to me to be needed; and in each to cultivate natural gifts and good qualities. I have sought, too, to encourage them at all times to be tolerant of each other. I love them all most dearly. But among my children I have no favourite.'

In a few months, he reminded them, they would see inaugurated provincial autonomy as the first stage towards all-India Federation. The success of this endeavour would rest very largely with them, and must in great degree depend upon their steadiness and forbearance. In the coming provincial elections it could in no circumstances be for him to advise them how to vote, for it was of the very essence of this system of government that in that matter they should decide of their own individual and unfettered judgment where it was that their duty lay; therefore the leaders of all political parties might rely implicitly upon him never wittingly to use language calculated to prejudice their lawful interests. It was quite true that those in opposition to the Government in the Central Legislature could never, in present constitutional conditions, be called upon by the Viceroy to form part of an alternative government. This, he pointed out, provided the best of all reasons for the change in the constitution laid down by the 1935 Act.

There followed a warning through which Linlithgow showed how keenly he realised his duty to be impartial and how clearly he foresaw his own position as a convenient target for political sniping. The successful working of a representative government, particularly in the formation period shortly to be entered upon, required, amongst other things, that he should as far as practicable be in touch with the leaders of all political parties as well as with the trend of opinion in the electorate. It must be understood plainly that when he granted an interview to the leader or leaders of this or that political party, that would in no way signify that he favoured such leaders or their parties above others. This rule and convention was well understood in Great Britain as between the Crown and political leaders. Its general acceptance in India was in his judgment essential to the successful working of representative self-government.

He pledged himself to co-operate just as impartially with the press and to feed them with facts as fully as he could – like the rest of them, newspaper men could not be expected to make bricks without straw.

He ended his broadcast with these words: 'In conclusion let me
say to you that of all those conditions which in great endeavours
make for a happy and successful issue, none is more essential than
that those who participate in them should both trust and respect
each other. All men are liable to err. I do not ask or expect that
all of you will at all times find yourselves in agreement with me.
Nevertheless, you may be sure that I shall never doubt your
sincerity or the integrity of your minds. I ask no more than that
you should favour me with the same whole-hearted trust that I
have promised to extend to you. For the next five years, without
let or stay, I will devote my mind, my heart, and such health as
Providence may vouchsafe to me, to the service of your country.
For this I ask you to remember me in your prayers. Let us move
boldly forward, with faith and courage, you and I, and with all
our strength strive to better the lot of her Peoples wheresoever
they may be and to sustain, in all its ancient fame and glory, the
great name of India over all the world.'

At the Viceroy's suggestion, the broadcast was immediately
repeated in Hindustani – a gesture greatly appreciated. He had
introduced himself to India in the best possible way, by being
himself. The first impression which he had given was of a man
who was wise and straight. It was an impression which the years
ahead with all their bitterness, disappointment and peril, served
only to strengthen.

The broadcast did much to encourage the rumours which were
already going through the bazaars. These were that the Viceroy's
political leanings were towards the progressive ideas of Lord
Irwin,[1] that he had been instructed to seek out Gandhi and find
a new basis for political agreement, and that the Indian Civil
Service would find in him a master rather than a servant.

From another quarter, however, the reaction was ominous.
Mahomed Ali Jinnah, President of the Muslim League, told his
followers that the new Viceroy's pledge of impartiality was a poor
reward for Muslim loyalty to the Government.

Certainly the nature of the duty which Parliament had laid

[1] Viceroy of India 1926–31, later 1st Earl of Halifax.

upon Linlithgow was clear beyond a doubt. It was to bring in
provincial autonomy at the earliest possible moment and to
follow up with Federation. He himself was to insist continuously
on the need to maintain momentum between the establishment of
the first and the launching of the second.

*

Within weeks of arriving in India the new Viceroy showed how
anxious he was about the threat to India from Japan.

A memorandum by the Committee of Imperial Defence had
dealt with India's defences, mainly on the historical basis of an
attack upon her north-west frontier. Japan, ran the argument,
was fully occupied with her policy of expansion in Eastern Asia
and did not want war. She had no friends except possibly Germany and was anxious for a political understanding with
Britain. In the event of a major war in Europe, she might adopt a
hostile attitude towards Britain either by way of furthering her
own policy or in return for German assistance against Russia. In
that case she would probably devote her main effort to action
against those British possessions nearest to her shores, but sporadic
action against India must be anticipated. This was thought most
likely to take the form of sea-borne attacks on ports and shipping
to induce us to lock up troops in India which would be better
employed elsewhere and to interfere with our trade. The only
action which India could take, primarily dependent as she was on
assistance from the Royal Navy, would be to provide for local
defences at her important ports and some aircraft for general
co-operation with the other services in coast defence.

Of a possible Japanese attack upon India overland there was no
mention. There was no reference to Singapore, none to Burma.
The Viceroy was far from reassured. In particular he was worried
by the intensive and highly suspect activities of Japanese 'fisher-
men' off the Burmese coast. He refused to be mesmerised by the
traditional obsession with the North-West Frontier and wrote to
Zetland on 26th April that it was not going to be entirely easy for
him 'to persuade the soldiers who have been scanning the North-

West Frontier for signs of Russians for so many generations to turn about and face S.E., but that nothing less than that manoeuvre will meet the case we shall, I think, find.'

He sent to his Commander-in-Chief, Sir Robert Cassels, an appreciation of the situation. The premise was as follows. Germany had attacked the U.S.S.R.: Italy's attitude was doubtful, necessitating the maintenance by Great Britain of naval forces in the Mediterranean: Great Britain, whether or not at war with Germany, had in home waters a naval force sufficient to keep command of the sea against Germany; she had detached to the Far East such naval forces as could be spared. Thus reinforced, the East Indies Squadron was based on Singapore with orders to operate as a containing force against the Japanese fleet. Relative naval strengths in terms of capital ships made it certain that the East Indies Squadron for years to come must be markedly inferior to the Japanese fleet.

In the circumstances envisaged, the Viceroy submitted that there was one operation open to Japan which offered her an immensely rich prize at a hazard of relatively small forces – the occupation of Burma. He gave reasons. There was no land communication between India and Burma: by sea the distance between Calcutta and Rangoon was 737 miles. In fertile Burma there was an enormous amount of rice available: nearly $1\frac{1}{4}$ million tons had been exported in 1935/6 (ten years earlier the figure had been over $3\frac{1}{4}$ million tons). At least twenty-one million acres now wasted were capable of cultivation. The country produced large quantities of oil: mineral fields existed in the north-east.

On the strategic side occupation of Burma would give Japan an opportunity to squeeze the western frontier of China. Its coast could provide excellent submarine and destroyer bases, so could the Andaman Islands and the Nicobars. Comfortably shielded from interference by the U.S.A. the Japanese, given air superiority, would be able to dominate from the air the whole of the lower Gangetic Plain in India and all her munition factories. The occupation of Tenasserim would present a powerful threat to the rear of Singapore Naval Base (the Viceroy was satisfied that the Japanese had for some years been systematically surveying the Tenasserim littoral). With Burma in Japanese hands Siam would drop into their lap like a ripe plum with French Indo-China following as an easy second crop.

Whether or not the operation had been preceded by a successful fleet action by the Japanese against the Singapore squadron, the Viceroy was by no means sure that a British fleet could prevent either enemy transports or individual ships like aircraft carriers or submarines from breaking through into the Bay of Bengal from the Pacific.

As he drew towards his conclusion he quoted the old warning from history that the Low Countries were a pistol pointed at the heart of England. Might it not, he asked, with equal truth be said that Burma was a pistol pointed at the heart of India?

Then he made his final point: the first and most vital precaution which it was within their power to take was the construction of communications between Bengal and Burma.

The Commander-in-Chief replied to the Viceroy by way of a commentary upon his appreciation prepared by his General Staff. Based as this was upon the question-begging assertion that the British Government had accepted the liability to provide adequate naval and air cover against the Japanese fleet it struck the Viceroy as thoroughly unsatisfactory. He minuted that it dealt with almost every contingency except that presented in his own appreciation. The argument continued for some weeks, the General Staff resting on its ability to move tanks, infantry and artillery across the Bay of Bengal, the Viceroy retorting that the transports carrying them would be sunk by Japanese submarines. Finally he felt he must give way to his experts but at least his initiative caused a detailed investigation to be made of the possibilities of building the road he wanted.

Linlithgow remained sceptical. One morning during the winter of 1937/8 his son Charlie found him lying on the floor of his study in New Delhi with a map spread before him. 'I believe,' he said, 'that our guns in Singapore are facing the wrong way.' He was to be dramatically justified by events.

3

The Viceroy's initial estimate of the Princes' attitude to Federation was optimistic but he was fully aware of the difficulties which faced him. In a letter to the King (Edward VIII) of 24th July, 1936, he gave his first account of his thoughts. The original enthusiasm of the Princes was, he believed, coloured by their feeling that under Federation they would be able largely to rid themselves of the control of the Viceroy and the Political Department and to behave pretty much as they pleased within the borders of their own States. When this dream was seen to be without substance their enthusiasm rapidly waned and some of the important Princes tried to destroy the whole plan of reform at a meeting held in Bombay in 1935. That attempt failed. Ever since then they had realised more and more clearly that Federation must come and that, whatever the hazards of joining, they and their descendants would have no future outside the Federation. Linlithgow thought therefore that he would get the required measure of support from the Princes, namely at least half of the total of 104 seats in the Upper House or Council of State available to them and the accession of States whose populations totalled at least one half of the total population of all eligible States.

The Viceroy's original plan, formed soon after his assumption of office, had been to call the Princes to a formal *durbar* in October at which he could talk to them of Federation and try to allay their suspicions. He had thought this course advisable in view of the 'miserable state' in which he found the Chamber of Princes. By June, however, he had changed his mind. He now thought that such a meeting would do more harm than good as one or two individuals might create among their colleagues a sense of difficulty and danger out of proportion to the issues. He therefore decided that it would be best to deal with individual rulers.

Linlithgow was disturbed to discover an impression in the minds of some of his civil servants – at least one of them in a senior position – that the India Office was half-hearted about the desirability of early Federation. He therefore instructed Sir B. J. Glancy, Secretary of the Political Department, to inform all officers that the sooner Federation came in the better it would be, and that the Viceroy looked to the Political Department for full support. In a letter to Zetland (15th June, 1936), in which he reported his action, he asked the Secretary of State for a strong statement of support for his view. He emphasised that there was no time to be lost:

'It is vital that the impetus of the new Statute and the consummation of Provincial Autonomy should carry us straight on into Federation. For indeed there would be grave danger in allowing any prolonged interval of time to elapse between Provincial Autonomy and the final phase. Federation has few enthusiastic friends. The Princes, I believe, for the most part regard it as inevitable but do not welcome it. Congress hate it, and Provinces will soon, whether as regards their bureaucracies or their public opinion, develop a degree of local patriotism, which would view with easy acquiescence the progressive weakening of central authority, such as would most certainly eventuate if the reconstruction of the Centre is unduly delayed.'

He urged that legal disputes between representatives of the Princes and Parliamentary Counsel and the India Office be quickly ended. Otherwise they would drag on and on.

The plan was that the States should be sent the model Instrument of Accession to the Federation and be asked, without deciding for or against, what limitations they would attach to their acceptance. The India Office would then collate the various limitations. If they were acceptable model drafts of the limitations would be prepared. Then draft Instruments of Accession for individual States would be prepared and States would be asked for a decision on that basis. Zetland felt that this final stage would be the time when a strong line should be taken with the Princes. He would be 'a little chary of pressing them too hard during the earlier stages lest we frighten them off.'

It had originally been hoped that the standard draft Instrument of Accession would be ready by spring, 1936. Linlithgow was convinced that the delay was mainly due to the fact that the States kept on appointing new legal advisers in London who knew nothing about the subject and had to spend their time learning.

The more closely he concerned himself with Federation, he told Zetland, the more he felt that if they were to succeed they must quicken the pace. They must also on every possible occasion make it clear to the Princes that Federation was the goal, that the British Government was committed to it and that it was in the interests of the Princes to expedite it. There was another reason why the Viceroy was so anxious to press on. He felt that the system of government at the centre was moribund. He knew that once a new system in great matters is on the move the old one begins to run down with disproportionate speed.

By the end of June the Viceroy had received from the Political Department a time-table for Federation. It contemplated that by the end of 1938 there might be some idea of the terms on which a certain number of Princes might consider accession. This was not good enough for him so he called for another plan. He accepted that he would have to allow the Princes six months for consideration but he meant to reduce the time spent on the scheme by the Government of India and the India Office. He recognised the risk, with its political implications at home, of being accused of bringing undue pressure on the Princes but was confident that it could be minimised with care and tact.

The Political Department came up with its new timetable. It still envisaged a longer period for examination and discussion than the Viceroy liked, but he saw that there were limits to the speed factor and accepted the plan. By it, all objections and limitations were to be raised by March, 1937. The government of India would need four months to classify replies and decide on maximum reservations permissible.

Discussions between the Secretary of State, the government of India and the States would be completed by 1st December, 1937.

The States would have detailed draft Instruments of Accession by 1st January, 1938, together with a formal question as to whether they would accede on the terms offered. They would have four months to consider. The Government would hope to have received enough answers by mid-1938 to show whether the necessary majority of Princes had agreed to federate.

By the end of July the Viceroy had decided to take further steps to expedite the process. He divided the States into three groups, each group to be visited by an emissary from his Political Department. The Viceroy found he had not a large field of really good men from which to choose his team, but he was well satisfied in the result. Three men of high quality were appointed, Courtenay Latimer, Arthur Lothian and Francis Wylie.[1] With them was to go Jeremy Raisman[2], whose grasp of finance was soon to gain him the post of Finance Member of the Government of India.

They were to tour their allotted States at the end of October. Linlithgow hoped their investigation would be finished by early December. He relied on them to come back with a definite indication of the reservations to be made and, if possible, of the attitude of the Princes towards the Instrument generally by the end of February or at the latest by the end of March, 1937.

When he had returned in August from his forthcoming tour the Viceroy would write personally to all major Princes explaining the duties of his three representatives. He was very clear that unless they pressed the Princes they would get no results, and that the majority of the Princes were waiting to see how the situation developed and closely watching the position of other Princes so as to make sure that they themselves would secure the maximum possible benefit.

*

[1] Sir Francis Wylie, G.C.I.E., K.C.S.I., Governor of Central Provinces and Berar, 1938-40, Political Adviser to the Viceroy 1940, 1941 and 1943-5, Minister to Afghanistan, 1941-3, Governor of the United Provinces 1945-7.
[2] Sir Jeremy Raisman, G.C.M.G., G.C.I.E., K.C.S.I., Finance Member, Government of India, 1939-45.

Arrival at Bombay "The Gateway to India"

Viceroy's House, New Delhi

Viceregal Lodge, Simla

Within four days of writing this report to Zetland, Linlithgow was in Ranchi on tour and spent an active morning investigating bulls, poultry and rice-growing. The streets were crowded with cheering people on his arrival and he recorded that he had never known so much vocal enthusiasm from any oriental gathering. He felt that the reason for this remarkable demonstration lay in the association of his name with agricultural development. He was right. His reputation in this respect, already strong when he arrived, grew rapidly. He was welcomed by one rural community with an archway bearing the delightful words 'Welcome to our cow-protecting Viceroy.'

Linlithgow identified himself from the outset with the culti- vators of India. He arranged for a group of them to be present at his inauguration and, within a matter of days, bought two Hissar bulls, to be maintained at his private expense and made available for breeding purposes to cultivators in the region of New Delhi. Incidentally the last syllable of his name means 'cow' in the Hindi dialect and he touched India's sense of humour when he stipulated that neither bull was to be given the name of Viceroy.

All through his viceroyalty Linlithgow made a point of personally visiting Indian villages whenever possible and of keeping himself in touch with the country's rural life at the grass roots. Also he decided within a few months of his arrival to launch an all-India Cattle Show. The first Show took place in 1937 and its immediate success showed that the idea had come to stay.

During his tour the Viceroy received the encouraging reply from Zetland for which he had asked, agreeing with his views and promising all support. He gratefully acknowledged the message and said that Zetland's support had strengthened his hand in dealing with the hesitant, whose numbers he found somewhat surprising. He added that he now saw no reason why Federation should not come in by 1st April, 1938.

c

4

The Viceroy was back in Delhi by early August. He now had his first interview as Viceroy with G. D. Birla, who had asked to see him. Birla, a rich industrialist and financial supporter of Congress, had for some years acted as a link between Gandhi and authority. Linlithgow came to doubt whether Birla knew Gandhi's mind as well as he thought he did, but this was an occupational hazard facing anyone in contact with the Mahatma.

Birla had been active in London in 1935. There he saw many members on both sides of politics. He himself recognised that the British were sincere in regarding the 1935 Act as a forward step but he warned that Indians looked upon it as quite the opposite. He said that the goodwill which he found in Britain was not shown by the Willingdon régime in India: it was the oppressive atmosphere in India which made Indians there believe that the reforms were a retrograde step: a better spirit was needed. As it was, he thought, both the Indian Civil Service and Congress were irresponsible: the first because they thought only of maintaining law and order, the second because they suspected every move by the Government. The result was that the right wing of Congress was getting weaker, its left wing was gaining strength and the Muslims were becoming demoralised.

Birla had met Linlithgow for the first time during his London visit. He described him as 'tall, well-built, not brilliant but capable and sound; no imagination, matter-of-fact, at the same time straightforward, frank and well-intentioned.'[1] His meeting with a group of Labour M.P.s headed by Attlee discouraged him. Almost all of them struck him as unintelligent and dull and he rather curiously accused them of making speeches with no intention of fulfilling promises. They suffered, he thought, from

[1] G. D. Birla, *In the shadow of the Mahatma* (1959), p. 186.

an inferiority complex and he noted he would rather have
Linlithgow as Viceroy than any of them.[1]

At their first interview in New Delhi Birla asked Linlithgow if
he would not send for Gandhi. The Viceroy replied that there
were limits to what he could discuss with Gandhi and he doubted
whether it would make any difference to the Mahatma merely to
be told that the Viceroy and Governors would interpret the
Constitution in a liberal spirit. He pointed out that he must not
act in any way which would seem to give comfort and votes to
the Congress Party. He could not therefore send for Gandhi, but
he emphasised that his door was open to all.

The Viceroy felt that Birla was trying to convey to him that he
should support Gandhi, who represented the conservative element
in Congress against the forces of the left wing. He made it clear
that while he was very conscious of the difficulties with which
Congress were faced, those difficulties must be solved by the
Congress themselves.

This was a significant interview as it showed that Linlithgow
could be flexible as well as firm. The metaphor of the open door
was not brought in at random. He chose his words deliberately
and he meant exactly what he said. Birla knew it, therefore
Gandhi would know it.

*

The Viceroy was under no illusions about the seriousness of the
Princes' difficulties but he was feeling increasingly optimistic as to
the outcome, which he thought would not be in doubt unless
there was a last minute stampede. He thought, too, that there
were signs of a marked softening in the ranks of Congress
towards the idea of early Federation. Officials at the Centre and
in the States were now co-operating satisfactorily. Thus, by the
end of September, 1936, he felt able to report that the general
political picture in India was very promising.

He asked the Secretary of State for a summary of the reactions
of the *Morning Post* and the diehard press generally to the federal

[1] Ibid., pp. 184, 185.

policy which he had announced. He wanted to be kept in close touch with the atmosphere in right wing quarters at home. The answer was that there had been no reaction in these quarters, while *The Times* and the *Manchester Guardian* had fully reported the procedure announcement. *The Times* was reserving comment until such time as the Viceroy might require Press support in meeting dilatory tactics or difficulties with the Princes.

Reasonably optimistic as he was about the political situation Linlithgow was not happy about the state of his administrative machine. This he saw as quite unfitted for the great tasks ahead. If the Government of India was to function properly after Federation he was convinced that there must be a radical re-organisation. All government departments were finding it difficult to get suitable officers. The trouble went back to a short-fall in recruitment during and after the first World War, which had led to a deterioration in the quality of I.C.S. recruits. Most seriously hit were the Departments of Finance and Commerce, where there was a real risk of administrative collapse unless the position was tackled at once. The men of special knowledge and experience who would be needed to cope with the future were simply not there.

The Viceroy asked for the recruitment of an expert cadre which could be given specialised training after the ordinary training in the Provinces. He strongly criticised the haphazard way in which vacancies had been filled in recent years. No fore-sight had been shown, so there was no continuous supply of qualified officers. In the recruitment figures for that year (1936) there was a shortage of ninety in the I.C.S. This, in a service which never reached an establishment above thirteen hundred, was a serious deficiency.

Linlithgow also felt that there was a strong case for setting up a Governor-General's Secretariat. There was nothing comparable in existence. His feeling was that, if the Governor-General were to disagree with a view put up by a department represented by a Member-in-Council, he would need independent departmental advice. He also felt it was necessary to build up such a secretariat before the federal Government came into being. Time would be needed to work out the many details concerned with personnel as well as with functions. If the scheme were not ready and working before Federation the Governor-General would be at the mercy of the federal minister who would have all the files as well as the loyalty of his department.

Most of the departments showed resistance to the Viceroy's plan. This was not surprising, springing as it did from a natural disinclination to give up existing powers. The Viceroy, however, went steadily ahead. All this time he was gaining increasing respect from his officials, who recognised his immense capacity for hard work, as well as his mastery of detail when necessary. For the first time in their experience they were seeing notes by the Viceroy on their files.

*

During the final weeks of his first summer season, the Viceroy applied his mind to various matters apart from the main problem of the federal time-table. In the field of education, for instance, he asked for the appointment of a commissioner to advise upon the reorganisation of primary education and the development of female education in the Provinces. For this purpose he wanted a man of high professional standing from Great Britain.

He also took the opportunity to speak to the youth of India. The occasion was the annual prize-giving ceremony at the Bishop Cotton School, Simla. In a short address on the search for truth he warned the boys that there was no more damaging weakness than self-deception – 'Nor is any one of those weaknesses to which we are all prone more difficult to put away.' Truth, he said, was the discipline that made our imagination our servant rather than our master: no-one could possess good judgment, which was about the same thing as an instinct for recognising reasonable probabilities, whose mind was not trained to follow truth: and in many of the most important things of life, reasonable probabilities were our only guide.

In September, 1936, the Viceroy gave his first address to the

members of both Houses of the Legislature. The Congress Party
did not attend. Information reached the Viceroy that at a meeting
of the Congress Executive nine had been in favour of attending
and only four against, but that orders were then received from the
top to stay away.

In his speech Linlithgow first reminded the Legislature that
there were two problems to which he attached the utmost
importance, public health and nutrition as affecting humans and
animals alike: he was already arranging for the establishment of a
Central Public Health Advisory Board: since he first took office
he had done all he could to stimulate rural development and he
felt already encouraged by the response. Moreover he set about
solving the malaria problem, so that within a year or two the
New Delhi region was free from this scourge.

Passing to the great question of constitutional development he
begged the Legislature to face up to the danger of delay once
provincial autonomy had been achieved on 1st April, 1937. He
did not minimise the intricate nature and difficulties of the federal
problem. He sometimes wondered, he said, whether those who
had laboured upon the scheme in so many Round Table Conferences and Committees and in Parliament itself were not in
some danger of finding themselves so engrossed in the multi-
farious details of the plan as to lose sight of the essential outlines of
the structure and, at times, even of the splendid vision that had
moved and inspired its inception. In a world where the rule of
force was threatening in so many directions he appealed to every
man and woman of goodwill to help for India's sake to bring in
those great changes which by their very nature involved nothing
less than the discarding of the old ideas of Imperialism for new
ideals of partnership and co-operation.

*

Linlithgow, worried like everyone else about the developing
world situation, was not satisfied with the information he was
getting from the Foreign Office in London. The printed reports
which were sent to him were too detailed and six weeks out of

date. He asked for a weekly résumé of events. He felt certain that
the outbreak of war in Europe would involve the East. India
would find herself confronted by an emergency in her defence
and internal security far more acute than any which arose in the
first World War. It was therefore of the first importance that he
should be kept fully informed of events in good time.

Palestine provided an example of India's sensitiveness to outside
events. The Muslims were showing signs of anxiety over the
disorders there and the Viceroy received a deputation from them
which raised the question of Jewish immigration. He was
presented with an address which he described to the King as
'couched in terms highly colourful and anything but compli-
mentary to the policy and actions of Your Majesty's Government
in Palestine.' But this was, he added, no more than politics and
there was no strong feeling behind the words. They parted good
friends.

Congress was meanwhile trying for its own ends to stir up
Muslim wrath in sympathy with the Palestinian Arabs.

The Viceroy and the Government of India returned from
Simla to New Delhi in October. This was always to be a welcome
moment both for him and for his family. They had not enjoyed
their first experience of the hill station and they were never to
take to it. Linlithgow felt the strain of the altitude and Lady
Linlithgow was often less than well there. On this first visit she
was laid up for a considerable time soon after arrival.

Simla, for all the beauty of its surrounding hills, was often
shrouded in mist. The house itself, Viceregal Lodge, was an ugly
Victorian mansion with none of the charm of the Lutyens house
in New Delhi.

One way and another it had not been a happy start for them.
Linlithgow himself had no time for nostalgia but his wife and
daughters were not over the home-sickness which had assailed
them very sharply. They did not, as a family, find their quasi-
royal status with its necessary formalities easy to adopt. This was
the part of his life which Linlithgow found most wearying
throughout his term. He was consciously short of the social

graces which had so distinguished Lord Willingdon. 'I can't do
this,' he said. 'He could.' But in fact he performed his social
duties with a simple and unaffected dignity and he looked the
part magnificently.

His first few months as Viceroy had established his reputation
as an exceptionally hard worker. He was often still at work at
one a.m. It is worth dwelling on this capacity for a moment.
Linlithgow felt, as soon as he had had time to look around, that
the administration was in bad shape and must be pulled together.
Much as he had liked Willingdon and admired his courage he
was distressed to find little evidence of his predecessor's reactions
to the papers submitted to him. He had not yet seen as much as
'W' on any file, much less on a minute. He felt also that some of
his officials needed waking up: 'As each head has appeared on the
skyline,' he wrote in a private letter, 'I have given it a good hard
spank and then kissed and made friends.' It was natural that he
should have his critics. One of them expressed the theory that
Linlithgow had always considered himself born to rule. The
shaft was ridiculously wide of the mark. The truth was simply
that he had decided a good deal was wrong and that he had not
much time to put it right.

One of his strongest critics in those early months was Sir James
Grigg, Finance Member of the Government of India and therefore
a member of the Viceroy's Council. Grigg was never a respecter
of persons, which nobody minded because everyone knew it.
'The trouble with P.J.', said Linlithgow, 'is that he thought he
was Viceroy when Willingdon was here and he does not realise
that now I am.' It is, however, right to record that the two men
became friends. When Linlithgow died, Grigg praised him as a
great man whom he had at first misunderstood.

The smack of firm Government did not stop at the civil
administration. Shortly after his first arrival in New Delhi, while
working at three a.m., the Viceroy heard an Indian army sentry
outside the window of his study having 'a most audible and
absorbed conversation' either with another soldier or a policeman.
He then saw the sentry throw away a cigarette. He ordered the

battalion to be relieved at once and forbade it to mount Viceroy's guard for three months. Linlithgow knew that his drastic action would be criticised but he was convinced that he had been right to take it. Referring later to the incident he pointed out that Viceroy's House was not Buckingham Palace. His study was on the ground floor and the sentries were literally there to guard his life. There was no more trouble of that kind.

5

By the end of September, 1936, the Viceroy was again pressing the Secretary of State on the question of speed in federal negotiations with the Princes. He had been in office for nearly six months and was therefore able to appreciate the situation from experience. Arrangements for the elections that would inaugurate provincial autonomy in the spring of 1937 were going smoothly enough. It was the following stage towards Federation which was making him increasingly anxious.

To quicken the pace the Viceroy wanted his three emissaries to the States to have authority to give rulings on certain questions put by the Princes on the effect of accession to the Federation. The Secretary of State restrained him. Zetland thought it would be a mistake to compress into one stage what had originally involved two. They might, he said, reach a point in their negotiations where more haste would result in less speed: the Princes might feel they were being rushed and take fright: let this particular series of visits remain exploratory. Linlithgow acquiesced. The emissaries should complete their inquiries in January, 1937. There should then be a general review, followed, if necessary, by further visits to States to deal with difficulties.

Although he agreed to defer to Zetland's caution Linlithgow took the opportunity yet again to urge that time was not on his side. He told the Secretary of State that experience had confirmed his early conviction that 'failing a formal approach such as I have made, backed by the whole weight of the personal influence of the Viceroy and of the Government of India, we could have no hope of reaching finality in any easily predictable time in this matter of Federation.' He expected to have a clear idea of the difficulties by early 1937 and he now hoped for Federation by 1st April, 1938.

So far the federal picture as it had been building up showed the Viceroy eager to force the pace and the Secretary of State restraining him. At first sight Zetland's caution seems out of character with the Government's policy. But he was watching the right wing of the Conservative Party. He wrote to Linlithgow that he had been warned more than once by Lord Salisbury and his friends that they would not necessarily acquiesce in the passage of Orders in Council dealing with Federation which they looked upon as the most dangerous part of the 1935 Act. Zetland had no doubt that everything done in furtherance of Federation would be scrutinised with a highly critical and jaundiced eye. The Secretary of State was not exaggerating the position. The opponents of the Act, in particular Churchill, knew that the Princes virtually had the power of veto on Federation and they were determined to see that it should prevail.

Linlithgow knew Churchill fairly well. They liked one another but they were never intimate friends. In these early months of his Viceroyalty he was doing his best to carry out the will of Parliament in the face of the efforts of Churchill and his friends to prevent him. He did not allow these efforts to upset him but he thought them misguided and dangerous. Like Willingdon before him he never ceased from his efforts to persuade the Princes that it was in their own interests to agree to Federation. He could only hope that they would listen to him rather than to Churchill.

*

There was a Conference of Princes at Bombay in October. It was clear that a number of those present would be glad to be rid of a Federation based on any except on their own terms but that they were not prepared to take the responsibility for a breakdown. The British-owned press in India was critical of the Conference's negative activities, holding that it was no good at this stage complaining that the issues were so complicated when discussion had been going on for the last five years. Those papers allied to Congress which were normally anti-Federation would have

supported the Princes in this context if they had merely stated
their objections to Federation. But the Princes demanded safeguards even beyond what the India Act provided. For instance,
one of them said the Act would reduce them from sovereigns to
constitutional rulers. The Indian press could hardly be expected
to share the Princes' dismay at this development.

Meanwhile reports from the three emissaries were coming in.
They showed the value of the Viceroy's decision to send the team
out. Wylie's report was particularly useful. He had been present
at discussions with eleven States. Not one had understood the
practical effects of Federation. Wylie had managed to dispel
many misconceptions and unreasonable fears. There were, of
course, genuine problems for the States but Wylie found that
they were suggesting every limitation they could think of, partly
at least because they did not want to overlook any possibility
which might occur to others. The smaller States were particularly
anxious. They could not afford expensive counsel and were
afraid that larger States would get better terms than they. Wylie
suggested that they should be reassured by a Government
promise to give all States equal terms as far as possible.

So far there had been no unconditional agreement to accede to
Federation although a few Princes had agreed in principle subject
to further discussion. Zetland wrote to Linlithgow that his plan
of the emissaries had proved itself and was a stroke of genius.

*

Towards the end of the year the Viceroy reacted strongly to a
proposal of the Government for increasing the pay and improving
conditions of British soldiers serving overseas. This had been
included as an incentive to recruitment, but the Viceroy pointed
out that it would cost India £2 million a year. This would
embitter Indian opinion because it would mean increased taxation
of several crores[1] a year. The money would be needed to increase
the pay of the British soldiers by more than the equivalent of a
peasant's whole income, to give him four meals a day as against

[1] A crore represented ten million rupees.

the peasant's one, and to give him ceremonial uniform while the Indian had one *dhoti*.

The political results of such a measure would, the Viceroy feared, imperil the new constitution. India's greatest service to Britain would be to bring the equipment and organisation of her own army up to standard. She could do it if she could be helped to the tune of £2–3 million a year.

Linlithgow took a very close interest in the army. When Field Marshal Lord Chetwode (Commander-in-Chief under Willingdon) wrote to congratulate him on his appointment as Viceroy, he had said in his letter of thanks that in his view the most urgent problem facing India was the Indianisation of the army and of the I.C.S.

*

On 11th November the Viceroy wrote what was to be his last letter to King Edward VIII. He told the King that news of His Majesty's intention to hold a Coronation Durbar had been extremely well received. He then gave an analysis of progress in the steps towards provincial autonomy. Political parties were busy everywhere with their plans for the first elections due to be held early next year. Congress had so far given no definite lead to its adherents as to whether, if they obtained parliamentary majorities, they should or should not take office in the provincial administrations. This failure to give a lead, he wrote, was due to differences of opinion within the Congress organisation. Many of their men would undoubtedly take office in their respective Provinces if given the opportunity. Their leaders, however, were mostly opposed to acceptance because they were against any course which might make the Congress machine less effective as an instrument for revolutionary agitation. They realised that, if the more active local leaders throughout the country were able to busy themselves executively with provincial affairs, they would be less and less willing to take their orders from Congress headquarters.

Within weeks King Edward had abdicated. On 21st December,

1936, the Viceroy wrote his first letter to the new King-Emperor, George VI:

'I do not feel, Sir, that you will wish me to say more about recent events than to tell you how deeply my wife and I have felt for Your Majesties and for the Royal Family in the distressing and most anxious times through which you have passed. The announcement of the abdication of King Edward and Your Majesty's accession to the Throne has been received by the public of India with all sympathy and respect. I cannot overstate the tact, moderation and restraint with which the public press has behaved throughout the crisis.'

The reference to the steadiness with which the public had reacted to the crisis of the abdication was justified. The moment was a grave one for the prestige of the raj. The deep and ingrained respect for kingship in an eastern country was essentially a personal emotion which was bound to be shaken by the discovery that the King could not do as he pleased. The constitutional side of the matter was not widely understood. Much of the Indian press treated King Edward as a hero who had sacrificed all for love. Nevertheless the expressions of loyalty to King George VI were widespread and sincere. The crisis soon passed.

It was hoped that the King would be able to hold a Coronation Durbar during the winter of 1937-8, but his doctors advised against it on the grounds of strain, coming, as it would, so soon after the Coronation in London.[1]

*

The Viceroy and his family went, as was the custom, to Calcutta for a fortnight at Christmas – sadly the first family Christmas spent without the sons. They attended the races, arriving in State in a coach which drove down the racecourse to the stands. It was a splendid sight. First into view came the bodyguard, scarlet and gold in the distance, then the coach with the Viceroy and Vicereine acknowledging the cheers of thousands who

[1] The Durbar had to be postponed again the following year because of expense, and the outbreak of war prevented King George from ever visiting his Indian Empire.

thronged the course to enjoy the fun. It was very like Royal Ascot but much more colourful owing to the bodyguard.

The season, happy as it was, did not pass entirely without a hitch. Linlithgow chose to attend his first public function at a club to which Indians were admitted as well as Europeans. Some of the business community disapproved. Such an attitude always distressed him and he sometimes wondered how there was any goodwill towards the British at all. The origins of this racial prejudice lay deep in the past, dating from the years when the British first brought out their womenfolk to India. There were, of course, many exceptions to it, especially in the administrative ranks of the raj, but there was enough to do great harm and cause much bitterness, especially in business circles and the army.

On the last day of the year the Viceroy had a talk with his naval Commander-in-Chief, Admiral Sir Alexander Ramsay. Ramsay was an outspoken sailor. Of this quality at least one memorable example survives. The naval Commander-in-Chief by custom spent Christmas and the New Year at Calcutta in his Flagship (Ramsay's was H.M.S. *Norfolk*). It was also traditional for the Flagship to give a ball in the presence of the Viceroy and the Governor of Bengal. The Governor (Lord Brabourne) lent Admiral Ramsay his house-boat, temporarily moored next to the Flagship, for the preceding dinner party, which consisted of some forty guests, including the Viceroy.

The guests were, of course, shown a seating plan before going into dinner, but on this occasion the staff officer responsible had delegated the actual placing of the name cards to another officer, who unfortunately went round the table in the wrong direction. The Viceroy, leading in the Admiral's wife,[1] went to the right place, as did the Governor and the Admiral with the Vicereine and Lady Brabourne. Otherwise there was chaos. The guests milled around in search of their places, the scene resembling a game of musical chairs as the band repeated its introductory music again and again.

Admiral Ramsay was understandably furious and he now let

[1] Formerly Princess Patricia of Connaught.

fly a broadside. Training his sights upon the elderly Bishop of Calcutta he bellowed at the top of his voice, 'Sit down, damn you!' The old man dropped on the instant into the nearest chair and everyone else followed suit. The action was over. The Viceroy had enjoyed every moment of it to the full. Such a welcome deviation from protocol seldom came his way.

When he saw the Viceroy on this New Year's Eve, Ramsay reported serious gaps in his port defences. He had no mine-sweepers, shore guns or searchlights. He also wanted a better Director of the Indian Navy in Whitehall. The Admiralty's reluctance to commit themselves on expenditure was, he main-tained, no excuse for any further delay as India could not count on unlimited time in which to put her house in order.

Activity in one further sphere must be noted before we leave the old year. There was trouble threatening in Waziristan on the North-West Frontier. The problem was not new but the Viceroy hoped that this particular running sore was showing signs of healing. He was to be disillusioned.

The leader of the tribesmen was the so-called 'Faqir of Ipi'. Although his attempts to embarrass the British were contained, he always managed to avoid capture – on one occasion by only a few minutes. He was a formidable antagonist. It was rumoured in the hills that he kept two pigs, one representing the Viceroy and the other the Commander-in-Chief. When in the mood to stimulate his morale he would cut a small piece from one or the other or both.

Top. A Garden Party at Viceroy's House, New Delhi

Bottom. The Viceroy with his butterfly net in Kashmir and with Madame
Chiang Kai-Shek in New Delhi

Mahatma Gandhi

Mohammed Ali Jinnah

6

In the early months of 1937 India went to the polls to elect its provincial governments, which were to take over on an autonomous basis on 1st April. In six Provinces Congress won a sweeping victory, Central Provinces, United Provinces, Bihar, Orissa, Bombay and Madras. They were unsuccessful in the Punjab, Bengal, Sind, the North-West Frontier Province and Assam. The extent of the Congress victories surprised the Viceroy less than some of the provincial Governors. Linlithgow had formed the view that, with the exception of the Unionist Party in the Punjab and of the Justice Party in Madras, the Congress Party was the only one worthy of the name, and certainly the only one possessing an active and widespread organisation in the constituencies.

The surprise of the Governors was well exemplified in the forecasts of Sir Hyde Gowan, Governor of the Central Provinces. Here Congress had claimed that they would win 65 seats out of 112. On 17th December, 1936, Gowan had called this 'an incredible boast.' On 4th February, 1937, he forecast, on the basis of his district reports, that they would win 35 seats. By 10th February his estimate was up to 60:

'The name of Gandhi is unquestionably one to conjure with among the masses in this Province – not for any particular political reason, but simply because he is Gandhi – and reports from several districts indicate that the one Congress slogan which has been universally successful is – "Put your papers in the white box and vote for Gandhi".'

On 7th March Gowan reported the final result. Congress had won 70 seats.

The Congress Party Working Committee was itself surprised at the extent of its landslide victory, especially in Madras where they won 159 out of 215 seats in the lower house and 27 out of 46 in the upper house.

As soon as the elections were over the question whether or not Congress would accept office came to a head. Ostensibly this turned on the potential use of the special powers of the Governors. The Governors of the Provinces in which Congress had secured a majority invited the provincial leaders to assist them in the formation of ministries. The leaders, acting under instruction from their All-India Committee, demanded an undertaking that they would not use the special powers vested in them by section 93 of the India Act of 1935. Obviously no such undertaking could be given. The Congress leaders therefore refused to take office.

This was an early setback for the Viceroy. He knew that the President of Congress, Jawaharlal Nehru, had been resolutely opposed to acceptance of office from the outset because, Linlithgow thought, if his lieutenants busied themselves with provincial politics they would become wrapped up in them and be of no further use to him in his plans for revolution on the grand scale. From Gandhi the Viceroy had hoped for better things. The Mahatma was both abler and more moderate than Nehru but he, too, was afraid of the divisive possibilities of provincial responsibility. Yet he realised that Congress would suffer loss of prestige if its members, having made lavish promises to their electors, declined to serve. He therefore made an issue of the special powers in an effort to throw the blame on to the Government of India for the Congress decision.

Meanwhile in the non-Congress Provinces the Constitution went ahead. The Punjab, Bengal, Sind, the North-West Frontier Province and Assam all equipped themselves with Governments claiming to enjoy the support of a majority of their Legislatures. The Punjab in particular had made a good start with a coalition under a most competent Chief Minister, Sir Sikandar Hyat Khan. The Viceroy hoped that the successful launching of provincial autonomy in these five Provinces would influence Congress towards reconsidering their attitude. Another factor which he felt

would encourage the same trend was the formation of minority
Governments in the Congress Provinces. Here the Governors had
succeeded in persuading appropriate members of their Legislatures to accept office without commanding parliamentary
majorities. This had infuriated Congress, which had confidently
looked forward to the immediate breakdown of the Constitution.
The minority Governments would probably be able to avoid
facing their Legislatures until June or July when they would have
to meet them in order to secure further supply. The interval
would at least give Congress a chance of second thoughts.

The Viceroy now began a long battle of attrition with Congress, knowing that if he could not get them to change their
minds the whole of the policy which he had been sent to India to
carry out would collapse. Although he was completely supported
in his attitude by the Governors and the Government of India,
there were to be times when he would feel very much alone
as far as his relations with the Government at home were
concerned.

The Viceroy gave a clear indication of how his mind was
reacting to the Congress challenge in a letter of 22nd February to
Sir. J. Hubback, Governor of Orissa. He was strongly against
dissolving the Assembly and seeking new elections if Congress
refused to take office. The majority party must be given every
possible chance to form a ministry. One by one the remaining
possibilities must be exhausted before finally the Governor had
to take over responsibility under the provisions of Section 93.
'What I feel very strongly is that we should at no stage lay ourselves open to any suggestion that we have failed to give the
utmost possible help in working, or trying to work the parliamentary system . . .'

The Governor of Madras, Lord Erskine, was hopeful that
Congress would accept office. His able Chief Minister, Rajago-
palachari, thought Gandhi was in favour of acceptance. The
Viceroy wrote to Erskine on 5th March:

'The right line is to give the utmost possible rope to Congress, of
course within the four walls of the Act . . . My general feeling . . . is

that we should take pains to dispel any apprehensions on the part of Congress that, if they take office, they may not get a fair deal from us or from the Services; and I would myself be disposed to err on the side of generosity rather than otherwise where there was any question of doubt.'

On 3rd March Erskine reported to Linlithgow an interview he had had on that day with Rajagopalachari, who had said that Congress would probably take office if they could get a public assurance about the use of the Governors' reserved powers. Rajagopalachari had just returned from Wardha[1] and he now suggested that it would ease the situation if the Viceroy were to see Gandhi and agree a formula with him. Linlithgow saw the trap immediately – and wired to Zetland. It would be of the greatest value to Congress, he pointed out, for them to be able to say that, far from acceptance of office being a climb-down on their part, they had taken office only in return for a specific concession by Government. It would be short-sighted in the extreme for the Viceroy or the Governors to give Congress an undertaking, whether written or oral, on the way in which the special powers would be used. Linlithgow asked for Zetland's support in refusing to follow such a course:

'We have abundant proof that the ultimate purpose of Nehru and Gandhi is to make for the overthrow of Government by the organisation of agrarian mischief on the grand scale. Our best hope of avoiding a direct clash is in the potency of Provincial Autonomy to destroy the effectiveness of Congress as an All-India instrument of revolution.'

They should do everything possible both in public and private to make clear to Congress that it could look for sympathy and co-operation in the working of the Act.

Linlithgow added that he thought that pressure from the Provinces would force Congress to accept office, but in any event he was quite clear that he would rather face an immediate breakdown and the use of Section 93 than agree to any limitation

[1] Gandhi's headquarters.

of his own freedom of action or that of the Governors as regarded special responsibilities or the use of safeguards.

*

On 12th March Birla saw the Viceroy. He said that Gandhi was most uneasy as he felt that Congress – except in Madras – would be either too weak or too rigid unless they were provided with a formula for their use in negotiating with Governors. Gandhi wanted negotiation at the centre between himself and the Viceroy. A few days later Rajagopalachari saw Erskine in Madras and put his own suggestion for a formula. Admitting that a Governor could not legally divest himself of his responsibilities if Congress took office Rajagopalachari wanted an undertaking that the Governor would not use his special powers of interference or set aside the advice of his Cabinet in matters appertaining to and within the legitimate scope of the provincial ministry. Linlithgow would not accept this for the obvious reason that the last phrase would be susceptible to infinite argument.

Rajagopalachari developed his idea further to the effect that the Governors and their Chief Ministers should agree to ignore the provision of the Act and leave it to the Secretary of State and the Viceroy alone to operate the safeguards. Linlithgow saw that this, too, was impossible.

The Muslims now took a hand in the game. Syed Wazir Hassan, who had been President of the last session of the Muslim League, issued a statement that the formation of minority ministries was illegal. He declared that Government should fall back upon Section 93. Linlithgow had no intention of doing so unless compelled by events, well knowing that nothing would please Congress better. He thought he might reply to Hassan's view unofficially. It would be wrong to do so formally because, since provincial autonomy, the constitutional position was that the Government of India was no longer directly concerned with the handling of the provincial situation by Governors. The point must be dealt with, if at all, by His Majesty's Government. This was done.

On 22nd April a telegram arrived from Zetland: 'A body of opinion here which it would be unwise to discount entirely is becoming anxious at continued deadlock and is inclined to take the line that Government having made the constitutional position clear ought to endeavour to find means of giving Congress opportunity of reconsidering situation which they apparently will not do in the absence of any move on the part of Government . . .'

Lord Halifax in Cabinet thought that Congress should be given a chance of making its position clear. He was attracted by a suggestion in the Press of Sir Tej Bahadur Sapru, the Indian Liberal leader, that the Viceroy should call a conference with the Congress leaders. Zetland, although he saw the difficulties of a conference, was afraid that, if a move of some sort was not made immediately, Congress might issue a manifesto which would make further attempts to remove the deadlock impossible. He therefore suggested that Linlithgow should make a statement that Government would not use its reserved powers in a legalistic way or to halt social reforms, but would adopt a sympathetic attitude to the proposed reforms.

The Viceroy replied by telegram next day. After a summary of the case against concessions to Congress he said that a conference as suggested was out of the question, given the existence of minority ministries. The non-Congress Provinces would demand association. 'We must also bear in mind not only the danger of disturbing minorities and driving the Muslims into the arms of Congress (I am aware that they are watching us closely and I do not wish to see a united front created in this area), but the un-desirability in view of the accepted policy of provincial autonomy of centralising discussions under the Viceroy.' There was nothing that Congress were more anxious to secure.

He recognised the strong desire in many quarters for his inter-vention now. But this would appeal to Congress as the best way of escape from the tangle into which they had got themselves. To Gandhi it would give an opportunity to re-establish his personal position, to enhance the prestige of Congress, to perpetuate the All-India solidarity of Congress by bargaining at the Centre on provincial matters and to open a sustained attack on the safeguards.

Linlithgow said he knew that some sections of opinion and certain newspapers were demanding an interview between the Viceroy and Gandhi as a way out of the impasse without any idea of how it would provide a solution. But Congress treated with contempt any expression of goodwill. They were simply out for a formula which would effectively nullify the reserved powers. For two reasons the Viceroy did not think it possible to contemplate any formula which attempted to define what Governors could or could not accept: first there would be the difficulty of interpretation; secondly a proposal, legislative or administrative, which might be harmless in ordinary times might in altered circumstances appear so inadvisable as to warrant a Governor exercising his special responsibility.

Linlithgow's message then gave Zetland a timely reminder:

'I hope Halifax appreciates the difference between circumstances in which he negotiated when reforms were at the stage of preliminary negotiation and those obtaining in which I and Governors are subject to a Constitution written in an Act the ink of which is hardly yet dry, and which is being satisfactorily worked in five Provinces.'

Finally he said that he was fully alive to the arguments on the other side but, after the closest observation of the position and weighing of the facts, he had decided that it was not yet time for him to intervene. It was wisest to allow matters to take their course until either the minority ministries were defeated or Congress made a move.

Zetland wired back that he thought Linlithgow's statement of his views convincing and he would support it. He had not wished to give the impression that he completely shared Halifax's point of view; the only specific suggestion he had wanted to convey was for a statement on the use of the reserved powers in connection with social and economic reform. He would bring the whole question before the Cabinet and anticipated no difficulty in getting support for what he described as his and Linlithgow's policy.

A few days later a curious situation arose over an item in the *Statesman*.[1] This took the form of an article dated 2nd May, which was headed 'Indian Impasse Deplored – Unofficial anxiety – Viceroy's silence unhelpful.' The text reported that the House of Commons was critical of the Government's attitude to the deadlock, that the Viceroy's advisers in India were unwilling to help Congress extricate itself from the impasse and that considerations of prestige on both sides could not be overlooked: the Viceroy's prolonged silence was increasingly noticed and regarded as unhelpful. Parliamentary opinion, the article continued, was most impatient of this attitude and held that unless the legislatures in the Congress Provinces were summoned officialdom would incur some share of the responsibility for any further deterioration in the situation. Those anxious to give vitality to parliamentary institutions should not flout a demand that the legislatures should be summoned.

Thus the *Statesman*. The message purported to come from Reuters. Reuters denied this. The Viceroy found that the evidence suggested that the message was sent from the *Statesman*'s London Office and inspired by its editor, Arthur Moore. Linlithgow met Moore, an impulsive Irishman, from time to time and always read his leading articles with care. But he thought him markedly short of ability and extremely slap-dash and impetuous in his methods. The article in question might, Linlithgow told Zetland, have very embarrassing reactions. If it really had been sent by Moore this would justify strong pressure on the board of the *Statesman* in London to bring him under control.

Zetland told Linlithgow that Moore was indeed the author of the article and had, when interviewed, seemed satisfied that he was well informed. He was disabused. The Secretary of State himself saw Moore just before the latter's return to India and found it difficult to understand his mind. When Zetland said that Parliament would not modify the safeguards Moore replied, 'Indeed I should hope not!' His efforts to explain his ambivalence

English-owned, under the control of a board in London of which Lord Catto was chairman.

suggested to Zetland's mind that Moore possessed singularly little
understanding of the mentality of the average Congressman.
His doubts as to Moore's judgment were confirmed when the
editor solemnly told him that he believed that with tactful
handling Jawaharlal Nehru could be led into the co-operation
fold. Zetland hoped, not in vain, for the support of Lord Catto,
Chairman of the *Statesman*'s board, in dealing with Moore.

The *Statesman*'s broadside coincided with a debate on India in
the House of Lords on 6th May, 1937. Lord Snell led for the
Labour Opposition. His speech was critical but temperate. The
deadlock seemed to him to be due for the most part to a clash in
temperament rather than to substantial material barriers. He felt
the time had come when they should ask both sides to make
another effort to agree. Let His Majesty's Government remove
any misapprehension which might exist. For instance, Mr Gandhi
seemed surprised that the Government of India and the India
Office did not see his words as he himself saw them. The Government should give an assurance that the reserved powers of the
Governors would not be used unnecessarily. To the Indian
leaders he appealed not to lead their people into the wilderness of
barren negotiation.

Zetland, replying to Snell, set out the case for the Viceroy's
policy clearly and with conviction. The diehards, too, made their
case, Lord Lloyd warning against any interview with Gandhi: in
the past these interviews had not been conducive to good relations
or good results.

Linlithgow wrote to Zetland that he was encouraged by the
debate as well as by the Secretary of State's report of a Cabinet
discussion of his policy. To the diehards he made a telling reference: 'Don't forget to remind them, if I get into trouble, that they
all supported provincial autonomy! And if you think it worth
while you may add, with my compliments, that the only ray of
sunlight on my horizon is the Federation that they conspired to
destroy.'

In the light of the Lords' debate Linlithgow again pondered the
question of inviting Gandhi for a talk. Again he decided this was

not the moment and again he was backed up in his view by all his advisers and the Governors without exception. Of course he recognised the value of personal contact with the Mahatma, whom he had not yet met. But he felt strongly that a failure following either an interview or even an invitation to an interview would be gravely embarrassing at this stage. He himself would have nothing to offer except explanation. On the issue of prestige his mind was clear. 'As you know,' he told Zetland, 'I am moved by considerations of prestige only where I think that of any political importance. But I cannot altogether eliminate the political importance of the prestige element and the risk of a rebuff, or an embarrassing breakdown, in this case.' There was another point to which he also gave weight. He did not want an invitation to be so timed as to make it appear that he accepted the claim of Congress to be an organisation parallel to Government and entitled to negotiate on behalf of India as a whole. As well as the minorities and the Princes, he must consider the effect of any action by him on the morale of the services and of the more conservative elements in India. He would, he said, attach little importance to these anxieties if a request for a talk came from Congress; they knew that the door was open.

The Viceroy's decision to stand firm remained unshaken. Nevertheless he thought that there were three contributions which could now be made from his end. First, Governors could intensify their efforts to keep or make contact with Congress leaders in the Provinces. Secondly, Governors could make further speeches repeating assurances and explanations. Thirdly, he himself might make a statement before the meeting of the legislatures. The Viceroy could not be sure that such an action would break the deadlock but he thought the time had come to make such a move. Obviously Congress would feel under increasing pressure to take office as the time approached for the legislatures to meet. In the event of a breakdown Linlithgow was ready for the consequences but he was under no illusions as to how serious they might be. They must be prepared to face a crisis of the gravest nature. If the authority of Governors were to be challenged it would be necessary to act with the utmost promptness and resolution. He had been reviewing the powers which could be employed in such an emergency and had found the various Provinces unequally armed. Indeed no Province was fully armed with all the powers which could and should be employed to crush a really dangerous attempt to overthrow the constitution. An Ordinance had therefore been drafted embodying all the powers which could be effective against a revolutionary movement. It would have to be issued by each Governor separately.

There were signs that Congress was becoming uneasy. The Congress President (Nehru) launched a strenuous propaganda campaign to break the solidarity of the Muslims by efforts to induce the left wing of the Muslim League to join Congress. It merely led to acrimonious controversy and an increase of communal tension. Communal riots broke out in the United Provinces, Bihar, Sind and the Punjab. Next Rajagopalachari came to Erskine with a change of formula. He proposed that, in the event of disagreement with ministers, a Governor should ask for their resignation. Erskine's correct reaction was that this was exactly the same as their dismissal and was unacceptable. What Congress wanted, of course, was a state of affairs where responsibility for the fall of a Ministry must always be seen to be the Governor's and never his Chief Minister's.

It will be seen from these events how surely Congress was poisoning the atmosphere against Federation – particularly by tactics which were absolutely certain to worry the Muslims as well as the Princes. The Viceroy had been working on the possibility of some concessions to the Princes in such matters as customs duties. Zetland thought he was in danger of committing himself to concessions which departed too far from the federal ideal. 'I have,' wrote the Secretary of State, 'the uncomfortable feeling that the market is at present against us. We appear to be dealing with unwilling sellers and are tempted to put our offers high in consequence. But so far as I can judge the States are unwilling to commit themselves until the political and financial future in British India is clearer. If they come to see that they will be safer inside the Federation than out of it – and otherwise the Federation cannot come into existence – then we shall be dealing with people who *must* sell and shall be able to make a better bargain . . . I am naturally as desirous as you to see the early establishment of the Federation, but I am most anxious that we should avoid imposing unnecessary burdens upon its resources from the outset . . .'

At the same time Zetland disagreed with a proposal of Linlithgow's to extend the life of the present Assembly. This might, he thought, lead to further extensions which would be difficult to justify. It might also lead to fresh elections, which might be more embarrassing than if they were held that autumn. He was aware that autumn elections would signify an admission that Federation was not now expected for some time – say two years from next January. But could they, he asked, as matters then stood, frankly anticipate that Federation was a probability within twelve or even eighteen months of January, 1938?

Linlithgow appreciated these arguments but he saw no possibility of autumn elections proving favourable to Government. He also thought that such timing would have a bad psychological effect on Federation, although he agreed that the delay in achieving it was now likely to be longer than they could wish.

7

At the beginning of June, 1937, Gandhi made a speech in which he professed himself very anxious that Congress should take office but only if the Government showed a willingness to conciliate Congress. The only obstacle he could see was the Congress demand that a Governor should dismiss his ministers in the event of serious disagreement. He said he would be satisfied if the Governor were to demand resignation (i.e. Rajagopalachari's formula). Zetland rejected Gandhi's demand. Governor and ministers might well disagree on one issue but be willing to carry on with the rest of the programme. A Governor could dismiss his ministers or ministers could resign, but the latter choice must be theirs.

Zetland's views were in line with Linlithgow's. To the Viceroy the very basis of the Act was the assumption of co-operation between Ministers and Government and the avoidance if possible of occasions of difficulty. He was aiming at a convention that the use of special responsibilities ought not necessarily to involve demission of office, although naturally the possibility could not be eliminated.

The situation was beginning to develop. The fundamental objection of Congress to the Constitution had been in no way weakened by recent events, but it was evident that there were Congressmen eager to take office. Congress's original demands in the matter of the special powers had been modified, if only very slightly. Suggestions were being made in some Congress speeches that the great need was for proof of British friendliness. Governors were doing their best to respond.

It was thought by some that the legislatures should be summoned within the next two months as the situation might otherwise deteriorate. This was the view of *The Times* of 11th June, expressed in an article by their Simla correspondent. He also stressed the merits of the prolonged silence of the Viceroy which, as we have seen, was strongly criticised in certain quarters. 'Much has been explained since the problem arose, and earlier intervention by the Viceroy might have done little to ease the situation and possibly much to complicate it.' But he added: 'that is no longer true, and Indian opinion now clearly looks to Simla for some authoritative action that will bring the issue to a climax.'

Meanwhile Rajagopalachari was having another tilt at Erskine. He said that Gandhi was only asking for dismissal of a ministry in a vital crisis. Congress had to make this condition in order to control their extreme left. If there could be some understanding arrived at, the Congress leaders could appeal to the honour of their followers to carry it out. The British Government, he pointed out, did not seem to realise that Gandhi was holding out an olive branch. If he was met on this matter he would agree to working his constitution normally and would not countenance petty tactics. Here was the chance to get rid of the civil disobedience mentality for good. Congress would not take office unless some agreement with Gandhi was reached. He alone could control Congress.

Zetland was unimpressed by all this. The hope of getting rid of the civil disobedience mentality he described as 'optimism run mad.' He suspected that Gandhi (who was, he thought, behaving like a 'saintly old sinner and humbug') was trying to trick either the Government or Congress itself in order to prevent a split in the Congress ranks. 'And to what end? . . . I can see no other end than to have his forces united when he considers that the moment has arrived for dropping the mask and launching a grand offensive against the British connection. Perhaps you will think all this the jaundiced view of one who has never been able to reconcile the claim of the little man to be the fountain head of righteousness with the tortuous cunning of his ways.'

*

The Viceroy for his part was concentrating less upon personalities

than upon the necessity to get Congress to accept office without
destroying the Act at the outset. He now drafted the statement he
intended to make in a direct attempt to break the impasse. He
would broadcast a message of friendship first and follow it
immediately with the statement. He gave his broadcast message
on the 21st June. In it he appealed for goodwill and stressed the
effects of interrupting the momentum of progressive political
reform. He referred to his experience with the Agricultural
Commission ten years ago. Here, he said, he had gained new
understanding of India's political problems from the Indian point
of view. 'This experience had brought about, I may truthfully
tell you, a profound change in my own outlook and opinions.'
The British were proud of their own patriotism, love of liberty
and liberal institutions of government, 'so it has seemed to me
that my countrymen should regard the growth in India of those
same qualities and aspirations, not as a matter for anxiety or dis-
quiet, but rather as an occasion for pride and as a call upon them
for their understanding sympathy and their ready help . . .' The
great aim, he reminded his all-India listeners, was to establish in a
unified India representative and responsible government.

The Viceroy's printed statement was issued next day. He went
in detail into the constitutional conflict, showing how Ministers
would work with Governors, and explaining the point of the
special powers and their bearing on resignation or dismissal of a
ministry. At the end he said he realised that for some people the
plan did not go far enough in the direction of self-government.
He gave the assurance that, in his best judgment and given goodwill on all sides, the Constitution would work and work well.
Then followed some words of deep significance:

'I am convinced that the shortest road to that fuller political life
which many of you so greatly desire is to accept this Constitution and
to work for it for all it is worth. Of their nature, politics are ever
dynamic, and to imagine that their expression in terms of a written
Constitution can render them static would be utterly to disregard the
lessons of history and indeed the dictates of common sense.'

He could not have hinted more strongly that this was the right

road to complete independence. On the practical side he proclaimed his conviction that the Constitution offered immense
opportunities for public service and that in its working lay the
best hope for improving the conditions of the rural population
and the poor.

Linlithgow was aware that his intervention might not achieve
what he wanted, but he felt hopeful that his timing was right.
He told Zetland that, having entered the arena, he did not
propose to make repeated appearances. He would be content to
deliver his message and retire again to a silence which had proved
a useful weapon in the last two or three months. He added: 'But
we are dealing with personalities whose reactions are frankly
incalculable, and one can do no more than make one's own
position clear beyond any question and hold steadily to the course
which has been set.'

*

Press reaction to the Viceroy's statement of 22nd June was all that
could be desired with the exception of the *Hindustan Times*, which
said that there could be no compromise of any sort. The paper
hoped that Congress would tell Government that if there was a
breakdown now the country must face the consequences (i.e.
civil disobedience). Gandhi's son Devadas was the acting editor
and it was thought that the article might be the result of pique
over the Viceroy's refusal to invite Gandhi to see him. In spite of
the favourable Press response Linlithgow could not be sure how
Congress would decide at its forthcoming meeting on 5th July.
But he believed that a refusal would strain party loyalties to the
limit.

On 28th June Zetland wrote to the Viceroy that it seemed
possible that Congress would not accept on the ground that
Government refused to meet them on a small matter. In that
event Government would be heavily criticised in Great Britain
and he would be under considerable pressure from Lothian,
Halifax and like-minded Ministers in Cabinet. He himself was
very conscious of the fact that this was a turning point. If the

decision was against co-operation the left wing would carry the bulk of the Congress with them. If Congress did co-operate the gulf between Britain and nationalist India would diminish because Indians would become absorbed in administration. When so much turned on the question of dismissal versus resignation was it right to be rigid?

'Gandhi's latest formula as I understand it,' wrote Zetland, 'is that he would be satisfied if we agreed that the Governors should dismiss their Ministers only if the disagreement was of a serious character. If this meant that the matter over which the disagreement arose was one of really first class importance, it might be possible for us to consider meeting them . . . ?'

Linlithgow was aghast at the letter's contents. He received it on 6th July, at the very moment when Congress were making their decision. He had made up his mind that he could not agree to any arrangement with Congress which could be seen as being made at the expense of the minorities. He had thought his Secretary of State completely supported him. Now, at this very moment, he found that Zetland was contemplating what he felt would amount to a stab in the back. He wired at once that if he was ordered to yield he would resign. Within hours of his sending his telegram Congress agreed to accept office unconditionally.

Zetland wrote on 7th July to say that Linlithgow must have read into his letter more than was intended – 'I should hate to leave you under the impression that I was prepared even to contemplate a set of circumstances which would make your position impossible.' He had only been letting Linlithgow know the trend of opinion and was thinking aloud to help the Viceroy. He was at a loss to know why Linlithgow was so greatly disturbed. If there had been any question of resignation he would cheerfully have resigned too. Zetland added that when thinking aloud on paper in future he would try to make it clear that his thoughts were not decisions or instructions but merely invitations for Linlithgow to match his thoughts with Zetland's own.

*

On 12th July Zetland wrote his congratulations to the Viceroy on Congress's decision which, he said, had been due in large measure to Linlithgow's patience and restraint followed, when the psychological moment arrived, by his message to the peoples of India. Linlithgow wrote back on 28th July and explained why he had been so shocked by Zetland's earlier letter. 'What was my position?' he asked. 'I had made it abundantly clear to you that in my view we ought not to give way upon any single point . . . and you in your turn having taken this matter before the Cabinet, were able to assure me of their support. Next we put together, you and I, the Section 93 Proclamation and the Ordinance, and we corresponded with Governors on the basis of the immediate passing into force of Section 93 in the event of Congress refusing office. Then came my statement in which I made it very clear that there could be no concessions, and that we could not go beyond your speeches and those of Governors . . . Congress knew exactly where they stood, and the minorities and parties other than Congress were at once steadied and pleased by the knowledge that we proposed to give nothing away . . . I had had no hint from you that you were apprehensive of any difficulty in the Cabinet or that, if a break became imminent, Cabinet might wish to reconsider the whole position . . . I felt then, and I feel with equal conviction now, that the least sign of weakness on our part . . . would have brought the whole psychological position which we had so carefully built up tumbling about our ears. Such was the position and such my attitude of mind when, at the very last and most critical moment, I got your letter of June 28th in which for the first time you told me that in your opinion Cabinet might take the view that they were not prepared to face a break with Congress upon the issue of dismissal versus resignation . . . I can only repeat here what I told you in my private telegram, that had Congress refused office on the terms laid down in my statement and had Cabinet decided in the sense indicated, I should have been bound to regard my position here as no longer possible.'

That could reasonably have been all there was to be said, but

Linlithgow had not quite finished. He ended generously: 'I for my part am anxious to drive ahead with the work in hand, with my confidence in my Secretary of State strengthened (if indeed that were possible) by the recollection of a good fight fought together to a highly successful conclusion.'

*

Let us now see what had happened on the other side of the hill. Reliable information reached the Viceroy from a source which had been in intimate touch with all those who were present at the vital meeting. Never had a statement from official quarters had such an effect on Congress as that created by the Viceroy's statement of 22nd June. There was criticism on a few points of detail, but the sincerity of the whole and the friendliness of the Viceroy's approach to Congress were universally acknowledged. Evidently members of the Working Committee of Congress and the provincial leaders were anxious not to provoke a clash for the present. Gandhi, it was thought, had some hope of achieving complete independence through working the Constitution although he hardly accepted this and was prepared for an unconstitutional movement whenever he saw fit. Of the other leaders the majority regarded a breakdown, followed by unconstitutional activity, as inevitable. But they agreed that Congress should show itself capable of governing the country for a year or two and then they would take stock of the position. Bhulabai Desai strongly advocated acceptance; he had gathered the impression on a recent visit to England that there would be more support there for Congress when the breakdown eventually occurred if they had meanwhile accepted office. This overwhelming feeling in favour of acceptance had been drilled into Gandhi before the meeting and the Mahatma then brought Nehru into line to the extent of persuading him to remain silent during the proceedings. The left wing hardly raised its voice at all.

It had been a triumph for the Viceroy. His judgment had been completely vindicated. Above all he had kept his nerve throughout the long ordeal. Lady Linlithgow wrote home in September,

'His stock is ever soaring and he remains calm and unmoved through all – he is never really free from worry of some kind or another.'[1]

[1] For instance, Waziristan had now developed into an extensive campaign with 25,000 troops employed.

8

Although the family had settled down by the summer of 1937, the Vicereine herself was still far from well. But her letters were full of spirit. She described with gusto the finding of a deadly Russell's Viper in the garden. An A.D.C. dispatched it with a curved sword snatched from the hall. Herself a brilliant painter of flowers, she was cheered up by the beauty of the Simla sunsets:

'The hills every colour – those nearest a dirty green, the near distance sepia, the far distance indigo blue with black shadows, and beyond the last range of hills you can see the plain 120 miles away pale cobalt blue and pinky mauve seared with silver bands which are the rivers in flood. And then the sky quite indescribable – last night the horizon was very pale green with fluffy clouds edged in gold, and then through all the colours of the rainbow to vivid orange and flame – All this with drifts of mist cupped in the hollows completes a picture which no artist could paint – Turner would have made the best job of it.'

The Viceroy had developed a new hobby during this summer. While camping in the hills with one of his daughters he saw, among other beautiful things, what she described as 'a navy-blue butterfly with a pink bottom.' This inspired him to give instructions for the assembling of all the gear necessary for butterfly hunting. He enlisted into the game the detectives whose duty it was to watch over his safety on his rambles in the hills. Each of them was supplied with a butterfly net and killing bottle, and they greatly enjoyed this rather surprising addition to their routine.

Two or three times a year the Viceroy would get away to the jungles of the Himalayan foothills for ten days or so. He was never happier than on these holidays with his family. He was a very good game shot and fisherman. He shot a few tigers because he had to, but he preferred his camera to his rifle where tigers were concerned.

His invariable companion on his jungle holidays was the remarkable Jim Corbett.[1] Corbett had worked on the railways in India as a young man. He lived in the Kumaon Himalaya and it was in this neighbourhood that he would often arrange a camp for the Viceroy. Corbett knew hundreds of square miles of jungle intimately and was famous as a killer of man-eating tigers. He became a great friend of Linlithgow and the whole family, who spent many unforgettable holidays under his guidance.

The jungle provided the perfect environment for the Viceroy, who loved to relax among its beautiful birds, animals and trees. The elephants, which provided the normal method of progress, always enchanted him with their ways, particularly their ability to find a shot partridge or quail in the dense grass and retrieve it with their trunks, handing it to the mahout over their heads.

The evenings in camp were delightful, with dinner in a large tent by the light of oil lamps. As often as not the Viceroy would have to work after dinner on papers brought in by dispatch rider during the day, and even on his jungle holidays he was closely guarded, a detachment of infantry being invisibly camped nearby.

Linlithgow enjoyed fishing as much as any sport. There were trout in the hill streams and mahseer (of the carp family) could be caught in the large rivers lower down. He once had an unlucky experience in the state of Mysore. One of his sons had arrived there on the day before his father was due and was shown the pool where a huge mahseer had been seen. He persuaded his reluctant host to let him fish there, feeling it was highly unlikely that he would catch the one fish intended for the Viceroy and knowing also that he was by no means the skilful fisherman his father was. By chance he struck with his very first cast and a

[1] Author of *Maneaters of Kumaon*, etc.

monster of seventy-six lbs was landed. 'You bloody boy, you've caught my fish,' was Linlithgow's laconic reaction to the news next morning, but he greatly enjoyed the incident. He himself had to be content with a fish of a mere fifteen lbs. There was, however, compensation; the fish disgorged a live turtle which the Viceroy took home, put in a tank and named Jonah. Jonah became quite tame and was kept in the Viceroy's room. He was still flourishing when the family left India.

In late July the Viceroy's monsoon tour took him to the Province of Assam. He went up the river Brahmaputra by boat as far as its junction with the Ganges. Scanning the shore – far distant at this point – with a telescope, he suddenly announced that he had seen a pink elephant working in a clearing. This bold claim, even by an abstemious man after a cup of coffee, was naturally disbelieved but he stuck to it. Having ordered the boat to put in at the next village he sent a reconnaissance party back along the bank. Sure enough they returned with the elephant and its proud owner. It was an albino of a definitely pink hue.

The journey to Shillong, the capital of the Province, was completed by car through magnificent jungle scenery. The Viceroy found the Governor, Sir Robert Reid, in good form and the position in Assam satisfactory. But he noted that rhinoceros had greatly increased and were breaking out of the game reserve there and damaging crops in the neighbouring countryside.

*

During this tour Linlithgow had been weighing up the question of sending for Gandhi. On the return journey he decided that the moment had come and he wrote to the Mahatma inviting him to New Delhi. Gandhi accepted and the first meeting between the two men took place on 4th August. Linlithgow wrote to the King:

'The interview was friendly in tone and its effect throughout India has been very useful in that it has contributed to the improvement of the political atmosphere and has tended to consolidate the good impression made by the decision of Congress to take office. I thought

Mr Gandhi attractive and extremely shrewd. He is courteous in his approach and frank in his expression of opinion, but I judge him to be implacable in his hostility to British rule in India, to the destruction of which he has dedicated every fibre of his mind.'

Their talk lasted for an hour and a half. It marked the beginning of a relationship of mutual respect and affection which was to last until it was eroded by war and then broken in the vortex of rebellion five years later.

Linlithgow never underestimated Gandhi's political ability. In his dealings with the Mahatma he saw more of this than of his saintly qualities. In fact Gandhi sent a refreshingly human reply to the Viceroy's invitation to their first talk. He wrote that he had in any case been intending to seek an interview on the question of the banning of Abdul Gaffhar Khan, a Muslim Congressman, from the North West Frontier Province. It was purely a formula to save face but none the worse for that, and Linlithgow would always have preferred humanity with all its weakness to saintliness in the matter of negotiation.

The Viceroy sent a detailed account of the interview to Zetland. Gandhi had first talked of the past, including the Indian Mutiny of 1857, and was inclined to be bitter about it. The Viceroy then did his utmost to dissuade him from his policy of forbidding official contact between members of Congress and the British. He failed to move him. He told Gandhi that, although he disagreed strongly with his policy on this point, he did not hold it against him personally. Gandhi replied in the same spirit but said that the dominant consideration with him was his apprehension of imperialism. Linlithgow warned him of the possibly un-favourable effect of his policy on British public opinion, which wanted to be friendly and fair to India. Gandhi took the point but would not yield.

They discussed Nehru. Gandhi praised him. He said that there was no gulf between them although he agreed that Nehru might fall short of the ideal in his advocacy of violence to achieve the just society. He had told Nehru that he ought to accept an invitation to meet the Viceroy but he was doubtful whether his advice would be taken because Nehru regarded the Viceroy as the leading instrument of imperialism in India.

Linlithgow thought that Gandhi was genuinely gratified by this invitation to meet him and said he could not have been more friendly or agreeable personally even though he was adamant about official contacts. He appeared to be in good health, he was mentally alert and his sense of humour was very keen: it was impossible not to be impressed by his general quality.

As to Gandhi's assessment of the Viceroy, Linlithgow thought that he had puzzled the Mahatma, but 'in that,' he noted, 'I have already been undeceived, for I have it on indisputable authority that he reported himself as having been up against one more conservative mind, very sure of all its bearings and in no way open to the weakness of receptivity.' Gandhi was later to qualify this first estimate with a tribute to Linlithgow's readiness to listen, which he thought greater than that of any other Viceroy with whom he had had to deal – even though he believed (wrongly) that his mind had always been made up before the listening took place. Linlithgow's infinite capacity for listening struck all who came in contact with him. There was no trick about it; he was a good listener because he wanted to hear.

*

The crisis with Congress had not deflected the Viceroy from the underlying problems of Federation. His correspondence with Zetland shows an undiminished sense of urgency. On 27th May he wrote: 'The more I reflect upon the political situation as a whole, the more impressed I am by the importance of achieving Federation as early as possible.'

The fact was that the Princes' fears were hardening. For one thing, Congress agitation in the States was increasing significantly. For another, some of the larger States whose accession to Federation was vital, were showing mounting anxiety lest, in the event of accession, their revenues should be forfeit to the federal Treasury. The Viceroy would have liked the Act amended to take account of their fears and to reserve certain excise duties to the States' Governments but the Prime Minister (Neville Chamberlain) was unwilling to contemplate a controversial measure which would be likely to revive divisions in the Conservative Party. Eventually the Viceroy's view prevailed but by then war had broken out and the issue was only of academic interest.

In November, 1937, Lord Lothian arrived in India for a long visit. He had seen Nehru and reported him as wholeheartedly opposed to Federation. Nehru said he would do everything possible to prevent it. He would not contemplate the responsibility of forming a government at the centre when most of the centre's revenue would be reserved for defence, leaving no money for carrying out reforms to which Congress was pledged: nor would he accept participation by the States in Government unless they adopted representative institutions. Lothian thought Congress might force a crisis over Federation.

Linlithgow was more optimistic. He felt that if he could keep Congress in office for another year they would not refuse to join the Federation. Nevertheless he saw the effects of Congress intransigence on the Muslims, who had now decided that if they were to hold their ground they must intensify their organisation of an effective opposition to the Hindu elements in Congress. He thought Congress had played their hand badly in several ways. For instance, they had tried to make the Hindu song *Bande Mataram* the national anthem of India. They wanted the Congress flag to be the national flag and they wanted to substitute Hindi for Urdu. There were other moves which the Muslims were bound to regard as pinpricks or worse. The Viceroy had not at this stage accepted that Congress was deliberately trying to sabotage Federation by its attitude to the Muslims but there can be no doubt, in the light of subsequent history, that the chances of a united sub-continent emerging as the prize of India's independence were receding as a result of Congress action.

*

How far this was in fact deliberate at that moment it is not easy, even in retrospect, to say. Nehru, as we know, was quite open in his opposition to Federation. He went so far, on a tour of North and North-West India in October, as to emphasise that the ultimate aim of Congress was the overthrow of the present Constitution and its replacement by one based on severance of the British connection. Significantly he forecast that a European war was inevitable and stressed the opportunity it would give to Congress to fight for independence. The most important aspect of the struggle, he declared, was not the acceptance of office but the organising of the masses and the instilling of 'mass revolutionary mentality' into them. Of equal importance was the recruiting of Muslims into the ranks of Congress.

Gandhi's position was not so clear, but it was certainly nothing like as extreme as that of Nehru. The Viceroy had an interesting talk with Birla, who came to see him in early December. Birla told him that Gandhi had personally cancelled a proposal that Congress Ministries should resign if Federation was implemented. The Mahatma shared the objections stated by Nehru to Lord Lothian. According to Birla, however, the Mahatma would not oppose Federation because of his objection to the States' position. He was more worried about the reservation of defence and external affairs. He wanted an assurance that essentially these two subjects would cease to be reserved to the centre. Linlithgow could only tell Birla that he would certainly want his federal Cabinet to advise him upon them.

Birla gave the Viceroy an encouraging account of his own views. He said he now recognised that the safeguards were essential for the present working of the Constitution and that Congress Ministers needed a prolonged period of political education in office during which they would need the patience and support of the Viceroy. Linlithgow replied that they would have that support provided that order was kept, otherwise he and the Governors would be bound to intervene.

Birla then said that Federation ought to be brought in without delay. Gandhi was ill and had been ordered three months' rest, but while he was alive he could make it possible to secure Federation even though Nehru was absolutely opposed to it for largely theoretical reasons. Birla's approach to the situation at this stage was that of an intelligent man with practical experience of affairs. As is so often the case with such men he did not speak for the politicians.

Linlithgow had followed up his meeting with Gandhi by inviting other Congress leaders and representatives of the Muslims to see him. He also invited leaders of the European community.

From Congress he asked Bhulabai Desai and Satyamurti (Deputy Speaker of the Assembly). Desai was not violently hostile to Federation although he felt that with external affairs and defence reserved to the centre there would be too small a field of activity left to the Federal Legislature. Like Birla he wanted Federation as soon as possible and he favoured a Federation of British India which the States could join when further developed politically. Linlithgow thought that this process, however sound in theory, might be too slow to be safe. The unity of India, he told Desai, was 'a very brittle thing' and he suggested that, all things considered (including opinion in Great Britain) the federal clauses of the Act of 1935 represented about the best scheme which had any chance of implementation in the near future. As for external affairs and defence the Viceroy repeated his assurance that he would take his Cabinet into his confidence over these subjects.

Linlithgow raised the question of the long-term aims of Congress – twenty, thirty or perhaps fifty years ahead. Did Desai think they would want to remain in the Commonwealth? They would be entitled to leave it if they wanted to. Desai said they would want to remain in.

The interview with Satyamurti was equally friendly. His objections to the federal proposals were the same as Desai's, as was his suggested solution. Again the Viceroy replied that any long process would threaten the unity of India. Was Satyamurti aware, he asked, of the strong movement of thought in the Punjab towards a federation of the north-west? Satyamurti blamed the system of communal electorates for this and told

Linlithgow that he would earn India's gratitude if he could do away with them. Linlithgow asked how this would be received in Bengal (where the Hindus were in a minority). Satyamurti saw the point. At the end of the interview he assured the Viceroy that, whether they agreed with him or not, Congress had high regard for him personally and he invoked a blessing upon the Viceroy's labours.

For the Muslims came Mohammed Ali Jinnah, President of the Muslim League, and Muhammad Yakub. Linlithgow admired Jinnah's cleverness but he was never to like him as he liked Gandhi, whose warmth Jinnah lacked. When he first met him the Viceroy did not foresee the hold which he would eventually have over the Muslims. 'I do not frankly feel any deep confidence in him,' he wrote, 'and I suspect that he is one of those political leaders who can play a personal hand but no other, and whose permanent control on the allegiance of their followers is frequently open to question.'

Jinnah took the line at their first interview that insufficient attention was paid to the Muslims and that there was a real risk of their being driven into the arms of Congress. More trouble should be taken in dealing with them both outside and inside the Legislature. Linlithgow thought there was something in this as far as the Legislature was concerned and that the government front bench had not made enough use of minority groups there.

Jinnah did not on this occasion come out unequivocally against Federation. Like the Hindu leaders whom the Viceroy had seen he thought they should start with a federated British India. The States could be admitted provided their representatives were elected on a wide franchise and on a basis of popular institutions.

Jinnah complained with some bitterness that Linlithgow had been unwise to see Gandhi as by doing so he had greatly raised the stock of Congress and thereby set back the prospects of the Muslims. Linlithgow let Jinnah do most of the talking and made little comment himself; for him this first meeting between them was a reconnaissance.

It was not many weeks later that the Muslim League held the meeting which caused the Viceroy to step up so strongly the tone of his warnings to Zetland. At this meeting Jinnah launched into a strong indictment of Congress for pursuing an exclusively Hindu policy which would result in chaos, bitterness, communal war and the strengthening of the imperial hold over India. The Muslims, said Jinnah, could expect neither justice nor fair play under Congress government and no settlement between them was possible.

At the same meeting Sikandar made what Linlithgow called a surprising and important move. He announced his decision to advise all Muslim members of his Unionist Party in the Punjab to join the Muslim League. The Premier of Bengal, Fazlul Huq, issued a statement in similar terms to the Muslims of Bengal.

The meeting also passed a resolution condemning the federal scheme and adopting independence as the ultimate aim of the League. It had been a real success for Jinnah. The League had undoubtedly gained significant strength and would now make rapid strides in extending its organisation. The Premiers of the Punjab and Bengal had clearly had their hands forced by Jinnah into decisions which, governing as each of them was with a Coalition Ministry, they must have taken with great reluctance. Communal bitterness was bound to be accentuated. There was immediate uneasiness among the Sikhs and Hindus in the Punjab over Sikandar's declaration.

*

For the rest, Congress had once again boycotted the Viceroy's annual address to the Legislature. Again this did not worry him although it did surprise him in the light of the acceptance by Congress leaders of his invitation to meet him. As before, there was known to be a division of opinion on tactics in the Congress Party, in which the decision to boycott was not widely approved. Linlithgow's speech announced that the present extension of the Assembly's life would end in October, 1938. This was interpreted as meaning Federation was nearer than had been thought. On the day following the Viceroy's speech (15th September, 1937) *The Times* correspondent in India noted the growing recognition of Linlithgow's deep concern for the fundamental problems of India. 'It is true to say,' he wrote, 'that at no time since his arrival in the country has the Viceroy's prestige been so high.'

An encouraging event meanwhile was the inauguration of the Federal Court on 1st October. Its jurisdiction was confined for the present to disputes between Provinces and on the appellate side to appeals from Provincial High Courts involving constitutional issues.

Apart from certain worries, such as a hunger-strike among prisoners in the Andaman Islands, the Viceroy was able to report that provincial Governments were settling down and there were signs that experience of administration was having a sobering effect. Congress Ministers were on the whole doing their best to check the tendency of some of their followers 'to do precisely as they please, including putting their tongues out at district officers and trying to bully the public,' as the Viceroy described it in a letter to the King (30th November).

In the same letter Linlithgow described a meeting of the All India Congress Committee held at Calcutta in November. There was a struggle between the two wings of the movement. Gandhi and the moderates were successful in protecting Congress Ministries in the Provinces from any too drastic criticism or interference by the centre; while Nehru, President of the Congress, who led the left in an attempt to strengthen the grip of the Working Committee over provincial Congress ministries, though defeated on his main objective, succeeded by some judicious propaganda in the press in saving his own face and in masking in some degree the fact of his discomfiture.

The Viceroy also referred to the question of the release of political prisoners. Gandhi had persuaded the Bengal Government to release many of them. The Governor had not felt called upon to intervene as he did not consider that these releases were a serious threat to the peace and tranquillity of the Province (the criterion for intervention laid down by the Act). Linlithgow

recognised that the releases would put a heavy burden on the
police but he thought it had to be recognised that no democratic
government could be expected for long to carry responsibility
for the forcible detention of a large number of persons not convicted of crime in the ordinary courts of the land. They must
hope that the lowering of political tension which had followed
the introduction of provincial autonomy might serve to direct
into constitutional channels the activities of those classes which in
the past had supplied the terrorist movement with recruits.

*

The Viceroy described his first visit to Lahore, capital of the
Punjab, in October.

'Walking and riding, we made our way through the glorious
scenery of the Kulu Valley to Mandi State, and thence to Lahore. This
being my first visit to Lahore since assuming charge of office, I entered
the city in State, and the next day held a durbar attended with all the
ceremony that ancient custom prescribes. Both occasions, and indeed
the whole visit, proved a great success. The crowds in the streets were
impressively large and very friendly, and wherever we went we were
given a very warm and courteous reception . . .

'I presented new colours to the 3rd Battalion, 17th Dogra Regiment.
Even the fact of a high wind and dust storm could not mar the very
high level of the drill of this regiment, the standard of which I can best
convey to Your Majesty by telling you that even with the assistance of
two ex-Adjutants of the Brigade of Guards who happen to be on my
staff, I was entirely unable to fault their performance on any single
point.'

The Viceroy and his family returned to New Delhi for a few
days and then set off for the State of Bikaner for the Maharaja's
Golden Jubilee. The Maharaja was a splendid-looking man with
his military bearing and impressive moustache. On arrival the
Viceroy took part in a procession of thirty elephants. His letter to
the King continues the description:

'I was much impressed by the warmth of our reception and by the
manifestation of affection for their Ruler exhibited by the whole

population . . . The State and public buildings and the hospitals in Bikaner are most impressive and do the highest credit to the Ruler's taste and public spirit. His Highness was immensely gratified at Your Majesty's recognition of the occasion of the 50th anniversary of his accession to the Gadi of this State by his promotion to the honorary rank of General . . .

'To touch upon lighter matters, I think you will be amused to hear that he took us out shooting in his high-powered car. When a black buck appears he stamps on the accelerator, takes both hands off the steering wheel and opens fire at the animal with his rifle. It is interesting to speculate as to whether or not he will resume control of the vehicle before it disappears into a thorn thicket at 40 m.p.h. . . .'

The Viceroy also referred to the retirement from Bengal of the Governor, Sir John Anderson, whose support he was sad to lose. Anderson had written him a charming letter of farewell (11th November) in which he had said, 'I realise something of the burden you yourself are carrying but, if I may be permitted to say so, I know of no one else who could carry it.' It was a high compliment indeed from a man whose integrity would never allow him to indulge in gratuitous flattery.

Anderson was succeeded by Lord Brabourne, lately Governor of Bombay. To Bombay came Sir Roger Lumley. It meant much to the Viceroy that there were in these two key places men upon whom he knew he could count (just as he could with Anderson) whether in the testing business of day to day administration or in any emergency that might arise.

Finally came a personal note which meant very much to Linlithgow:

'I hope, all being well, that we may be a united family for New Year's Day. It is almost two years since I have seen my sons and I am much looking forward to their coming out.'

The family was reunited on New Year's Day, 1938. One son had arrived in time for Christmas. The other reached Calcutta on 1st January with Linlithgow's brother Charles Hope and his brother-in-law and sister, Lord and Lady Herbert.

The new arrivals were driven straight from the station to the great maidan or plain where the annual Proclamation Parade was to be inspected by the Viceroy. Their first sight of the Viceroy was of his tall figure riding into view to receive the Royal Salute.[1] He was wearing a black frock coat from which there shone the orders of the Star of India and the Thistle.

His sons had not seen their father for eighteen months and they wondered how they would find him. They were not surprised to find him more tired than when he had left home, nor to hear that he was thought rather stiff and unbending on first acquaintance. One observer noted that, though possessed of a great sense of humour and fun, he hardly had time to let it appear and he took a lot of knowing. Once people knew Linlithgow, however, they found him easy to relax with. He always got up from his chair to greet visitors, including his departmental secretaries at their weekly interviews, with a friendly welcome. Laithwaite never forgot one particular visit of Gandhi's to Viceroy's House. He had to interrupt the proceedings with an urgent message. As he entered the study he was astonished to see the Mahatma perched on his chair with his legs drawn up in the Indian fashion. Gandhi had asked the Viceroy if he would grant him a great favour. The Viceroy, expecting some impossible request, said that he would if he could. Gandhi then asked if he might sit like this as he was tired.

On one occasion the Viceroy gave an interview to one of Lumley's Ministers in the Bombay Government. This man had been imprisoned for some political offence before Linlithgow's time and had escaped through the window of a lavatory, as the Viceroy knew. When he took his leave at the end of their talk the Minister made for the door of the Viceroy's lavatory. 'No, not this time, Minister!' said Linlithgow, directing his visitor to the right exit. The Minister himself reported the incident to the Governor on his return with great delight.

Inside the house at New Delhi one was soon aware of the admirable way in which formality, unavoidable as it was, never

[1] He had bought his large horse from a dealer in England and had it given a course at the zoo before shipment to get it used to elephants.

subdued comfort. There were servants everywhere, sitting at
intervals along every passage. The complete silence in which they
moved – barefoot on thick carpets – unnerved the occasional
guest at first. Lady Linlithgow had made charming the rooms
used by family and guests. In the State rooms, she removed some
infelicitous additions which her predecessor had imposed upon
the architect's design. Her achievement in this field met with the
deep appreciation of Sir Edwin Lutyens himself, who presented
her with a glass goblet inscribed with these words:

> To Her Excellency
> The Marchioness Linlithgow
> Whose Presence dignifies
> Whose sovereign touch repairs the wounds
> Inflicted by mistaken zeal upon
> The Viceroy's House at Delhi
> This goblet is humbly offered
> As a token of gratitude
> By him who has most reason
> To be grateful.
>
> E. L.

Among first impressions of the Viceroy's New Delhi home
none made a stronger impact than the garden. Designed by
Lutyens in Mogul style, it was a paradise of flowers and lotus-leaf
fountains. It was a very large garden and gave full scope to Lady
Linlithgow's skill as a gardener. In the main part she went for
masses of single colours in their different shades. Mixed colours
she used in a little sunken garden at the far end which she made
particularly her own. It was here that she and her husband would
sometimes sit for an hour at tea-time. They could not often be
alone together and they cherished these moments of peace in the
short Indian evening. The only sounds to break the silence were
the twittering of parakeets as they flew over the garden in green
flocks to their roost and sometimes the distant singing of a
bullock-cart driver on his way home at the end of the day's
work.

The Viceroy's working day began at breakfast. For the first year or so he and his wife had breakfast together but pressure of work became so heavy that he eventually had it alone with Laithwaite. The rest of the morning would normally be taken up with interviews. He saw the Minister in charge of each department, also its Secretary, regularly once a week.

Whenever possible lunch was a private family occasion but there were generally two official lunch parties each week. The same applied to dinner. The Viceroy's band played every evening in a room adjoining the dining room. The party always went into dinner to the strains of 'The Roast Beef of Old England' – a custom going back many years. It is a good tune and the family sometimes sang it in rousing chorus when there were no official guests present. No one ever bothered about the words, which are clumsy to a degree; it was the harmony that mattered. The band soon got used to vocal accompaniment.

The official dinner parties were preceded by an impressive introduction. When the guests had assembled and been drawn up in line for presentation, curtains opened at the end of the room to reveal the Viceroy and Vicereine standing side by side. The National Anthem was then played and they came forward to meet the company.

Of State occasions the most splendid was the annual investiture, at which the recipients of honours were invested with them by the Viceroy. The ceremony took place in the Durbar Hall in Viceroy's House, which gave a marvellous effect of mirrors and black marble. Here is the account of an eye-witness:

'We dined at 8 as the Investiture took place at 9.45. Everyone dressed up in their finery, and we took our places in the Durbar Hall to the left of the Throne. The Bodyguard lined the corridors. A fanfare announced Their Excellencies, who processed in, led by the Staff in scarlet and gold uniforms, their trains carried by 4 little Indian Princes. Dressed in pale blue coats, trousers and turbans – jewels flashing from their necks, ears and heads – they looked sweet and very solemn. Hopie looked magnificent in Privy Councillor's uniform over

which he wore the mantle of the Star of India – pale blue velvet.
Doreen in white with a diamond tiara and necklace.

'66 people, English and Indian, men and women, were invested with
their different orders . . . and about 400 people filled the Hall as
spectators. It was impressive and solemn . . . It lasted until 11 p.m.
when the procession re-formed and hand-in-hand Hopie led Doreen
out, to the accompaniment of the National Anthem.'

9

Early in the New Year, 1938, Linlithgow toured Madras and Hyderabad in the south.

In Madras he had a long discussion with Rajagopalachari, who said he fully realised the force of the arguments for Federation but that the Muslims were strongly against it. Congress and the Muslims were, he observed, discussing the question at that moment. As long as these talks were in progress and there was any hope of a favourable outcome Congress could not commit itself to Federation because of possible destructive effects on communal feeling.

The Viceroy reported to Zetland (13th January) that these Hindu–Muslim talks were news to him but he doubted whether they would have any lasting result. He took the opportunity yet again to urge haste upon the Secretary of State:

'I do increasingly feel and would like to put formally on record my own strong feeling that the situation in this matter is deteriorating, and that if we can in any way overcome the difficulties it is of vital importance to us to lose no time . . . I remain entirely unconvinced that the market will improve with delay . . .'

Linlithgow arrived in Hyderabad on 18th January. The State was the largest in India and its ruler was uniquely styled His Exalted Highness the Nizam. The Moslem ruler of a mainly Hindu community, he was in a vulnerable position. The opposition press was doing its best to frighten him and he was extremely sensitive on the question of Federation.

The Viceroy reported to the King that he had established friendly relations with his host. The Nizam's was not a forthcoming personality and it had been an uphill task:

'We dined and lunched with His Exalted Highness sitting between us for a whole week. The labour, Sir, of this was not inconsiderable and I only hope that the fruit thereof may be good.'

The Nizam's wealth had always been a legend. He was reliably reputed to be the richest man in the world with an unequalled collection of jewels which never appeared. He spent money generously on services in the State and helped Britain handsomely in both World Wars, but in lesser respects he was notoriously mean. On the occasion of the Viceroy's visit he was never without an old walking stick which had been broken and bound up with string. This delighted the Viceroy, who, as he said farewell, offered to give him a new stick next time they met. The Nizam appeared to see the joke and smiled slightly.

In his letter of 10th February Linlithgow also described to the King the significant increase of Hindu-Muslim tension over recent months. He wrote that Jinnah had become alarmed by the defection of a growing number of Muslims from the Muslim League to Congress. This was because they were seeing Ministers in a position 'to help their friends and to inconvenience their opponents.' Jinnah's reaction had been to rouse the Muslims with the cry that the growing power of Congress threatened Muslim culture. This was a success and reinvigorated the League.

The Viceroy had seen Sir Tej Bahadur Sapru, leader of the Liberal Party, as soon as he returned to Delhi from Hyderabad. Sapru told him he had warned Lord Lothian, with whom he had recently discussed the situation, that he wanted to democratise the Princes too fast. If action to that end was to be stepped up, the point would be used against government that it had yielded to Congress at the expense of the Princes over a matter on which government had never even asked the Princes to meet it. This would simply have the effect of frightening the Princes off Federation.

Linlithgow asked Sapru whether he thought there was a satisfactory alternative to the scheme of the 1935 Act. Sapru replied that they should stand fast on the Act and the federal plan embodied in it. It was not ideal but at this stage it was the only practical answer and should be implemented with all possible speed.

A few days after Sapru's visit Birla came to see the Viceroy. He thought that Congress was moving towards acceptance of Federation. Gandhi was not over-worried, said Birla, by the reservation of defence and external affairs to the centre, but was concentrating on the method of choosing the States' representatives. Birla wanted the Viceroy to help Gandhi by persuading a number of Princes to move towards democratic election of representatives. Linlithgow asked him if either he or Gandhi had thought of the difficulties. Birla answered that Gandhi did not worry about details but concentrated upon fundamentals:

'I said that no doubt was a splendid position from which to view the world, but unfortunate people situated as I myself am situated who are responsible for working out these schemes . . . were perforce bound to think out in every detail and in all its consequences every proposal of the kind he had in mind.'

The Viceroy particularly wondered whether Gandhi had considered the effect of the suggested action upon the Muslims. They would at once demand that a proportion of the States' seats at the centre be reserved for Muslim candidates. Linlithgow told Birla that insistence on these conditions would probably postpone Federation for twenty years, which might be fatal to an all-India Federation. It would encourage the already strong movement for a Federation of the north-west, comprising the Punjab, Sind, the North-West Frontier Province and the Punjab States. Such a scheme, he warned, was by no means academic. It might interest Birla to know that certain very influential persons in the Punjab had not only declared their preference for this plan but had openly advocated it before a Muslim conference in Lucknow in private session.

Birla said that the communal position in India was getting rapidly worse. Congress was aware of it and its leaders were deeply anxious. He then suggested that the best course might be to let the Muslims have their Federation of the North-West. This astonished Linlithgow, who thought at first that Birla was teasing him. When he saw that the suggestion was serious he asked Birla whether he envisaged the perpetuation of British military power to keep the peace between Muslim and Hindu Federations:

'If so, I recommend him to pursue his reflections a little further. For my part, and having regard to the military power at the disposal of the Muslim Federation, I thought that no more serious danger could be conceived, whether to the future unity of India or to the peaceful evolution of a Hindu confederacy further South.'

Birla then said that the only chance for Federation lay in agreement between Government and Congress and the best hope of this lay in discussion between the Viceroy and Gandhi.

This was a most interesting conversation. It showed clearly Linlithgow's dread of partition and therefore his shock at encouragement for it coming from a Hindu. There was, of course, nothing surprising in the Viceroy's view. For him, as for the raj throughout its rule, the unity of the sub-continent was the crown of British achievement.

In the same month of February, 1938, there occurred the first major constitutional crisis since Congress agreed to take office. It arose over the matter of the political prisoners. The Governors of the United Provinces (Haig) and Bihar (Hallett) had, with the Viceroy's approval, been occupied with their Ministers for many months over the question of their release. A considerable number had already been freed. The Governors insisted upon two provisos: each case must be examined on its merits by Ministers and the Governor together and no release would take place under pressure of hunger strike or any form of organised indiscipline in gaol.

On the eve of their departure for the annual meeting of Congress at Haripura the Chief Ministers of the two Provinces suddenly demanded the immediate release of all political prisoners without individual examination. In Bahir the demand was for release within three hours and in the United Provinces it was almost as abrupt.

Neither Governor felt that wholesale release could be held to constitute a grave menace to the peace and tranquillity of his Province and they referred the matter to the Viceroy. It was clear to Linlithgow that his own special responsibility was involved. He saw that general release of prisoners convicted in the courts of crimes of violence must prejudice gravely the fabric of law and order in India and damage the prestige and morale of the judiciary. He also knew that the objective of Congress was to weaken the Government of Bengal by engineering a drive for the release of 387 'political' prisoners within its jurisdiction. He had to watch, too, the position of the Punjab Government, another coalition to which Congress was hostile. The Viceroy therefore ordered the two Governors to decline the advice of their Ministers. Both Chief Ministers thereupon resigned.

On 22nd February the Viceroy issued a public communiqué. He set out the facts, pointed out the dangers involved and made plain that he was concerned to preserve the principle of discriminating clemency. On their return from the Congress meeting both Ministers withdrew their resignations under instructions from the Congress Working Committee, the Governors having informed them that they were prepared at once to resume individual examination of cases recommended for release.

What had happened at Haripura was, apparently, that the two Chief Ministers were told by Gandhi that they had made a blunder and must get back into office. The incident was a boon to the right wing of Congress. No one talked of anything else so that the attacks planned by the left upon the policies of the moderate element in the Working Committee never matured and Gandhi and his supporters were able to have their way.

The effect of the whole incident had been salutary. Vital principles had been vindicated. Congress had learned for the first time that the Viceroy and the Governors would not hesitate to use their special powers when necessary. Moreover the resignation of two Congress Ministries had failed to disturb the other five – it was known that several of these had made it clear to the Working Committee that they were strongly opposed to resigning in sympathy.

In Bengal, too, the results were good. Gandhi went there some weeks after the crisis and was known to have negotiated the release of political prisoners without pressing for that of convicts.

Linlithgow was relieved at the outcome of a crisis which might have developed into a situation of the utmost gravity. He had felt it would not be easy to present his case to Parliament and the public at home. He knew that he would have been criticised for making an all-India question out of something which, it would have been said, should have been left to the Governors and Ministries concerned.

*

Early in March, 1938, Linlithgow felt for the first time real doubt as to the chances of Federation. He wrote to Zetland that he was increasingly conscious of the great difficulties in the way of success. If they should find themselves confronted with unanimous opposition from the Provinces he did not now feel that even whole-hearted support from the Princes would be enough. The actual position facing the Viceroy appeared to be that the Provinces, the Muslim League and the Princes were all against Federation on the present terms. If this state of affairs remained they would have to come down to bargaining terms:

'Given Gandhi's survival over the next two years, and provided we are able successfully to mobilise that large, but largely silent body of moderate and responsible opinion in British India which understands the strength of the case for comprehensive reform at the Centre upon an all-India basis, I am not without hope that the thing may yet be successfully put through . . . but delay, I repeat, plays every day into the hands of the other side and however little responsibility for it can properly be attributed to either of us, it may well prove that it has already been so great as materially to prejudice our prospects of putting through the existing scheme.'

To add to his worries Linlithgow was faced with two serious problems which were looming up. The first, which had already caused him anxiety, concerned the strain on his administrators. Sir Hyde Gowan, Governor of the Central Province, had to resign because of ill health. The Viceroy thought the risk of further breakdown even greater than he had been fearing for some time:

'Seeing as I do in growing measure the shortage of really competent men of sufficient seniority and experience to hold high and important posts and the almost entire absence of men who are not overworked, I cannot but feel uneasy at the position which will confront us if we are faced with a sudden and prolonged crisis . . . one cannot improvise policemen or civil servants of 20 years service, more particularly for work in the districts. Nor is there any source on which we can hope to call for men on any scale that would be of the least value to us.'

He wanted the European intake increased. He stressed the danger of leaving things as they were:

'I should regard the nervous and physical exhaustion of any appreciable proportion of the senior British members of the I.C.S. as a matter of extreme gravity, and one involving risks for which neither you nor I should wish to shoulder responsibility.'

The Viceroy very much wanted to choose younger men for the higher posts because their energy and initiative were not sapped by the strain of heavy work in the Indian climate as was apt to be the case with older men. But he was forced to move with great care in this exercise since he could not afford the resignation of senior officials on being superseded by their juniors. He simply had not got the reserves of manpower to enable him to take the risk except in an exceptional case.

Linlithgow himself was to be allowed home on leave in the summer. He had asked for leave this year rather than in his third year (the customary moment) because the burden of the last two years had been so exceptionally heavy following closely on his exhausting experience as Chairman of the Joint Select Committee. He was physically sound although he knew that the strain and pace of his work had made a heavy call on his constitution. He proposed coming home on duty and not for reasons of health; it would be a help to discuss Federation with Zetland face to face.

The second problem confronting the Viceroy concerned the

army in India. There were two facets to it. First Linlithgow discussed with his Commander-in-Chief the new War Office policy at home of lowering the age of senior army appointments. The Viceroy found that General Cassels was not inclined to follow the War Office lead. He himself felt differently and he proposed to keep an eye on the situation. He asked Zetland for private information on the policy,

'for with the possibility of a major war one not to be discounted, and with the strain which falls on the higher command and on higher staff officers under modern conditions of warfare, I cannot help feeling that the age level, especially in this climate, is much too high, and that it may be proper that I should bring pressure to bear on the Commander-in-Chief, in considering future appointments, to reduce it.'

At the same time the War Office was again on the attack with proposals to increase the pay of British troops as an incentive to recruitment. This would mean a very heavy immediate increase in the annual cost of the British garrison in India. This could not be met unless India either abandoned high priority measures for re-equipment already announced or suspended her programme to reorganise the British cavalry and infantry, which had already started. This in its turn would seriously affect the military efficiency of the defence forces in India. On the political side the Viceroy again warned that there would be 'a political crisis of the first magnitude' as Indians saw themselves required to pay more for what they considered already to be an extravagant element in the forces in India.

Linlithgow's view, which he pressed strongly, was that if the pay increases were to be announced the home Government must at the same time agree to discussions in London on the whole aspect, strategic as well as financial, of India's defence. He wanted the discussions to be held above the level of the War Office, which he did not trust in this context. They must be attended, from the beginning, by a financial representative from India. Further, the Government must give an unequivocal assurance that, pending the result of the talks, further concessions to British troops would not involve further expenditure by India.

The Secretary of State's reply greatly disturbed the Viceroy. Zetland cabled to him a War Office suggestion that the financial problem raised by increased allowances to British troops should be met by the temporary reduction of these troops by two battalions. This merely led the Viceroy to retort that the War Office was apparently trying to blackmail him into the acceptance of their ideas – and this in a situation where India was quite unprepared for war.

The Viceroy's firmness won him a respite and he looked forward further to tackling the Government on the spot when he came home on leave.

*

With the military crisis temporarily out of the way Linlithgow felt the moment was approaching when he might usefully see Gandhi again and discuss Federation. This time he saw other leaders first. At the end of March he had a talk with the editor of the *Hindustan Times*, which represented Birla and his interests.

The Viceroy went into the federal problem with complete frankness, speaking of the difficulty of reconciling the Princes' views with those of Congress. He asked the editor if he thought the general desire was to take the present scheme, imperfect as it might be, and hope for political development in the acceding States, or to postpone unity until the States had achieved some measure of popular government. The editor replied that the wise course was to take the present scheme with such modification as could be secured. The Viceroy said that with all the detailed work to be done they could not now hope for Federation before 1940. He carried away from the conversation 'a definitely hopeful impression.'

This was not the only contact Linlithgow had at that point with the *Hindustan Times*. The paper employed an able cartoonist called Shankar, who was about to visit Britain for six months to improve his technique. The Viceroy commended him to Zetland:

'He is, I would judge, of quite unusual quality; he is witty; has great fertility of imagination; a keen sense of humour; is never in bad taste and on the technical side is very quick at catching a likeness. Personally he is a charming little man with excellent manners.'

The personal trouble which Linlithgow took on Shankar's behalf (Lady Linlithgow, too, was to give him introductions) was characteristic. In fact Shankar's cartoons were often bitingly critical of the Viceroy but they were always enjoyed by the victim. On one occasion Shankar portrayed him with two enormous chins. Linlithgow had a personal message sent to the cartoonist pointing out that he had three chins, not two. That the shape of his face was the result of polio was irrelevant for this least vain of men.

The Viceroy saw Jinnah on 6th April. The Muslim leader refused to support any scheme which would produce a Hindu majority in a federal India. His star was in the ascendant and he had moved away from the position he had taken at their first interview. His reorganisation of the Muslim League had brought about a marked stiffening of the communal attitude even in a Province so remote from communal disputes as Madras. The intensity with which the two communities were watching each other was even more marked than in the past.

A few days later Linlithgow saw Bhulabai Desai. Desai now wanted Federation postponed until the States had progressed politically; he thought the process would take two to three years. The Viceroy said this was a serious under-estimate and there was no hope of building up electoral machinery in the State in so short a time. But Desai thought things were moving in the States faster than people thought, and that pressure upon the Rulers would grow. Again the two men parted on extremely friendly terms.

Then came the Viceroy's second interview with Gandhi (5th April). Zetland had been worried by accounts of the Mahatma's health. He wrote that he himself thought that Gandhi's death at this juncture would be a calamity, but that this view was not exactly universal in Great Britain. The Viceroy found Gandhi in good form. He was glad that he had taken the initiative with the invitation as this had pleased Gandhi.

They came quickly to the question of Federation. The Mahatma said he wanted to break the Act. He realised that the Government could not be expected to pass important amendments so soon but he insisted on acceptance by the States of the principle of democratic election of their representatives at the centre. He said it would be a great mistake to assume that if their condition were not met Congress would work the Act and merely grumble. The Viceroy dealt with the point about the States, as he had met it with the other Hindu leaders. He did not get the impression that Gandhi had thought out the problem in detail. 'But,' he wrote, 'the more I see him the more I am convinced that he is the only man in that party who can deliver the goods, though I by no means underestimate his capacity . . . to drive as hard a bargain as he can.'

Linlithgow's last interview before leaving New Delhi on tour was with Sapru. The Liberal leader referred to the increasing communal tension. He said the fight was no longer a religious one – 'cow or pig' – but was essentially political. Congress had shown a lack of foresight. He also complained of a tendency shown by Congress Ministers to remit sentences, thereby undermining the prestige of the Courts. He was generally pessimistic and saw a deterioration of the machine of government so marked that things could not go on on the present basis.

*

On this less than cheerful note the Viceroy set out for the North-West Frontier Province, arriving at Peshawar, the capital, on 19th April. The Governor of the Province was Sir George Cunningham, one of the great governors. The Viceroy reported later to the King (8th June):

'I am glad to tell Your Majesty that Sir George Cunningham's Ministry were on the station platform to receive me. They also attended a banquet at Government House, and indeed behaved in an exemplary fashion throughout the period of my visit to the Province.

As you know, Sir, the government of the North-West Frontier Province is at present in the hands of a Congress Ministry with Dr Khan Sahib as Chief Minister, and the attendance of these Ministers on public occasions was therefore a welcome and significant sign of some importance. Incidentally, I may mention that Mr Gandhi arrived in the Province very shortly after I had left, and that rumour has it that he reprimanded Ministers for their attendance upon me. Lately, however, I have learned that Dr Khan Sahib held to his point and that the Working Committee of Congress has relaxed the extreme strictness of its injunction forbidding the attendance of Congress Ministers upon ceremonial occasions and at official entertainments attended by the Viceroy or by the Governors. I regard this as a great point gained, and I think the change . . . should contribute materially to an improvement in the relation between Governors and their Ministers.

'I was on the whole favourably impressed by the Chief Minister and his colleagues. The whole environment of the Province is very different from that obtaining in any other Congress Province, one essential difference being that the population of the Province is almost entirely Muhammadan.[1] Then again, the propinquity of the tribal areas and of Afghanistan constitute conditions peculiar to the Frontier Province which must most profoundly affect its political future. The Ministry, which consists of three Muslim Pathans and one Hindu, is disposed to be far less subservient to the orders of the Congress High Command than is any other Congress Ministry, and it will be a matter of much interest to observe their future development.'

From Peshawar Linlithgow went east to Dehra Dun in the United Provinces, a favourite haunt of his, for a few days' fishing and shooting. His holiday had barely begun when he had to change all his plans because of a crisis in the State of Orissa.

The Governor of Orissa, Sir John Hubback, was due for leave. In his place there had been appointed as acting-Governor the senior official in the State whose name was Dain. The appointment had sparked off a row before the Viceroy left Delhi and Gandhi had in fact referred to it after his interview with Linlithgow. Congress maintained that it put the Orissa Ministry in an impossible position to have placed over them as Governor an

[1] The electoral success of Congress in this Muslim region was probably due to widespread resentment against local landlords.

officer who had been the Ministry's servant. The Chief Minister, supported by Gandhi, now threatened to resign if the appointment went through. The Viceroy was reluctant to admit the principle for which Congress contended. There were few men of the right calibre from whom such an appointment could be made in a Province and for such a man to be automatically barred from the acting-Governorship was an obvious waste. On the other hand Linlithgow was bound to admit that there was substance in the objection advanced by Congress. In the end, after a warning from Zetland that the Cabinet would view with 'extreme disfavour' a real crisis over the point, the Viceroy gave way. Hubback's leave was postponed and Dain came home pending retirement.

It had been an unfortunate episode for all concerned. The I.C.S. saw its officers' chances of high service diminished. Hubback could not take a much needed rest. He was nervously unwell after a trying time with his Chief Minister, Biswanath Das, to whom he was unable to speak without being gratuitously offensive – Zetland wondered what relations with India would be like if all Governors carried on like that. The Viceroy had Hubback up to Simla for a week and reported that the rest and cool air, coupled with some wise advice, had done him good. By the time Hubback went home in August an officer from Madras had been found to fill the temporary post. Hubback came back refreshed and carried on until 1941.[1]

*

During the spring of 1938 there had been a disturbing rise in communal tension. Each side was manoeuvring for position. On the Hindu side there was serious rioting in Bombay and other cities. The Muslim League held meetings in Calcutta, at which Jinnah and Fazlul Huq made strong speeches. Huq not only criticised the Viceroy for having seen Gandhi but also accused him of going out of his way to express to Gandhi his satisfaction that Congress Governments were functioning in seven provinces.

[1] He lived to be 90.

There was no basis for this last accusation and Huq was told so. He was contrite and offered to make amends. The Viceroy replied that he did not ask for a public apology (he felt this would weaken the Bengal Government); he asked instead for a private letter from Huq pledging himself that it would not happen again. Huq wrote accordingly.

In May the Viceroy had reports from some of the Provinces that Congress Ministries seemed to be preparing a campaign to resign if they could not have their way on various issues. He thought this was probably a sign that they had found their feet and might now try to extend their field of interference by threat of resignation.

Aware that he might be faced with an awkward situation, Linlithgow planned his tactics. No alternative governments were possible in the Congress Provinces. The issue would therefore lie between giving way, or standing firm with the probability of having to fall back on Section 93. The Viceroy was determined to continue his policy of the utmost patience but he would fight if confronted with a really major issue. The very last thing he wanted was trouble, but if there must be another contest it must be fought on good ground. Fortunately the crisis did not come to a head.

*

Three weeks before his leave started, Linlithgow saw Sikandar. He did not find the Punjab Premier constructive. Sikandar pleaded for postponement of Federation on the grounds that a Congress majority at the Centre would result from early implementation and would immediately attack the reservation of defence and external affairs. This would undermine the privileged position which the Punjab enjoyed on army recruitment. Sikandar proposed the partitioning of India into six or seven regional groups, one of which would be Pakistan. On top of this he wanted a complicated system of central representation designed to prevent a Hindu majority in the All-India Legislature. The Viceroy listened and then implored Sikandar to try to dissuade

Jinnah from committing the Muslim League to complete opposition to Federation.

Linlithgow now came to an important conclusion on the question of whether to continue pressure for amendment of the 1935 Act or not. He had canvassed all the Governors. Their views varied but the weight of their advice was to leave things alone for fear of exacerbating a situation already bristling with suspicion. There might be certain minor adjustments which the Secretary of State needed to make, but the Viceroy's opinion was that the whole Bill had better be postponed. Pressure from the States and from British India to amend it in their respective interests must be resisted.

This course would avoid the need to consult Provinces and would therefore prevent any agitation on the subject by Congress. Over the Princes, in particular, it represented a change of mind, but it was a decision reached after painstaking consideration by a man who had tried with exceptional patience to find a sign of co-operation somewhere in the task which Parliament had laid upon him.

❧ 10 ❧

Linlithgow set out with his family for home and a much needed rest on 25th June, Brabourne assuming office as acting-Viceroy on that day.

Linlithgow enjoyed the first few weeks of his holiday in peace, spending most of the time at his beloved Hopetoun. In July he was in London, for there was work to be done.

His first engagement was with Jawaharlal Nehru who, it will be remembered, had refused to see him in India. He knew that Nehru was in London and thought he might accept an invitation to lunch privately, so he rang him up on the chance. Nehru accepted and the two men lunched together on the following day (19th July). The conversation was general and extremely friendly and they did not get down to Indian politics. Needless to say this meeting and also an interview which Nehru had with Zetland caused suspicion among the Muslims, who at once believed that the British Government was negotiating with Nehru.

Linlithgow had two talks with Zetland at which they returned to the possibility of amending the 1935 Act. Then the Cabinet discussed the matter on 27th July and authorised Zetland to go ahead with the offer to the Princes. They now agreed the proposal to permit the Princes to retain part of the proceeds of excise duties. Sir Samuel Hoare, who had piloted the India Bill through the House of Commons with tireless energy and skill, argued in Cabinet that the proposal was unjustified on its merits. This had always been Zetland's approach, too, but the Secretary of State wrote to Brabourne that unhappily they were in the hands of the Princes and could not deal with the matter on its merits.

'So far as I am concerned I have accepted Hopie's assurance that without this concession the Princes will not come in, and once that view of the situation is accepted there is really no more to be said.'

So Linlithgow was back where he started, and in a better position. Hoare was anxious to postpone Federation for as long as possible because he feared opposition by either the Princes or Congress once the system was under way, but Zetland deployed Linlithgow's constant theme that time was not on the side of the Government. The Cabinet supported him. Zetland added in his letter to Brabourne:

'The average member of the Cabinet looks upon memoranda by the Secretary of State for India as tiresome if inevitable intrusions!'

This remark is more significant than it might appear. Zetland's words in fact described what had long been the reaction of the average Englishman to events in India.

The remaining subject to be discussed in London between Linlithgow and Zetland was the thorny one of Indian defence expenditure. Certain concessions were made to the Government of India's point of view and the Cabinet also decided to send out immediately a committee under the chairmanship of Lord Chatfield to review the defence position in India. Grigg fulminated from Simla against the committee's appointment. For some reason he considered it an insult to the Commander-in-Chief, who shared the objection.

Linlithgow had done his best to get the Treasury to move further and even saw the Prime Minister. He was satisfied there was no more to be gained for the time being; the Treasury had come a considerable way towards him in the space of a week, which was fast going for that department.

In August Linlithgow returned to Scotland, where he enjoyed the rest of the summer with his family. He took in his stride the news that the Congress Working Committee had rejected all the Muslim League's demands. These had been made at a series of talks between the two communities. Jinnah now denounced Congress in public and declared there could be no compromise. He had then seen Brabourne, to whom he expressed the fear that

Zetland and Linlithgow were negotiating with Congress on the federal question. He then suggested to the acting-Viceroy that the Central Government should be kept as it was, that the British should protect the Muslims in the Congress Provinces and that the Muslims in return would protect the British at New Delhi. The Muslim leader was far too intelligent to believe for an instant that such a solution was possible but it suited his tactics at that point to propose it.

Congress was also putting increased pressure on the States by propaganda and incitement. In the small State of Dhenkanal (on the Orissa border), for instance, the situation was near to open rebellion. Troops had to be sent to stand by in case of complete breakdown.

*

The Viceroy resumed office on 24th October. His first task was to assess the attitude of Congress in the event of war breaking out. The Munich crisis had enabled Brabourne to see how Gandhi was reacting to the position. The Mahatma appeared generally depressed and preoccupied by the internal political situation. Congress and his closest associates were puzzled by his behaviour. Brabourne thought the probable reason was that Congress Ministries were becoming increasingly interested in administration and showing signs of resistance to central control (as Linlithgow had expected they would). Privately, and occasionally in public, they recognised the help they were receiving from the Governors and government officials. Moreover Congressmen were increasingly disposed to pay no more than lip-service to Gandhi's creed of non-violence. All this was clearly not to Gandhi's liking. There were those who thought he might already have decided that Congress had nothing more to gain by staying in office and that he would shortly force a crisis.

As to what attitude Gandhi himself would adopt in war Brabourne could not be certain. He thought, however, that the Mahatma's mind was moving, by the end of the Munich crisis, towards the position that a non-violent Congress would not co-operate in a war and that any demand for active help would be met with refusal.

There was undoubtedly a strong feeling in political India that the country had much to gain and little to lose by a war in Europe. There was indeed reason to believe that the Working Committee were in favour of bargaining with the British Government for constitutional favours in return for co-operation. It would be surprising if this had not been the case when its advantages were so obvious. But such an attitude would cut clean across Gandhi's belief in non-violence at any price. His policy required complete detachment. If it were to prevail, Congress Ministries would not be able to remain long in office because a war would quickly require positive activities in the Provinces. Meanwhile the Chief Minister of the Punjab, Sikandar, whose Province recruited most of the Indian Army, pledged unstinted support for Britain.

The Viceroy saw his Commander-in-Chief as soon as he was back in office. He pressed General Cassels to reduce the age limit in the case of senior appointments. Cassels was unwilling to comply. He said that he could not face the injustice of passing over deserving officers because of their age. Linlithgow reminded him that things were moving in this direction in England and asked him why the difficulties should be any greater in India. He thought he shook the Commander-in-Chief a little but that the battle would be a long one.

The Viceroy also found Cassels reluctant to co-operate with him in another matter. The Chatfield Committee would arrive very soon and Linlithgow felt that this could provide an opportunity for action on which he was extremely keen. 'I am more and more convinced,' he wrote, 'of the importance of associating Indian political opinion in the Assembly in some way with defence questions and have, I think, since I came back made some impression on the Chief's reluctance to contemplate this.' His patient approach even in a matter of urgency like this affords a good example of the power of the Commander-in-Chief in India. The Viceroy had to carry his Chief with him as far as he could. An unco-operative Chief could, as Defence Member of the Viceroy's Executive Council, make things awkward. This was no time for awkwardness but Linlithgow had to work with the tools with which he was provided. Cassels was a nice man but not of the calibre needed at the time. It would have been much better, certainly in modern times, if the Defence Member of Council had not been the Commander-in-Chief. He would then constitutionally have been in a position to give orders to the Chief.

*

The Viceroy was at once busy again on the federal front. Just before his return from leave Glancy had reported on the reactions of the major States. With the exception of Hyderabad these were as favourable as could be expected considering the serious misgivings aroused by what the Princes regarded as inadequate security for States' rights. They had further misgivings over Congress hostility to them.

The moment was approaching when the final offer would reach the Princes. It would contain such alterations in the States' favour as were thought necessary for success, to be implemented in a subsequent amendment of the Act. It would be final. Grigg had by this time expressed the view that everyone responsible for Indian policy was blind to the trend of events which were undermining the morale of the services 'at breakneck speed.' Linlithgow did not minimise the experimental nature of the whole scheme but could detect no grounds for Grigg's pessimism in his reports from Governors, the secret service, responsible Indians or the press. Basically his answer to Grigg rested on the realities of the situation:

'To endeavour to put back the hands of the clock seems to me as impracticable as it would, in my judgment, be unwise. For good or for bad, we have taken the decision we have and, failing quite decisive evidence to the contrary . . . which in my judgment does not at this stage exist, we have no alternative but to apply ourselves with all the energy at our disposal to the implementing of the policy which H.M.G. have laid down.'

The Princes received the Government of India's offer at the end of November, 1938. They were asked to reply within six months. Each ruler was to declare his attitude to the offer; the actual signing of the instruments of accession would not be asked for until all the replies were in and the results assessed. The offer was not to be published since negotiations were constitutionally a matter between the Crown and each individual ruler.

The Viceroy saw the editor of the *Hindustan Times*, who surprised him by expressing the opinion that Federation would go through. But when Linlithgow touched on the possibility of closer association of Indian political opinion with defence, the editor said the Congress would not accept anything less than a radical amendment of the Act which would break the reservation of defence to the Governor-General. The Viceroy replied that there could be no question of this. Congress ought not to miss the opportunity of Federation because there was 'the almost certainty that, once the system started working, they could within ten or fifteen years look to the realisation in practice of most of their desires in the matter of defence and the like.' If Congress turned its back upon Federation and insisted on the establishment of parliamentary institutions in the States, or a particular convention on defence, they took a grave risk 'and the growing interest in issues such as Pakistan left the very strong impression on me that other parties, too, were looking to the future and making their plans.' The Viceroy made it clear that he would do his utmost to further the policy with which he had been entrusted by Parliament – to establish India as an organic political unity. Anyone in his position who did not face up to that would bear a heavy burden of blame.

Another interview at this time was with Miss Agatha Harrison, one of a small group of Quakers who kept in close touch with Gandhi and the Congress leaders. Linlithgow, reporting the interview to Zetland, told him that Congress used her as a 'conduit pipe' to him. He thought it useful and even valuable to listen to people like Agatha Harrison, who occasionally passed on something worth having, although the time taken over these particular talks was considerable. He reported Miss Harrison as being 'well-primed by Congress on mis-government and oppression in the Indian States – she was almost in tears about it.' She gave Linlithgow a message from Gandhi that he did not ask for the Viceroy's intervention in the States, only for his restraint. It would be easy for him to do nothing in opposition to Congress there and monstrous to use British force to 'bolster up' wrongs in the States. Miss Harrison asked the Viceroy if she could take a message back to Gandhi. 'Give him my kindest regards,' he said, 'and tell him I understand.'

Pressure upon the Viceroy over the form of government in the States was mounting from various quarters which were friendly to Congress. Linlithgow had constantly to remind these people that there would be no Federation unless the States came in and nothing would be more certain to keep them out than action by him such as was asked for. Nevertheless he knew how badly some of the States were administered and he issued instructions to all Residents in the States that the Government of India must now take more active steps to encourage good government and raise standards of administration, especially in the smaller States. These steps must be taken whether or not the Princes acceded to Federation because the problems of their administration vis-à-vis British India would remain whatever the circumstances. The decision was the result of several months of careful consideration by the Viceroy of this very point. But he was anxious about the extra strain which would inevitably fall upon his political officers, confronted with a new problem of observation and supervision over a third of India.

*

At the end of November Linlithgow took an important initiative in the agricultural field. He opened a conference of Ministers on agricultural marketing.

He emphasised, from his own experience, the necessity for adequate preliminary surveys and careful economic reconnaissance. He made a plea for standardisation and explained what he meant:

'Standardisation, the determination of grades, is more than agreement on convenient categories of physical attributes – size, colour, purity, water or fat content, and the like. Standards must be very definitely related to the requirements of the consumer. An efficient marketing organisation should be the grower's intelligence bureau. Often you will find that the cultivator, who cannot himself be in touch with distant and overseas markets, will prefer a crop because of its agricultural advantage . . . because it is easy to grow or because it matures at a convenient moment in the seasonal routine of the holding, or appears to give a particularly heavy yield. . . . But the marketing officer, who knows the requirements of the ultimate markets and the prices ruling in those markets, is frequently in a position to advise the cultivator that he will increase his prospects of profit by growing some variety other than that one which seems to possess the highest agricultural advantage. . . . Consider how much loss may be spared to the grower if his marketing organisation is able to provide him with very early warning of . . . a change in demand. . . .'

A Viceroy, of course, had not the time to draft most of his speeches in detail, but these paragraphs bear the stamp of Linlithgow's own painstaking work, springing from his deep knowledge of the subject.

Early in December Linlithgow paid a visit to the independent kingdom of Nepal on India's northern border. It was a goodwill visit and took the form of a tiger shoot in the border country known as the Terai. The Viceroy wrote to the King on the eve of his entry into the country:

'I hear from my camp that four nights ago a wild tusker entered the elephant lines where over 300 elephants are standing, and choosing a likely looking young lady elephant took her away with him. Quite unabashed she returned to duty next day.'

The Christmas stay in Calcutta was as usual full of engagements for the Viceroy. He noted a mood of questioning anxiety among the European business community as to the future of British policy in India:

'I don't doubt that this mood is encouraged in some degree by the flood of anti-British articles which fill the nationalist newspapers, and which – under a democratic constitution – it is not easy for the Ministry to check. These signs of anxiety are, I think, due to the fact that the large European community in Calcutta has all along kept itself very aloof from Indian society; while its experience of politics has consisted in great degree of an uncomfortable oscillation between periods when terrorism in Bengal has loomed large and those in which by ordinance and other measures of a positive kind, the power of Government and the prestige of the European have been forcibly restored. These experiences, however inevitable in face of the unhappy history of Bengal, have not been those which were likely to imbue the European community with the spirit of political tolerance or to prepare it to face with equanimity the process of handing over the reins of government to Indians. These circumstances apply with equal force to European members of the Civil Services in that Province, and the effect has been to produce in Bengal a degree of uneasiness and even anxiety as regards the future which is not to be noticed in any other Province. . . . In Bombay, where the Parsee [Persian] community has for long stood as a bridge between Indian and European, the feeling between communities is excellent, and one comes across little or none of the anxious outlook which I have elsewhere mentioned as prevalent in Bengal.'

In fact Bengal was reacting to a major increase in anti-British propaganda in the Province. In the last nine months of 1938 there were eight times as many cases reported as in 1935. This had its effect on the services, on loyal Indians and on students (ninety-five per cent of whom were Hindu). The general line of the propaganda was that British rule was on its last legs and would be out within five years, to be replaced by Congress rule.

Linlithgow addressed the Associated Chambers of Commerce in Calcutta. He stressed that the first consideration in framing the federal scheme was the dominant importance of Indian unity: upon unity depended India's international prestige and economic well-being: it was even more important now than it had been three years ago for two reasons: first, the background in Europe had changed, secondly, provincial autonomy had worked so well that the danger of fissiparous tendencies was developing and could threaten this unity which all who cared for India's future longed to see consolidated.

In these words he set out both the achievement and the intention of the British Raj. It was his last message to India in the last full year of peace before the second World War was to put both to the test.

11

Early in 1939 there was sadness. Linlithgow came into his wife's sitting room one morning when she was discussing the day's arrangements with their family. He went over to the window and stood looking out over the garden in silence as he sometimes did when he was worried. Then he said quietly, 'Poor Brabourne is dead.' The Governor of Bengal had died of cancer after a short illness. The Viceroy wrote to the King:

'I know how grieved Your Majesty will be at the very sad news of Brabourne's death. His loss to Bengal at this time is indeed irreparable. Both he and his wife were immensely popular in both Bombay and Bengal, and they made an excellent impression during the four months that Brabourne acted for me last year. I had the highest opinion of his judgment and skill, and shall greatly miss his unfailing support and wise counsel. I am sure that Your Majesty will feel that you have lost a devoted and valuable servant.'

Linlithgow felt his friend's death deeply. Apart from the affection he felt for him he regarded Brabourne as by far the best man to succeed him as Viceroy.

*

The Congress attack upon the States was increasing in strength. The Viceroy's task was not a simple one. He wrote to the King:

'It is not an easy or comfortable business to handle, because certain of the States under pressure are not administratively in too good shape, nor are all their Rulers well equipped, either by character or experience, to stand up to so formidable a challenge.

I have to be extremely careful, in stimulating the Chiefs to undertake necessary administrative reforms and the removal of any real grievances agitating their subjects, not to put upon them more than they can bear, lest I should reduce them to a state of despair or even of resentment. Your Majesty of course knows that many of the smaller Ruling Chiefs are really no more in substance or importance than considerable landlords. That they were given ruling powers which were withheld from many landlords in other parts of India whose status and possessions are frequently far greater, has been due largely to historical accident and the policy in vogue at the time of the subjugation of the regions in which their ancestors flourished. But great or small, efficient or the reverse, the same principles are at issue whichever of the Indian States is assaulted, and when they are attacked we are bound to give them countenance and, if necessary, protection. Naturally Congress seeks to find the weakest spot in the defence, and I am therefore left at times to conduct an awkward campaign with allies some of whom are none too staunch or reliable. . . .'

The Viceroy had here described clearly the dilemma of British rule in India. Gandhi never let him forget it. Even if the Mahatma was prepared to see the point of the Viceroy's wise reminder that no generation can be held responsible for history he hammered away with his accusation that the Princes were a British creation – an unhelpful generalisation and not entirely accurate.

Linlithgow went on in the same letter to tell the King why he thought that the campaign against the States was so vicious at this moment:

'. . . the immediate intensity of the attack on the States is due in part to the internal difficulties which at present confront Congress. For the first time Gandhi's absolute authority has been challenged by the refusal of Subhas Bose, the outgoing President of the Congress, to withdraw his candidature for re-election in favour of the Mahatma's nominee (Rajendra Prasad). The "Old Guard," with Gandhi at its head, had become so accustomed to complete obedience from the whole organisation that it never occurred to them that Bose would refuse to toe the line. They had themselves chosen a candidate little known to the wider public and had taken no pains to canvass his claims. This, I think, is much more the real explanation of the affair than any very substantial diminution in the authority of Gandhi, or widespread drift to the left by the rank and file. The position is not yet clear, but it is plain that Mr Gandhi and his friends have been rendered extremely cross by what has happened. I do not doubt their capacity to take their revenge in due course. Meantime I expect both parties to the struggle will pick a quarrel with my Government in order as far as possible to conceal their own domestic differences.'

Linlithgow went on to mention a successful visit to Bombay in January. He had been amazingly well received by very large crowds and his programme was a heavy one. He did some official entertaining there as he felt that Calcutta should not have a monopoly of viceregal entertainment outside New Delhi. He also broke new ground in another field. The Indian Merchants' Chamber (a left wing body) had presented an address to him – its first address to a Viceroy since 1921. This was confined to highly controversial topics and expressed views directly opposed to the Government of India. Linlithgow proposed to give an oral answer. This horrified Grigg, who tried to dissuade him. But his instinct was that in a case like this it would be right to 'give a courteous but entirely firm reply; and that I propose to do.' He did.

At the end of February the Viceroy toured Rajputana. He was captivated by the beauty of the States of Jaipur, Jodhpur and Udaipur. He was also determined to keep up the momentum of his drive to face the Princes with the facts of life and in each State he took the opportunity in a public speech to emphasise the importance of administrative reforms. But his visit to Udaipur was cut short and he had to return to New Delhi to deal with a crisis which had come to a head in this very context.

Trouble had been brewing in a small State in Western India called Rajkot, the ruler of which was known as the Thakor Sahib. A powerful Congress leader in the west of India, Vallabbhai Patel, had persuaded the Thakor Sahib in December to agree to the appointment of a committee to draw up a scheme of reforms. The committee would consist of three officers of the State and seven non-official members to be recommended by Patel and nominated by the Thakor Sahib. A week later Patel sent in his list. The Thakor Sahib objected to certain names upon it and, after a short interval, announced the names of the seven himself. Only three of them were Patel's.

A few weeks later Gandhi entered the lists. He accused the

H

Thakor Sahib of a breach of faith as well as of ill-treating political prisoners. He arrived in Rajkot himself and was at once given every facility to inspect the State's prisons. He was accompanied by three officers of the Western India States Agency, who reported that no trace could be found of ill treatment. Then, on 2nd March, Gandhi sent the Thakor Sahib an ultimatum that he would fast until the breach of faith was repaired. He imposed conditions concerning the constitution of the committee, the time by which it was to end its deliberations and the release of all *satyagrahis*[1] within twenty-four hours. The Thakor Sahib rejected the ultimatum and Gandhi began his fast on 3rd March.

The Viceroy now intervened. Having received a request from the Thakor Sahib for the loan of a Government official to preside over the reforms committee he replied that he would try to find one. He also sent a message to Gandhi. In this he said he hoped that the appointment of one of his officials as chairman would meet Gandhi's anxiety to ensure that the Thakor Sahib carried out the undertaking given in December. The Viceroy also expressed regret that Gandhi had not consulted him before deciding to fast and asked him to come and talk things over with him as soon as possible. If there were misunderstandings this might clear them up 'and on personal grounds, too, I should greatly deplore any decision on your part as arising out of such misunderstandings to continue a fast which cannot but be a great strain on you.'

Linlithgow followed this message with a telegram to Gandhi in which he said he realised that what counted most with the Mahatma was the question of breach of faith. Acknowledging the existence of doubts in the matter of the December agreement he suggested referring them to the Chief Justice of India, Sir Maurice Gwyer. The Thakor Sahib was agreeable. Gandhi accepted the Viceroy's offer. 'I have great regard for you,' the Mahatma replied; 'I feel there is a sympathetic bond between us. I feel, too, that I should rely on your honour . . .' On condition that political

[1] Those who practised *satyagraha*, a word coined by Gandhi in South Africa, meaning non-violent civil disobedience.

prisoners were released – the Thakor Sahib agreed to this – he abandoned his fast.

The Viceroy had discussed the situation with his Council before sending his telegram to Gandhi. Grigg was strongly against compromise and thought the time had come to hit Congress hard. The Commander-in-Chief was inclined to agree with Grigg. No one feared to take tough measures less than Linlithgow when he felt it right. On this occasion, however – and it belies the impression of critics who did not know him that he was an inflexible man – he was convinced that toughness was not the answer.

'I felt very strongly,' he wrote to Zetland, 'as days went by the phenomenon with which you with your Indian experience will be familiar . . . of the rising tide, a very rapidly rising tide, of strong emotional feeling in this country; a feeling so strong indeed that it seemed perfectly clear to me that it was no good our endeavouring to score debating points or to win on technicalities or even, within limits, on the merits; for the Mahatma's death would undoubtedly have released a torrent of criticism and of recrimination which it would have been very difficult indeed to resist.'

The Indian members of Council shared the Viceroy's view and so did Sir Reginald Maxwell (now Home Member of the Government of India), whose balanced judgment and personal knowledge of Gandhi were of the greatest service.

The opinion of the Chief Justice went in favour of Gandhi. Gandhi then overplayed his hand. After an interval he returned to Rajkot to maintain his pressure on the Thakor Sahib. It appeared that Gandhi had earlier promised the landlords and the Muslims of Rajkot that he would secure for them representation on the reforms committee. He then found that he could not implement his undertaking without destroying his own majority on the Committee. He temporised but the parties concerned sought to hold him to his promise and challenged him to take this case also to the Chief Justice for settlement. At this point Gandhi gave in, proclaimed publicly that his fast had been a misguided one and apologised to everyone, including the Viceroy, for the trouble he had caused. The Viceroy noted that the Mahatma put up 'a tremendous smoke screen of almost metaphysical argument to conceal his withdrawal.'

In spite of the damage which Gandhi had suffered from his defeat, the Viceroy believed that he had largely offset this by defeating Subhas Bose's attempt to capture the high command of the Congress Party for its revolutionary elements. Bose had managed, despite Gandhi's opposition, to get himself elected for a second year to the presidency of the All-India Congress organisation. Linlithgow admired the ability with which Gandhi succeeded in ousting Bose although his methods were 'of the most questionable constitutional validity,' and getting his own nominee, Rajendra Prasad, elected in Bose's place.

Linlithgow had told Zetland, even before Rajkot blew up, that nothing in India had moved more quickly than the States-Congress situation. He was sure they would have to work hard to keep abreast of it and he was doubtful of the adequacy of the Political Department in this connection. He thought that they might have to reorganise it drastically:

'I feel sometimes that nothing short of a shake-up of this kind will purge the Political Service of their mediaevalism, the consequences of generations of experience in the Indian States. We are faced with a radical change in a situation of the first importance, and we may be driven to consider equally radical changes in our machinery for dealing with it.'

As events turned out there was no time to work out the sort of scheme which might have met the case. Anyhow, the shortage of men of first-rate quality would have made a solution extremely difficult.

Meanwhile the Viceroy had conveyed to Birla and Mahadeo Desai[1] his surprise at the contrast in tone between Gandhi's personal letters to him and the kind of statement which the Mahatma was making in public. On being assured that he need not take the latter remarks too seriously, as they were meant to appeal to the public, he suggested that Mr Gandhi might reserve

1 Gandhi's private secretary.

his sharper arrows for his private correspondence and appear in his more human and gentle guise in the statements he released for public consumption.

Mahadeo Desai paid the Viceroy a remarkable tribute for his handling of the Rajkot affair. He wrote to Laithwaite (7th March):

'How can I be adequately grateful to His Excellency for his sympathy – I was going to say charity – and the deep understanding he brought to bear on this supreme occasion? A truly Christian Viceroy saved the situation in 1931.[1] Another truly Christian Viceroy has saved another graver situation today. True godliness will suffer no praise, and I will offer none. I will simply say – let God be praised.'

Birla added his own commendation. In a letter to Laithwaite of the same date he wrote:

'I have not the words to describe the magnitude of the part played by H.E. Lord Linlithgow. It is no exaggeration to say that his great act opens a new era in our history . . . Lord Linlithgow will long be remembered with affectionate gratitude. . . .'

Rajkot had put great strain upon Linlithgow and reinforced in him a determination to try to reduce the pressure of work both upon him and upon his chief administrators. He found the amount of detail which he had to decide in addition to the greater matters of policy quite ludicrous. So it was. It is a matter for wonder that he endured four years of war and its crises on top of what he had already had to bear, with his nerve and stamina unimpaired. He was aiming at a twenty per cent reduction, he told Zetland, and he laughed as he wrote in the knowledge that the exercise would prove impossible.

*

Within a few days of the end of Gandhi's fast the Viceroy was addressing the Chamber of Princes. To the full Chamber he gave assurance that Great Britain would stand by her treaties to the Princes. At the same time he warned them that a heavy obligation lay upon them to adjust themselves to changing conditions. They

[1] Lord Irwin.

must live in their States (some were hardly ever there), limit their
privy purses, provide popular institutions and be active in
remedying the legitimate grievances of their subjects. Smaller
States, he urged, should unite their administrations, for instance in
police matters and education. He was surprised to hear that his
audience felt encouraged by his speech.

He followed up this address with a meeting at which he spoke
to sixteen of the most important rulers in private, including the
Standing Committee of the Chamber. It was a remarkable
speech. It seems a pity at this distance of time that he did not
make it in public but he was speaking at a moment of extreme
delicacy when the very last thing he wanted to do was to cause
panic in the Princely Order, panic which Congress would be only
too ready to encourage by quoting, or misquoting, him.

The Viceroy said that political agitation in the States was not
caused by the prospect of Federation. It was a part of a great
upsurge of political activity which they might trace right across
the face of Asia from the Nile to the Yellow Sea of China and it
had been evident in India for the last twenty years. They would
fail to understand this movement if they thought it was mainly
directed towards the termination of British rule in India. 'Essentially the movement is everywhere one directed towards a
liberating of political institutions and towards the progressive
recognition of the rights of the individual subject . . . and the
change has come to stay . . . the fact is that the old order has gone
for ever.' The Viceroy advised the princes to face the facts: 'My
own instinct is conservative, but when change is plainly and
inevitably coming, I would not advise my friends to wait for it in
complete inaction. Far better to go out to meet it, and to mould it,
while it is still malleable, to your own purposes.'

Shortly after the Viceroy's meetings with the Princes, Gandhi
came to see him. The Mahatma said that he had been impressed
by the Viceroy's efforts to move the Princes in the direction of
reform. Following up this acknowledgement Gandhi instructed
his followers to suspend civil disobedience in the States.

*

On the eve of the Rajkot affair Linlithgow had had a long talk with Jinnah. The Muslim leader said that he did not reject the federal idea, but the Federation must be one which would ensure an adequate equipoise between Muslim and Hindu votes so that there would be an adequate balance between the communities. The Viceroy asked him how he would secure this. Jinnah had in mind the manipulation of territorial votes and the adjustment of territorial divisions. He was seen to blush when the implication of these suggestions was pressed but said he preferred his ideas for the carving up of the country to Sikandar's.

The Viceroy then asked Jinnah if he thought that this equipoise could be maintained if the British left India. Jinnah said it might be very difficult. Did he then want the British to stay? The Viceroy wrote to Zetland:

'He admitted with some reluctance that it looked very much as though that was the position which was going to emerge; but he added that many were losing faith in us. It was perfectly clear that we had not yet made up our minds whether we were going to go or not; and the only possible course for the Muslims to take in these circumstances was to continue to abuse us as loudly as possible in public, partly because we were so clumsy in our handling of the situation, and partly because the Muslims must show the public that they were as good nationalists and as good Indians as any other community. Behind the scenes they might adopt a more co-operative attitude – so long, that was, as we did not intend to clear out.

If on the other hand we really had it in mind to abandon control of this country then it was quite obvious that Muslims must bestir themselves and be ready to fight, and he felt quite sure that in doing so they could also look for the help of Congress.'

Linlithgow asked Jinnah if he seriously contemplated that His Majesty's Government

'should now go back to Parliament, after ten years of endeavouring with the help of Indian opinion, and with the utmost publicity, to devise a workable scheme, and after two years' experience to suggest that in the Provinces the scheme devised admitted of being worked; say that the idea of the transfer of responsibility to Indian shoulders for which we have been working was all mere nonsense, and that something completely different, on the lines which Jinnah now indicated would have to be devised? Why should we carry that baby?

'Jinnah said that that was precisely the position. He quite recognised that it was not attractive from the point of view of His Majesty's Government, or to the British in India, but if we carried the advantages we must also carry the burdens, and so long as there was any shadow of authority in India exercised by His Majesty's Government we might be perfectly certain that we should be landed with every possible responsibility by Hindu and Muslim alike.'

The Viceroy found this an extremely informative interview. Even allowing for Jinnah's defensive tendency to exaggerate, his words did link up with the feeling of uncertainty about the future in various quarters.

In the same letter Linlithgow told Zetland that the Commander-in-Chief was seriously worried by the combination of a threatening international situation and deterioration in India. Cassels wanted the Government of India to force the issue with Congress and hit them hard. The Viceroy probed this question with Cassels, Grigg and Maxwell. Grigg supported Cassels; Maxwell opposed them, as did the Viceroy. Nevertheless Linlithgow was worried by the position as set out by the Commander-in-Chief. He wrote:

'We may, of course, find as neither you nor I have ever concealed from ourselves, that the whole system to which we are working is wrong; that breakdown and confusion in the Provinces, either because the personalities available in politics are not up to the strain, or because doctrinaire ideas are allowed to have their way too fully, are inevitable as things are now shaping; and that a radical change of policy cannot be avoided. But I remain unshaken in the view I have expressed so often that if there is to be a breakdown we must be prepared to go, if necessary, almost to dangerous lengths to give the present system every trial and to establish beyond question that any collapse is due not to any fault of ours, but to some inherent vice or weakness in the material; and that we must be able, with a clear conscience, to feel and to say that we have spared no effort to make a success of the only apparently workable scheme that the best experience available could devise.'

Zetland was puzzled as to why the pessimists saw defeat in the Government's present Indian policy: the purpose of the 1935 Act was to give India self-government and therefore to relax control by Whitehall and New Delhi: no one could expect that administration would be as efficient as before. The logic of Zetland's argument was perfectly sound but the cause of the anxiety for the future which was making itself felt lay in the deep doubt over Great Britain's exact ultimate intentions. Was there to be unrestricted self-government for the old Dominions under the State of Westminster but a restricted sort for India with Britain bent on keeping the reserved powers of defence and external affairs as defined in the 1935 Act? Neither Indians nor British people in India were sure.

Linlithgow himself was in no doubt that complete self-government for a unified India was the ultimate goal but, like most of those who understood the complexity of the situation, he saw the final step as a good many years ahead.

Meanwhile he was trying his hardest to carry out his task of federating India. He reported a significant talk which Laithwaite had had with Agatha Harrison on 14th March. She spoke warmly of the Viceroy's handling of Rajkot and had told Gandhi that the Government of India could not be expected to intervene and save Gandhi's life and continue at the same time to be criticised and abused by Congress. It was a naïve expectation. Miss Harrison then told how she had urged Gandhi to associate his leading colleagues, Nehru, Patel, Bose and so on, with him in his discussions with the Viceroy. Gandhi made it clear that he was determined to handle the situation on a one-man basis. Miss Harrison reported him as anxious to co-operate and come to terms.

There had been a Congress conference at Tripura in Bengal which had shown a wide gap between the right and left wings of the party. Bose, himself a Bengali, was, of course, on his home ground and there were scenes of rowdyism which came very near to violence. Bose and his extremist followers suffered a bad defeat at the conference, which the Viceroy thought might precipitate more direct action in Bengal. Indeed during the proceedings Nehru had been disturbed to notice a group of Bengali delegates gathered on a hill, some of them armed. There were fears that an attempt might be made to assassinate Gandhi and his hut was surrounded by plain-clothes police.

*

Through the spring of 1939 the Viceroy was naturally concentrating hard upon the problem of the Princes. Their replies to the great question were to be in his hands by the end of July and he knew how unwilling many of them still were to face up to the course which he knew was in the best interests of their Order. He wrote to Zetland on 21st March.

'Were the issue not so serious, there might be some amusement to be gained from the thought that at a time when there are so many indications that Congress want Federation and will not be prepared to die in the last ditch over preliminary conditions prior to entering it, the Princes, who certainly stand to gain very substantially . . . should take fright and declare that they cannot face the risks involved. But if the Princes do intend to turn down Federation, then I am very clear that the full responsibility for doing so must be placed fair and square on their shoulders.'

Linlithgow had been impressed, before writing this letter, by a talk with a distinguished Hindu, Raghavendra Rao. Rao had governed the Central Provinces for a period in 1936 and had just returned from a tour of British India. He told the Viceroy that he thought Congress would work Federation and would not stand out for too long on preliminary conditions although they would get what they could. Nehru was tipped as Prime Minister; Rajagopalachari and Pant were the candidates for the Finance Ministry. Rao added that Congress knew that no party could form and maintain the first Federal Government without the constant support of the Governor-General.

A few weeks later the Viceroy had more support for his hopeful view of the attitude of Congress. Birla told Laithwaite that the settlement of Rajkot and the degree of personal contact between the Viceroy and Gandhi which that affair involved had materially affected Gandhi's attitude. He (Birla) found him more prepared than he had ever found him before to believe that there was a genuine desire on the part of Great Britain to co-operate with India and he believed also that a mental process was developing inside the Mahatma as regards civil disobedience.

Linlithgow thought there was probably a good deal in what Birla had said

'though we should be unwise to cease to sup with a long spoon when we are with him [Gandhi].'

Meanwhile the Viceroy had kept up his search for a way in which the Assembly could be associated with defence problems:

'I am perfectly certain that the inability of the Central Legislature to discuss defence, and the segregation of the Legislature from defence represents a state of things that is more and more unsatisfactory. With the approach of Federation I feel that the existing practice can hardly be defended.'

Of course he must retain control as the Act directed and he could not allow the establishment of any conventions which might hamper him in the discharge of his responsibilities, but he could not help feeling that 'some half-way house must be practicable.' He had in mind an informal Defence Committee consisting of leaders of the parties in the Legislature. The Commander-in-Chief was not keen on the idea. He felt it might be used to embarrass the Indian Army. Linlithgow saw his point but felt strongly that some contact must be made. He proposed to take soundings.

If the chances of a co-operative attitude by Congress towards Federation seemed more promising, this was not true of the Muslims. Jinnah had, under threat of resignation, forced the Muslims in the Assembly to abstain in the division on a new trade agreement for India, thus causing an important defeat of the Government. Constitutionally this did not make any difference to the outcome because the Viceroy used his powers of certification to restore the necessary provisions, but tactically the move surprised Linlithgow. It also annoyed many prominent Muslims throughout the country who criticised Jinnah strongly. The Viceroy was told that Jinnah wanted a year in which to try out the policy of supporting neither the Government nor its opponents in the hope that each would be convinced of the value of Muslim support and would bid for it.

Linlithgow reported an hour's discussion which he had with Jinnah, mainly on the subject of Muslim grievances. They talked about the political position generally. Jinnah then turned to the Viceroy and said that he would frankly confess that he saw no solution and that he did not now believe that this country was competent to run a democracy; that he and others who had advocated a reformed system of government had, he felt in the light of practical experience, formed a wrong judgment of the capacity of India to run such a system. Jinnah thought that propertied Hindus were coming to the same conclusion. Everybody had been carried away by a natural desire for home rule and by an objection to government by aliens,

'but he was satisfied now, he thought, that the present system would not work and that a mistake had been made in going so far. He concluded these observations by reminding me that the country depended on us.'

Linlithgow replied to Jinnah that if this was true he and other Indian political leaders had bluffed His Majesty's Government and the British electorate into thinking that their scheme for self-government under the Act was a good one. In any case to what form of government should they revert? Jinnah did not like this question and made no positive suggestion for carrying on the government of the country if the present scheme broke down.

The Viceroy had no doubt that the Muslims were becoming increasingly uneasy at what Jinnah described as 'Hindu arrogance' and more and more apprehensive of the fate of a minority – even a minority of ninety million people – under the scheme of the Act. He felt there was some foundation for Jinnah's allegations of unfair treatment of Muslims in particular Provinces although investigation had never borne these out:

'But in Jinnah's case, as in that of other critics, I feel that at this stage there is nothing for it but to hold on and test the scheme further with a consciousness that it may break down or may prove impracticable and that if it does we shall have to think again. It would of course be the greatest mistake in any way to discount the importance of expressions of opinion of this character, particularly from a man of the standing of Jinnah: and we must give full weight to them. But the stage has not yet been reached at which any case has been established for going back to Parliament . . . And the problem of the alternative has not been touched . . . by any of our critics.'

Zetland's reply was to the point:

'It is at least refreshing to find Jinnah admitting an error of judgment in pressing for parliamentary government for India and saying further that the situation depended upon us. I should, however, be not a little surprised if he proved willing to say the same thing in public. Indeed I should be more surprised if, in the event of our even suggesting the possibility of our having to consider the imposition of any restriction on the free play of democratic forces in India, Jinnah did not shout as loudly against us as the most rabid Congressman!'

Zetland was becoming increasingly pessimistic over the growth of communal tension. There were bad reports coming in from both the United Provinces and the Central Provinces. The Secretary of State thought that tension would continue to grow at least until the issue of Federation was settled. If the Muslims would not play and the Princes were to shy off they would seriously have to ask themselves what should be the next step.

Linlithgow himself felt that the Muslims would come in provided the Princes gave him a platform from which to launch the scheme. He was just as aware of the difficulties as Zetland but more optimistic of the outcome as far as the Muslims were concerned. He did not believe that they alone could stop Federation.

A touch of light relief was supplied by a letter to the Viceroy from an Indian in New Delhi. Linlithgow quoted it as an example of the consolations of his office. The writer said that war could be averted if the Viceroy would fly to London with the Congress President and Gandhi 'to cool dictatorships with love and a give-

and-take policy.' If Gandhi could not go because of his health, let Miss Slade[1] go. If she refused, 'my wife, who is now lying seriously ill in Ambala, as she is imagining a grave war and is almost running mad over it, could perhaps be persuaded to go when she is slightly better.'

[1] Miss Slade, the daughter of an English admiral, was a devoted disciple of the Mahatma. She was popularly known as Mira Ben.

12

Exchanges of view between the Viceroy and Zetland on the Muslim problem continued until well into the summer. Linlithgow traced the course of the argument as it had developed during the three Round Table Conferences and the sittings of the Joint Select Committee which had preceded the 1935 Act. He wrote that neither of them should be surprised that the near approach of Federation had brought Muslim fears to the surface. During those earlier discussions the Muslims had made demands of the most excessive character but at no stage had the British Government been able to go further than in the scheme of the Act. They had not felt justified in doing so either on the merits of the case or as a matter of practical politics, given the legitimate claims of other communities and the necessity to get them into any workable scheme. The root of Muslim apprehensions, said the Viceroy, lay in any system of responsible central government. No plan for Federation based upon representative government could be acceptable to those Muslims who contemplated the future course of Indian politics as an unending communal contest. But the Government were agreed that an all-India Federation was the only practical line of constitutional advance as also was it the necessary corollary of provincial autonomy.

Linlithgow continued:

'I do not think that the Muslims have it in their power to prevent the attainment of Federation, or to make it unworkable – unless they can discover means to prevent a sufficient number of Rulers from acceding. Indeed I shall be most surprised if, when the test comes, Muslims do not work the federal constitution to the best of their opportunities. I have always felt too . . . that it is in the achievement of Federation that there is the best hope of some alleviation of existing tensions. I shall be very greatly mistaken if we do not find that the two communities will work much more closely together with the degree of responsibility at the centre which Federation involves . . .; and that with the Hindu-Muslim problem transferred in an active form to the Central Government the chance of leaders in either community bringing a greater influence to bear on the rival ambitions . . . in individual Provinces is a real one.'

In the same letter the Viceroy referred to a speech which Sir Firoz Khan Noon, the Indian High Commissioner in London, had made to the 1900 Club on 3rd May.

Firoz was a Muslim from the Punjab. The 1900 Club was composed of right-wing conservatives and the diehards were present in force. Firoz surprised them by saying that it would be dangerous for the British Government now to put Federation in the melting pot as India would blame Britain for vacillating and would claim that Federation was never intended to work. The best policy was the Viceroy's policy of begging India to accept Federation. If India failed to respond it would be plain that it was not the Viceroy's fault.

It was an important speech and it naturally encouraged Linlithgow. Some weeks later he received further encouragement from the Governor of the Punjab. Craik informed him that Sikandar's secretary had stated that the Muslims would accept Federation if it were imposed.

On 1st May Congress passed a resolution against supporting a war forced on India without the consent of the Indian people. A few days later Gandhi was again complaining to the Viceroy about the situation in some of the States. He wrote a letter which began, 'I purposely restrained myself from troubling you whilst you were touring and taking part-holiday.' The Viceroy noted that he was profoundly grateful for this. Gandhi continued:

'I must say that my experiences of the working of the Political Department are not happy. I observe that the Viceroy, no matter how strong he may be, is not powerful enough to carry out his intentions even as the Congress President is not with his voluntary departments. You will not mind the comparison. A knowledge of our little difficulties enables me to send out my sympathy to you instead of blaming you for what appear to me to be innumerable pin-pricks.'

It was an astute letter as well as showing that Gandhi had a sense of humour.

In June there was a meeting of some of the leading Princes and their ministers at Bombay. They resolved that they regarded the terms of the federal offer as fundamentally unsatisfactory and unacceptable in their present form. The Viceroy was surprised at their decision to come out into the open so early and definitely, thereby taking a great risk of responsibility for the breakdown of the federal scheme. He had expected them to defer a decision and ask for better terms. Meanwhile they had, he thought, made more remote the possibility of a compromise acceptable to British India.

Linlithgow's dilemma was acute. He had asked to be allowed to put pressure on the Princes before the Bombay meeting – pressure in their own interests. But Churchill and the diehards were in determined mood. Having insisted successfully at the outset that the Princes should not be pressed to accept they were not going to draw back now. Their tactical position was strong for they themselves were applying all the pressure they could muster to dissuade the reluctant Princes from acceptance. As Linlithgow pointed out to Zetland, the Government had allowed its hands to be tied. Of course he understood why, but the fact remained. All that he felt could further be done to counteract it was to remind the Princes that publication of the terms of the offer to them was inevitable and public opinion would see how narrow was the margin left for further concessions.

The course of the Bombay conference was not without its irony. Opposition to the federal offer had been led by Bikaner and Bhopal, the two Princes who had been the protagonists in favour of Federation. These two took hold of the discussion and ran it as an anti-Federation demonstration. They smothered all opposition and controlled the agenda and proceedings. The Jam Saheb of Nawanagar, Chancellor of the Chamber of Princes, was no more helpful. The opinion of the Princes' legal adviser, Judge

Morgan, that they would be wise to accept the offer, was suppressed. After the meeting the Jam Saheb circulated a letter to all Princes bringing pressure to bear on them to comply with the Bombay policy. It contained many inaccuracies and in its turn suppressed Morgan's opinion. Linlithgow described it as 'a thoroughly objectionable document.'

Whatever the ethics of these Princes' behaviour at Bombay, the main force behind their intransigence lay in the genuine fears activated by the Congress attack on the States the previous winter. Zetland was told this by the Mysore representative at the conference and there can be no doubt of its truth. Congress was reaping where it had so impetuously sown.

The Viceroy asked the Jam Saheb to correct the inaccuracies of his circular letter. The Jam Saheb said he had no power to alter it without consulting his Standing Committee, which would take ten days. The Viceroy therefore took steps himself to tell the Princes the truth, especially about Morgan's advice, through the appropriate political officers. Meanwhile one of the more important rulers, the Maharaja of Indore, had already gone to California for his health so that he could not be reached for some time. His health was genuinely bad but it was known that he did not wish to be interested in the problem.

In spite of the Bombay set-back Linlithgow knew that some of the Princes were ready to accept the federal offer and he wanted to strengthen their hands by making plain that His Majesty's Government were determined to stand by their policy. He therefore asked Zetland to make this clear in public as soon as possible. The Secretary of State replied rather weakly that he had no engagement in the near future which would provide a suitable platform outside Parliament. As to a debate in the House of Lords or an arranged question in the Commons, he was afraid that either course might carry him a good deal further than either he or the Viceroy would wish to go. The diehards might be stimulated to encourage the Princes in their resistance and it was 'most difficult to get speakers to support the Government view . . .' Meanwhile some States had joined the number ready to accede, notably Bahawalpur. Linlithgow had been hopeful of this State but was not sure of it. On receiving the good news, he said it was like landing his first salmon.

On 21st August he addressed the Standing Committee of the Chamber of Princes at Simla. While he reiterated that the decision was for the Princes to take he told them he thought the federal offer was very favourable to them. They would have one third of the seats in the Lower House and two fifths in the Upper House. This, he told them, had always seemed to him to be a bloc which, if the Princely Order were wise and held together, no political party could afford to ignore.

If the Princes stood aside, the Viceroy continued, it was not for him to predict the direction which political development in British India might take. But development there must be; it would be contrary to all the teachings of history to imagine otherwise. The Princes must see, as was evident to any skilled observer, how difficult it would be to retain the so-called 'irresponsible Centre' indefinitely. Whether it would be likely to help the Princes to remain outside future developments they themselves must judge. He himself was concerned to do what he could to prevent the injury that must follow from the collapse of the federal plan and of the welding of India's unity caused by the abstention of the Princely Order. Leading members of the Order had after all been directly responsible for the emergence of the ideal as a result of the Round Table Conference.

The Viceroy then referred to the suggestion that a Prince who rejected the federal offer would be showing thereby his loyalty to the Crown. There could, he said, be no more fantastic or improper suggestion: he would not have mentioned it had there not been a reference to it in two of the replies from the Princes.

Finally Linlithgow reminded the Princes of all the care which had been taken over many years of deliberation and discussion before the passing of the 1935 Act. No one could reasonably expect to secure all that he might reasonably wish in this world.

It is hard to see how persuasion could have gone further than this or what more Linlithgow could have done within the limits

enjoined upon him by Parliament. He was fighting a pretty
lonely battle but he was not entirely alone. Sikandar at the end
threw his weight loyally behind the Viceroy's efforts and told him
that he had warned Bikaner and the Jam Saheb that they would
be most unwise to bear responsibility for the breakdown of the
federal scheme. They would find themselves in an infinitely
worse position if this happened and he had strongly advised them
to face up to facts.

*

Although the Viceroy's overriding problem was the Hindu-
Muslim question, he had never minimised the importance of
British opinion in India. Zetland reported to him a conversation
with the leader of the business community in Calcutta, Sir
Edward Benthall, with whom Linlithgow had also been in touch.
Benthall said that the uncertainty felt by the European community
was caused mainly by divided counsels at the Centre. He referred
to the two schools of thought which were known to exist in the
Government of India. What he called 'the big stick' school found
its most powerful exponent in Grigg. Grigg, however, had now
left India and Benthall thought opinion in official circles would be
less divided. He said the average European did not look far
ahead, being concerned mainly to avoid interference from Government and to be free from lawless disturbances. Zetland told
Benthall that British people in India would have to face up to
realities in the not too distant future; the purpose of British rule
was to confer the benefits of democracy. Benthall replied that
when this was put to the average Englishman in Bengal he found
it reasonable enough.

   Sir James Grigg's recent departure was certainly calculated to
improve the atmosphere although Linlithgow later wondered
how much of a nuisance his late Finance Member might be to
him at the War Office, to which he was to be appointed as Secretary of State in 1942.

   During that last summer of peace the Viceroy was busy, as
always, on matters beside Federation. With the strong probability

of war in his mind he had carried out a detailed review of the position on the North-West Frontier. He gave much personal attention to this. Zetland complimented him on the resulting survey. Its production amidst so many other preoccupations stamped the achievement as 'a really remarkable one.'

Towards the end of July the Government of India received a request from the Chiefs of Staff for the loan of India's Anti-Aircraft Battery. This may sound an odd statement, but it is literally true. Linlithgow's comment to Zetland was a masterpiece of moderation:

'We shall, I feel certain, come under sufficiently heavy criticism here if the emergency finds us with one A.A. Battery only. If it finds us with none, the position would be difficult to a degree.'

If history were ever to doubt the pacific nature and intentions of the Empire it would need little further reassurance than this incident.

Linlithgow had been Viceroy for nearly three and a half years when war broke out and the moment is right for a summing up of his record so far.

Parliament, it will be remembered, had sent him to India with a two-fold task, first to inaugurate provincial autonomy and then to launch the federation of the country on an all-India basis.

The first part of the mission was now successfully completed. In spite of early protestations by the Congress high command that they had accepted office in order to destroy the constitution from within, the provincial Ministries had shown a steadily increasing awareness of their responsibility and a readiness to undertake it. This had indeed resulted in two resolutions of the All-India Congress Committee. The first resolved that a Provincial Congress Committee should not interfere in the day-to-day administration of the Province by the Ministry; the second that Congressmen should not offer *satyagraha* against the actions of a Ministry without proper authority. There had also been at least one case (there were probably others) where the Ministry had been instructed by the High Command to refrain from raising constitutional issues with the Governor.

On the communal front it is true that tension had seriously increased. The point to mark here is that Hindu-Muslim relations were worsening as the prospect of self-government for India drew nearer to realisation. Thus the accusation that communal tension was the deliberate invention of the British to bolster their claims to remain paramount was shown to be as false as un-prejudiced men both in India and Britain had always known it to be.

In the matter of Federation Linlithgow had not been able to mould events as he had wished because his hands were tied. But his tireless efforts to bring the Princes round and his persistent warnings to Zetland from the beginning that time was not on his side show how ludicrous was the criticism levelled against him years later that he had dragged his feet over Federation. In fact when the outbreak of war put an end to this scheme nearly two fifths of the States had expressed their readiness to join, some of them making accession conditional upon protection of their treaty rights. This represented twenty seats out of fifty-two and a population of eleven millions out of thirty-nine millions. Linlith-gow himself believed that he would have secured Federation, had war not supervened, by July, 1941.

*

The coming of war brought personal anguish to the Linlithgows, as it did to thousands of other parents whose sons were of fighting age. For them the blow was heavy. They could not expect to see their two sons again before the end of the viceroyalty whenever that might be. Moreover Charlie had only just married (in July) and Linlithgow had never met his daughter-in-law. Charlie went to France almost at once in his father's old regiment; his brother was serving in the Scots Guards. Their father wrote them each a cheerful letter saying that he had confidence in them and he could now only hope for the best.

The Viceroy and Zetland had agreed on the steps to be taken in the event of war being declared. These were that Linlithgow should issue a statement to the Assembly on the Empire's war aims and that he should then see the party leaders individually and discuss the situation with them.

India's constitutional position was clear. With Britain at war India was at war automatically. No declaration by the Viceroy could initiate this, or gainsay it. It was a fact. The Viceroy was later criticised both in India and by certain elements at home for not asking the Assembly for their assent to India's entry into the war. At the moment when he made his statement he was not criticised by Gandhi or by any other responsible leader. That was to come later. On the merits of consulting the Assembly, quite apart from the constitutional position which he could not avoid, Linlithgow later asked where he would have been if Congress had refused his request (as they certainly would have done) at a moment when the whole of the Punjab had backed the allies and the Princes had 'thrown themselves at the feet of the King-Emperor.'

As for Federation both the Secretary of State and the Viceroy agreed that further steps towards it must now be postponed for the duration. The Hindus, who had so foolishly let slip a golden chance to help in its realisation, now regretted the position. The Muslims were delighted. The Princes felt relieved.

13

Directly after the declaration of war Linlithgow asked Gandhi to come and see him. Gandhi did so on 4th September and the two men talked for nearly two hours.

Linlithgow asked Gandhi where he stood. The Mahatma told him that he himself was in favour of India giving full and unconditional support to Great Britain although he could not speak for his friends. He said that, although he stood for non-violence, he had in the past given moral support to recruitment and was ready to do so again in his individual capacity. Gandhi showed 'great emotion' when he spoke of the possibility of the bombing of Westminster Abbey or Westminster Hall and said that he contemplated the war 'with an English heart.'

The Viceroy made clear to Gandhi that he would do all he could to keep him in touch with the war situation and he made arrangements for a senior staff officer to visit him with maps and up-to-date information. Concerning the internal position he stressed his anxiety that the Congress Ministries should stay in office. He could not hold out any prospect of statutory changes but that did not mean that there could not be the closest consultation such as the two of them were having at that moment; he told Gandhi of his strong wish for a link between Government and Indian leaders, particularly in the sphere of defence. In short, anything he could do to help he would do, and he would keep an open mind as far as his constitutional duty allowed him. Gandhi appreciated this approach. He agreed that matters could not be hurried and said that as long as the Viceroy's mind was not closed he was content.

The Mahatma then raised the communal problem and the Muslim fears of Hindu dominance. The Viceroy, he said, could make a very valuable contribution by moving the Muslims, who were impressed by his powers, towards greater co-operation with Congress. This ought to be done as it was the only direction of true advance. Gandhi then threw in the old canard that communal differences were the fault of the British. He said that it was impossible for Britain to work for a unified, self-governing India and at the same time to exploit Muslim anxieties and communal differences in order to stay in India.

Gandhi asked whether the British were sincere. Linlithgow replied that he could say at once that those who had had personal experience of these matters and had been associated with the Act of 1935 were entirely sincere. At the same time, he added, he was bound to recognise that there was a large group of conservative opinion both in India and at home which had not yet fully faced the issue as presented by Gandhi, and which had not fully realised that it was impossible to have it both ways. But one could not hope to move diehards by telling them not to be diehards. What was needed was patience.

They parted on the most friendly terms. Linlithgow had been deeply touched by the emotion which Gandhi had shown, even if the Mahatma evinced 'the same disinclination to trouble about minor or subsidiary issues as I have always noticed in him.'

On the same day the Viceroy saw Jinnah. Before the interview he had received a message from Sikandar, who asked that nothing should be done to inflate Jinnah or make him more difficult to deal with. Sikandar also repeated what he had already said in public, that the Punjab and Bengal were wholly behind the Government in the prosecution of the war whatever Jinnah and his friends might say.

Linlithgow felt it wise to be patient with Jinnah and to try to lead him in the right direction. If he could help the Muslim leaders to get more together he was, he had said, determined to do so. He told Jinnah, as he had already told Gandhi, of the need to suspend federal negotiations. Jinnah said he regretted that Sikandar had rushed in front of his colleagues in the Muslim League to pledge co-operation. He had no feelings against Sikandar, but Sikandar alone could not deliver the goods.

Jinnah asked the Viceroy to strengthen his hand. He wanted something positive to take back to his followers, preferably a complete re-shaping of the constitution. Linlithgow asked him if he wanted him to turn the Congress Ministries out. 'Yes! Turn them out at once. Nothing else will bring them to their senses. Their object, though you may not believe it, and though I did not believe it till two years ago, is nothing less than to destroy both you British and us Muslims. They will never stand by you.'

The Viceroy asked Jinnah to explain a statement he had recently made in public that he no longer believed in democratic government for India. How was India to obtain self-government if not by democracy? Jinnah replied that the escape from this impasse lay in partition – which was not an answer to the question.

This conversation, too, had been friendly although Linlithgow got the impression that he had upset Jinnah's tactics by the decision to suspend Federation. He believed that Jinnah had planned to offer the co-operation of the Muslim League in return for the abandonment of the scheme.

The Viceroy saw various Princes during the next few days. The Nizam of Hyderabad had spontaneously issued an appeal to the Muslims of India to support the war effort. Several Princes had already made substantial contributions of money to the tune of over twenty *lakhs*[1] of rupees.

*

In spite of Gandhi's own attitude the Working Committee of Congress lost no time in attacking the Government. The Viceroy's information was that Gandhi held fast to the view which he had expressed to him and that he urged the Working Committee to offer unconditional co-operation. But the Committee was less far-sighted than Gandhi. It announced that the British Government had flouted Indian opinion by declaring India a belligerent nation. The issues of war and peace must be decided by the Indian people, who could not permit their resources to be

[1] A *lakh* represented 100,000. The rupee was then worth 1s. 6d.

exploited for imperialist ends. Co-operation must be between equals by mutual consent. India could not associate herself in a war said to be for democratic freedom when that freedom was denied to her.

Linlithgow thought it 'a tragedy in many ways that we should have in so important a position a doctrinaire like Nehru with his amateur knowledge of foreign politics and of the international stage.' He did not propose to rush into any decision on tactics until the picture was clearer. He could see that the most common demand was for an assurance of Dominion Status at the end of the war and for the constitutional association of Indian politicians in its conduct. But he was surprised at the curious failure to realise, even in well-informed quarters in the Press and elsewhere in India, that they were tied by the Act and that anyhow they could not produce at a moment's notice some constitutional device within the Act's terms which would meet the contradictory demands put forward while avoiding all the thorny controversies which had bedevilled every effort at constitutional advance for the last thirty years.

Moore of the *Statesman*, for instance, was urging Federation at once. He was confident that, if only the leaders could get together, the whole thing would be solved and a workable scheme devised in the course of a day or two. Linlithgow's reaction was that he and Zetland could but sigh at the thought of such optimism as this. They had struggled wearily through years of discussion and of search for a way, knowing all the facts and having to face them:

'The tiresome thing is of course that the public, less well informed, and with less adequate background, tends to get the general impression that an easy solution is at hand and that it is only the stiffness of neck of yourself and myself which prevents it from being adopted.'

The Viceroy was under no illusions about the long-term challenge which was bound to face the raj at the end of the war. Even before the Working Committee's statement he was suggesting to Zetland that it would be wise to make generous allowance of leave to officials during the war. He foresaw that the raj would find itself confronted 'not merely with the ordinary aftermath of war on its conclusion but with the necessity for swift and courageous action in the constitutional field.' It was therefore of the greatest importance that they should have reserves to fall back upon and that the team should not by then consist merely of overworked and tired men.

This boldness of vision is not inconsistent with Linlithgow's more cautious assessment of the immediate possibilities of action; it is complementary to it. He was fully prepared for boldness at the right time. His immediate duty was to hold India together for war.

On 21st September, 1939, he set out, in a telegram to the Secretary of State, his views of the developing situation as he saw it and the possible ways of meeting it. The pace, he began, was becoming a great deal faster than he had anticipated at the beginning of the month. The Muslim League was offering conditional co-operation, demanding that the Government retreat from the 1935 Act. Congress for its part had rejected Gandhi's plea for unconditional co-operation, and were now bargaining hard.

Swift decisions, the Viceroy warned Zetland, might have to be taken on issues of great importance and he was anxious to clear the ground. There were three possibilities. First, if Congress would not co-operate except on unacceptable terms the Government must face the situation and allow Ministers to leave office. Secondly the Government could pay the full price of co-operation whatever the cost. The third possibility was to aim at a middle course, enabling both Congress and the Muslim League to keep in line with the Government of India in an effort to secure their co-operation, or at least their friendly neutrality; the provisions and scheme of the Act would be maintained.

The second course they could rule out at once. There would be no chance of reconciling the claims of Congress, the Muslims and the Princes either in the matter of Dominion Status or that of defence. Apart from that Linlithgow felt strongly that Britain

must not enter into any commitment which she might not be able
to honour in the event:

'. . . this type of blackmail once started is apt to continue, and you are
well aware of the fissures within the Congress itself and the difficulty of
satisfying all parts even of that party.'

The first course might have to be faced but it might involve the
collapse of the Act, international misunderstanding and the
slowing down of the war effort owing to the strain on an under-
manned machine. Moreover, large numbers of British troops
might have to be kept in India against the possibility of civil
disobedience. It would, however, be possible to carry on somehow and the Muslims would probably support the Government.

Linlithgow recommended the third possibility. He suggested
that he should meet Gandhi and propose the creation of a Defence
Liaison Committee. If that were not accepted he would ask
Congress for suggestions and would propose an all-party meeting
which would at least bring out the obstacles in the way of con-
ceding what Congress demanded.

*

Before the end of September Linlithgow was applying his mind
to a problem which was to cause a good deal of misunderstanding
both in India and in Britain. What should be his attitude, now
that India was at war, towards viceregal ceremonial, tours, parties
and so on? His own instinct suggested that he should keep in
touch with important centres but should dispense as much as
possible with what he called 'external trappings.' He took
soundings in various quarters and found that there was general
agreement with his view but he was advised not to cut down too
dramatically in case of a disproportionate effect on public morale
in an impressionable environment. In the result he decided that
there would be no more state balls but he would continue with
dinner parties and the occasional garden party with the sole
object of keeping in touch with both Indians and Europeans
whom he would not otherwise meet. 'I think,' he wrote, 'there is

probably a good deal of importance in retaining even in times of stress such as these a sufficient degree of public appearance to indicate that we have not retired into our shell and sunk into the depths of depression.'

On 16th September the Viceroy saw Gandhi. He was the first of no fewer than fifty-two leaders of various kinds whom Linlithgow saw, the series being carried through without a pause. It was an exhausting task but he could have chosen no more thorough way of hearing a cross-section of opinion at a vital moment.

Linlithgow told Jinnah he had sent for Gandhi and asked the Muslim leader to come too. Jinnah replied that he was too busy to come until after 1st October. This haughty response much annoyed some of Jinnah's colleagues, including Sikandar and Zafrullah. It was not untypical of his manners. He was, for instance, often late for his interviews with the Viceroy, whereas Gandhi was always meticulously punctual.

Linlithgow went ahead and saw Gandhi alone. He found the Mahatma very friendly and much more at home than when they first knew one another. After wishing the Viceroy many happy returns of his fifty-second birthday (24th September) he gave an account of what had happened at the Working Committee. The Committee had been very critical of his (Gandhi's) attitude after his last meeting with the Viceroy. In the light of the general feeling shown he had decided that he could not do without Nehru and that he must hand over to him completely the task of drafting the manifesto.

Gandhi then asked the Viceroy for a declaration by Government of what he called 'a really satisfying kind': Congress were in a special position and could alone achieve results.' He wanted a declaration of British intentions and an arrangement by which Congress could share power at the Centre with the Government.

Linlithgow set out the position as he saw it. He could hold out no prospect of any amendment of the Act at this stage, nor could he accept that Congress alone spoke for India; he could not disregard the legitimate claims of the Muslims and the Princes. He realised that underlying the demand for Dominion Status was the issue of control of defence, including recruitment to the army and the desire for the elimination of the reservation of defence to the Governor-General and the consequent appointment of an Indian Defence Minister.

The Viceroy said that he had been thinking of all possible ways of easing the situation. He had thought of an All-Parties meeting. He was perfectly conscious, he explained, that by exposing the internal differences between the great Indian communities and by bringing to notice the bitterness of the communal feeling and the incompatibility of the demands and policies of Congress and the Muslim League he would save himself a great deal of trouble. But that was not the proper approach to such grave issues. The most real contribution that could be made to India's future lay in sparing no effort to remove communal differences. 'Whether one liked it or not those differences existed. They were deep and real; and I was bound to remind him that to most thinking men they appeared to make the attainment of Dominion Status, or of complete self-government difficult to a degree, if not wholly impossible at this stage.'

About Gandhi's two specific demands, for a declaration and a share of power by Congress at the centre, Linlithgow felt he could not be encouraging. On the declaration point he said that it was just possible that His Majesty's Government might be persuaded to say that at the end of the war they would reconsider the position under the Act. As for the demand for a share of power now he felt that this presented serious constitutional difficulties and that they could not combine cabinet government as in Britain with the departmental system as practised in India without putting an unacceptable strain on the administrative machine. He also pointed out the weakness of a Cabinet not responsible to the legislature. At the first signs of internal stress there would be resignations. Good government must come first at this time.

Gandhi's reply was that Britain should hand over to Indians

themselves the problem of achieving unity: war demanded the
opening of a new chapter. There had, of course, for years been
nothing to prevent Indians themselves from uniting except their
mutual suspicion. This was Gandhi again falling back on the old
myth of 'divide and rule.' The Mahatma followed up, however,
with a statement of vital significance to the story of those days.
He said that as a private individual he regretted that the Viceroy
had failed to achieve Federation after his long labours. He (Gandhi)
had discovered, he admitted, that the Act of 1935 was capable of
expansion to satisfy the full requirements of national life in India.
If Congress had been wiser it might have been possible to implement the Act and in that event the difficulty of the Muslim and
the princely positions would have been less. But Congress, like all
others, was fallible and it was no good crying over spilt milk.
There, in Mahatma Gandhi's own words, lies the refutation of
charges against Linlithgow over the failure of Federation.

Gandhi thought that an All-Parties conference should be avoided
at all costs. He also felt that the idea of a broad-based consultative
body would satisfy no one; there would be extreme difficulty over
choice of members and discussion would almost certainly
degenerate into communal wrangles. Linlithgow asked him if he
would prefer a Parliamentary Committee and he said he would.
But on the big things it was a question of all or nothing. He saw
violence arising all round. If the Viceroy could make the right
sort of declaration in time then it was possible to scotch this
danger, but it would be a very close-run thing. It was essential to
secure for Congress a proper share of responsibility at the Centre.
Linlithgow asked what sort of body he was thinking of. Gandhi
said he thought he meant a 'named' body but that frankly he was
not yet quite sure or clear in his own mind. Linlithgow pursued
the matter in detail. Did Gandhi contemplate representation on
such a body of the Muslims and the Princes? The Mahatma held
out at first for representation being confined to Congress Muslims
but abandoned that narrow position and reluctantly agreed to the
wider scope including the Princes. Proceedings of this body
would be open; it need neither meet often nor vote when it met.

The Viceroy, whose Council would continue in being, would take its views and advice into serious consideration.

Such was Gandhi's brittle concept. What he was after was a way out for the Working Committee so that it could make a hopeful declaration on co-operation. Linlithgow saw what he had in mind but found his approach unconvincing. The Viceroy wanted to advance by experience; Gandhi agreed it would be unwise to go too far too fast but said that the Working Committee must be able to give their people some hope. There the meeting ended. The two men saw each other's difficulties and each thought the discussion had been valuable. Gandhi by way of a post-script begged Linlithgow not to consult the Muslim League over the declaration. They had talked for over three hours.

The Viceroy's conclusions from the conversation were not hopeful. He thought that Gandhi himself was anxious to help and would not impose too stringent conditions. But he thought also that the Mahatma no longer felt strong enough to hold his people together, that the pressure from the Congress Left was increasing and the Right might not be able to keep to an agreement with Government even if one were reached.

'It is clear too that the depth and reality of the communal fissure is more apparent to them than ever; and I should have said that they feel a growing doubt as to their capacity for holding the situation in that regard, or for achieving what is no doubt their objective of tying the Muslim community and the Princes tight in constitutional bonds imposed in the first instance with our authority and maintained thereafter in their original rigidity by the majority community.'

Linlithgow felt certain that Congress Ministers would leave office with great reluctance but he was in no doubt that they would have to obey the order to resign if it came. By way of preparation for the worst he impressed upon Governors the need for parting with their Ministers on the friendliest possible terms and of leaving the door open for later reconciliation. If the break had to come they must be resolute and make it clear that they would stand for no interference in the government of their Provinces. It was essential to reassure the various services and the many thousands of loyal Indians of this. At the same time the Viceroy was well aware that whatever was to happen in the short term there would be Congress Governments in power again at some stage. He felt certain that the only wise course was to try to keep all parties and their different sections together as much as possible.

'There is no other way in which we can achieve the unity of India, and any suggestion that we were endeavouring to divide and rule, or that the Secretary of State, the Governor-General and the Government of India were taking sides in matters of this nature could only be . . . damaging to a degree.'

Linlithgow saw Prasad and Nehru next, on 30th September. He repeated to them the gist of his conversation with Gandhi and then immediately stressed how strongly he felt that the great aim must be the ultimate unity of India. They must take the utmost care not to prejudice this prospect in whatever course they took in connection with the war. Dominion Status, therefore, must depend on the achievement of the federal stage. He could not contemplate any amendment of the controversial parts of the 1935 Act in wartime, nor could there be adjustments in government without the support of Congress, non-Congress Hindus, the Muslims and the Princes. He said that he could not, in his forth-coming declaration, promise Dominion Status after the war because this would at once provoke the Muslims and the Princes to active opposition and bring open conflict between the com-munities. As for defence, which the Act left in British hands, neither Muslims nor Princes would be prepared to see it in the hands of Congress.

The Viceroy acknowledged the negative nature of these con-ditions but he emphasised that they were the result of patient and conscientious reflection. He was genuinely anxious to help. He thought the consequences of a break would be deplorable and would most readily and earnestly consider their suggestions.

Prasad then replied to the Viceroy. In a carefully prepared address he said that India could put heart into the war only if a declaration were now made envisaging complete freedom for her.

The Princes should not be allowed to stand in the way with their out-of-date systems of government. The Muslim attitude could not be allowed to hold up the whole business of constitutional advance for India. He said that he did not suggest amendment of the 1935 Act. Congress was not really opposed to Federation as such, only Muslims were. Nor did he consider that the Muslim League represented the mind of Islam. As for an All-Parties Conference, he was resolutely against the idea.

Linlithgow privately reflected on Prasad's 'lamentable reluctance to face realities.' He told him it was easy enough to generalise. The difficulty lay in working out the details. They could not keep out other political parties. Prasad's proposals, he said, were heading in the direction of a fourth Round Table Conference. Prasad 'visibly shuddered at the possibility;' he said he did not desire it at all as it would lead to an immediate struggle between the communities.

Now it was Nehru's turn. He dwelt at length upon the immense changes likely to follow the war. The Government must think in terms of sweeping changes, not of gradual steps. Congress must be prepared for courses which the Government might regard as revolutionary but which seemed inevitable in the context of India's world environment. The declaration should promise absolute freedom to India after the war and the right of India to draft her own constitution through a Constituent Assembly.

Nehru, too, was against an All-Parties Conference, which both he and Prasad thought the Congress would boycott. He wanted a general election now. This might be difficult in war but it must be faced. They should then draw upon the new Legislature for a new Government. Its powers would be wielded by consent rather than by law. Some prominent officials might be added to it. This popular body would then be combined with the existing Government at the Centre so as to provide a single machine. Nehru admitted that he had not worked out the details; these were his general ideas. The Viceroy's idea of a Defence Committee of the Legislature appealed to him as being all to the good.

The Princes could join it, but otherwise they must be coerced by any popular government in India. Revolutionary action was needed in the States.

Linlithgow told the two Indians that it would be difficult to accommodate their views with his own but he would not criticise in detail what they had said until he had considered it carefully. He still hoped they might find some basis of agreement short of their general demands which seemed to him to be founded largely on speculative hypotheses. He told them that they were galloping ahead like two spirited chargers. His progress might seem to them more like that of an old *gharry* horse. But he must beg them to be patient if that was the case; since while they were free, he constantly had the cart behind him.

Linlithgow found in both his visitors 'a sad decline from the standard of the Mahatma,' with Nehru's mind obviously closed to any argument and Prasad seeming unable to exercise any independence of judgment although reasonably open-minded. He felt disturbed at the prospect of India's largest party passing into the hands of men of this calibre. He thought Nehru was going to be 'the chief nuisance' in this business:

'I found him doctrinaire to a degree, with all the indifference of a man who had never had himself to carry the burden of administration to the importance of detail . . . Gandhi having, with whatever hesitations as to the soundness of Nehru's policy handed his mantle to Nehru, no doubt feels bound to go a very long way in supporting and advocating policies commended by Nehru which would never have commended themselves to the old man himself had he still been in sole and effective charge.'

Linlithgow was on the mark in his feeling that Nehru's influence was growing in relation to Gandhi's but he was assured by Vallabbhai Patel, whom he saw next, that matters really lay between the Viceroy and Gandhi. The Viceroy took to Patel, who had a sense of humour, a shrewd and active brain and a strong personality. Patel clearly saw the point about avoiding speculative hypothesis as a basis of argument.

Before he saw Jinnah the Viceroy sent for Gandhi again. He

told the Mahatma of his talk with Nehru, who had 'soared above the mundane matters with which I was trying to wrestle and lifted us all with him into the airy heights of his brilliant imagination . . . he showed no signs of the least interest in the practical aspect of the Indian problem.'

Linlithgow then dealt with an equally soaring message which Gandhi had sent to the *Manchester Guardian* about freedom for India and the test which Britain must not fail. He said he wished to make the strongest appeal to Mr Gandhi to return to realities and 'keep both feet upon the firm ground of practical politics.' The divisions between the communities were deepening and communal passions were rising while they watched. He begged the Mahatma to help him. India's status and her constitutional goal stood to be reached by co-operation with Britain. Her ruin politically would probably flow from the other course.

The Viceroy asked if his intuition was right, that Nehru did not really want a settlement but had made up his mind to face a break. Gandhi replied that he was in part correct. Nehru, he said, from the moment when the Viceroy had sent for him (Gandhi) on war being imminent, had been inclined to the view that there was no hope of a settlement and that the British, whom Nehru knew so much better than anyone else, would not offer anything which could be accepted. Gandhi had challenged Nehru and told him he profoundly disagreed. He had moved him and thought that Nehru would now work whole-heartedly for a settlement.

The Mahatma now came to what he really wanted to say. He felt, in growing degree, doubt as to whether his belief in non-violence was compatible with his continued association with the Congress. Matters had come to a head only last evening in the Working Committee when Nehru said that India would need a first-class army if she did win her freedom. Gandhi had said, 'If that is where Congress is leading India, it is clear that I can go no further with you.' He had therefore parted from his friends and was alone. Prasad and Patel might follow. He himself would preach again the doctrine of non-violence. He wanted to be clear on one point: the Viceroy might not like the results. He would tell India that 'she should not return poison gas for poison gas though the Germans might do their worst.' The British must do as they thought right. He did not know what the Viceroy personally might feel. Certainly he expected no immediate change in his view. The Viceroy was, as it were, in the Scotch Express, and could not alight with safety to himself at least until the next stop. How many would follow the Mahatma he could not say. But whether a few millions went his way or he marched alone he would not look back, for he was bound to fulfil his destiny.

Gandhi said he had wished, since the Viceroy and he had come so close together, himself to tell him these things in advance. Meanwhile he hoped the Viceroy would go quietly ahead on the line he had already taken. If by chance the greater part of Congress were to follow Gandhi, then of course his own path and perhaps the Viceroy's also would be greatly eased.

It was the end of a most remarkable conversation. Linlithgow thanked his visitor and said no more. They parted on the understanding that he would send for Gandhi if he wanted to see him again, when the Mahatma would at once respond.

The Viceroy saw Jinnah on 5th October and found him more friendly and co-operative than before. Jinnah began by thanking Linlithgow for helping to keep the Muslims together and Linlithgow replied that it was in the public interest for the Muslim point of view to be fully and competently expressed. The Viceroy said that he had not made much headway with Congress and that it would be difficult in any declaration to go further than to promise possible modifications in the existing constitutional scheme at the end of the war. But it was of no use to proclaim the intention of granting Dominion Status on the coming of peace if the essential preliminary, which was Federation, was not agreed in form by the two major communities.

Jinnah did not like the idea of a declaration as it would only increase communal tension. He saw no chance of unity unless Congress gave up the claim to speak on behalf of all parties and recognised the Muslim League as spokesman for the Muslims. He said he had failed to move Nehru on this.

The two men discussed various possible ways of associating Indian opinion with the direction of the war effort. Jinnah did not think that an expanded Council could be held together; he preferred a broadly based group of representatives, connected with Departments through the Viceroy.

The Muslim leader then pleaded for more protection for the Muslims. The Viceroy replied that he had examined the position carefully but could find no specific instances of oppression. Jinnah said that the Hindus had 'a subtle intention' to undermine the Muslim position, as for example in the instruction issued in the North-West Frontier Province for compulsory teaching of Hindi.

Linlithgow had not agreed with Jinnah's assertion of organised Congress persecution of the Muslims but he received a disquieting account from Dr Ambedkar, leader of the Scheduled Castes.[1] Ambedkar, whom the Viceroy thought 'as impressive a figure as in the past,' told him that his people had never suffered more than they were suffering now from Congress and that there was an organised persecution designed to drive them into the Congress camp.

Linlithgow was still in the process of interviewing the fifty-two when Mr Attlee, Leader of the Opposition, launched an attack upon his policy in a debate in the House of Commons. The Labour Party, including its leader, had long been a carefully measured target of the Congress Party and had been subjected to a clever stream of propaganda which concentrated upon their unique claim to speak for India. The theme, couched in greatly over-simplified terms, was a plea for freedom from the imperialists with their diabolical invention of the myth of communal hatred in India. Attlee in the Commons criticised Linlithgow as being out of touch with realities and as lacking 'imaginative insight' – a phrase which he was fond of repeating in this context.

Attlee's criticism, of course, attracted much attention to India. Linlithgow reacted by observing that, while he was not unduly

[1] The official name for the Untouchables or Depressed Classes.

sensitive about this sort of thing, he did think it unreasonable to a degree.[1] He had kept in the closest touch with Gandhi. His sending for him immediately on the outbreak of war – criticised by Attlee – had been part of an arrangement already agreed with the Mahatma. Attlee might be reminded privately that Muslim opinion had to be considered and the Government had to weigh any proposal for changes in the system of government in India in the light of the fact that the army was largely Muslim. Furthermore tribal areas and the Afghans were sure to react unfavourably to any increase in Hindu authority at the Centre, a consideration of the utmost significance in time of war and with the attitude of Russia so uncertain.

[1] Linlithgow personally liked Attlee, whom he had got to know as a member of the Joint Select Committee which framed the 1935 India Act.

14

The Viceroy had finished his exhausting series of talks with the fifty-two by the middle of October. On the 17th he issued his awaited statement. Zetland had had difficulty in persuading the Cabinet to go as far about future intentions in India as Linlithgow wanted. In the event the statement reasserted that Dominion Status for India was Britain's aim. The Viceroy added that at the end of the war the Government would be willing to consult with representatives of the several communities, parties and interests and with the Princes over the framing of such modifications in the 1935 Act as might seem desirable. Full weight would be given to the views of the minorities. He appealed for caution and practical judgment in estimating the pace of constitutional progress.

As to Britain's war aims, the Viceroy said it would be unwise to give them precise definition at so early a stage. But that did not mean there was any real doubt in the minds of the public, whether in India or in Britain, as to the motives for which they were at war. They were fighting to resist aggression whether directed against themselves or others. They were aiming beyond victory at a better international system under which war would not be the inevitable lot of each succeeding generation.

On the question of associating India more closely with the prosecution of the war,[1] the Viceroy announced that it had been felt best to establish a consultative group which would be representative of all the major political parties and of the Princes. The Governor-General himself would preside over it and he would start consultations about its formation in the very near future.

Predictably the declaration was at once condemned by Con-

[1] The Viceroy had already requested the Government at home to make suggestions as to how best he could help them with the war. He received no answer until March, 1940.

gress. Gandhi, who had so very recently informed Linlithgow that he had parted from his Congress associates, showed that he had rejoined them with a vengeance. The declaration, he said, made it clear that there was to be no democracy for India if Britain could help it and Congress could not be a partner with Britain in her war with Hitler. Linlithgow had long since learned to be surprised by nothing where Gandhi was concerned, but in his own unwavering sincerity he was deeply disappointed by the completeness of the Mahatma's *volte-face* after so short an interval, and by his evident inability to match his private opinions with his public utterances. So much for the sympathy, so much for the friendship built up and valued between the two men, so much for the Viceroy's earnest plea to Gandhi for his help in that critical hour. But he would never give up trying, he would never be bitter.

On 22nd October the Working Committee passed a resolution rejecting the declaration as 'an unequivocal reiteration of the old Imperialist policy' and calling upon the Congress Ministries to resign. Gandhi, in a further statement, said that further action would depend on Britain's handling of the crisis; 'the Congress has left the door open, it is for Britain to amend the mistake.' Both he and Nehru claimed that communal differences were no obstacle to what Congress wanted but were being used by the British as a 'bogey' (Gandhi) and a 'screen' (Nehru).

The Muslim League's reaction to the declaration was polite but equivocal. In their resolution they appreciated that the British Government had emphatically repudiated the Congress claim to represent India and noted 'with satisfaction' – but without accuracy – that the Government also recognised that the League could alone speak for the Muslims. They could not wholly accept the Viceroy's account of events leading up to the passing of the 1935 Act but did 'not think it necessary to enter into a controversy regarding those inaccuracies, historic and otherwise.' While recognising that they had always stood for an independent India, they sought a clear answer to their previous demands that there should be no change in the constitution of India without the agreement of the League. If their doubts could be removed they would then authorise Muslim support of the Government in the war.

On the day following this pronouncement the Chief Minister of Bengal (Fazlul Huq) refuted Gandhi's charge that the British Government wished to hold India; he said 'it is Indians themselves who by their internal dissensions and quarrels are forcing the British to remain in India as the paramount power.'

The reaction of the Liberals was disappointing. In September the National Liberal Federation had passed a resolution that India should unconditionally support the democratic powers: this was not the time for bargaining, though India's grievances were grave and many. The Federation had then appealed to Britain to create conditions such as would lead to a general political appeasement and ensure complete co-operation from India – a request which was unaccompanied by any constructive suggestion. Now they joined the popular throng and passed a resolution condemning the Viceroy's declaration but again offering no solution.

The extreme Hindu Mahasabha, maintaining its hostility to Congress, supported the declaration.

By November, 1939, it seemed that all the Congress Ministries would resign. Linlithgow was determined to press on. If Government had to be carried on by decree he meant to be resolute in his responsibility for law and order but at the same time he deeply regretted the necessity:

'I am profoundly influenced by my conviction that a reactionary policy in India is not practical politics and that a struggle now . . . while doing much mischief at a most critical time, must in the end give place to a return to something like the scheme of the Act.'

The Viceroy now suggested an important move. The Commander-in-Chief might be replaced in his Council by an Indian Defence Member. The Cabinet turned the idea down, but after a long discussion they agreed with his proposal to invite Gandhi, Prasad and Jinnah to come and see him together.

The joint meeting took place on 1st November. The Viceroy

proposed to his three visitors that to ensure harmonious working at the Centre they should try to reach a basis of agreement between themselves in the provincial field. If this were achieved they could then make proposals for representatives of their two organisations to participate in the Central Government as members of the Viceroy's Executive Council. One or more representatives of other groups would be added. This arrangement would be for the duration of the war and would not prejudice the constitutional reforms to be considered after it.

Prasad rejected the proposal next day, using the same arguments as those employed against the declaration of 17th October. Jinnah said that he had been unable to discuss the proposal because of the refusal of the Congress representatives to do so.

The Viceroy published the relevant correspondence a few days later and said that he would continue his efforts for agreement. This brought forth a statement from Gandhi that it was the Government's 'divide and rule' policy that had made agreement impossible. He and Prasad and Nehru then repeated the point that the communal question was unimportant and was used deliberately to conceal the main issue. At the same time the Mahatma sent a message to the *News Chronicle* that 'to fling the minorities question in India's face is to confuse the issue.' These posturings by the Indian leaders were, of course, believed by the left wing in England, but nobody in India who knew the true position was taken in for a moment. In fact the Viceroy's obvious sincerity and goodwill were strengthening his own position. It was at this point that a Congress newspaper carried the following paragraph:

'Lord Linlithgow is no Don Quixote riding a rickety bull. Make no mistake, he is a very astute Viceroy who has put Congress in the most difficult position in which they have been for 20 years.'

Shortly afterwards there was a further meeting in New Delhi, this time between Gandhi, Nehru and Jinnah. Nehru stated later that the talks had removed many apprehensions and that he was unaware of any disagreement on fundamental issues such as had been referred to by the Viceroy. The Working Committee passed a long resolution which included an attempt to define a constituent assembly. There would be adult suffrage and the number of members in the Assembly should reflect the numerical strength of the communities, which meant that there would be no 'weightage' as between the communities.

In reply to all this the Secretary of the Muslim League delivered a rousing attack upon Congress on 6th December and Jinnah announced that 22nd December would be observed as a 'day of deliverance and thanksgiving as a mark of relief that the Congress Governments have at last ceased to function.' Again the Secretary of the League let fly, accusing for good measure British imperialism of combining with Congress to make life intolerable for the weak.

Vallabbhai Patel joined in to declare that each Congress Chief Minister had invited the Governor of his Province to intervene whenever he felt that the attitude of the Provincial Government towards minorities was wrong, but that the Governors had found Jinnah's accusations unsubstantiated. In fact there had been no such invitation. It was true, however, that the Governors with one exception had reported to the Viceroy, in answer to his inquiries, that they had not found any examples of unfair treatment by their Governments. Lumley in Bombay, whilst acquitting his Ministers of oppressive action, considered that one of the causes of Muslim fears was the arrogance of Congress, about which there had been complaints from many Hindus as well as from Muslims. This arrogance was seen in the Legislature but its main impact came from the attitude of the Congress rank and file in the villages and towns, where the local Congress bosses had sometimes made it plain that they intended to make things uncomfortable for the Muslim minority. Lumley had been given examples of this by a Congress Muslim who had been one of his Ministers.

Jinnah returned to the attack with a demand for a Royal Commission to be set up by the British Government consisting of High Court Judges to inquire into his complaints.

The acrimony of the communal situation and the intransigence which it left in its path were depressing. Zetland told Linlithgow that Sir Stafford Cripps had written a letter to Nehru telling him to stand firm upon his position and not to give way an inch. This the Secretary of State tolerantly called 'very naughty' and he felt, not unreasonably, that the attitude of the Labour Party was the reverse of helpful.

*

Linlithgow's patience in the face of disappointment was unshaken. On the failure of Gandhi, Prasad and Jinnah to agree to any provincial settlement whatever he wrote to Zetland:

'There remains today entire disagreement between the representatives of the major parties on fundamental issues. All I will say now is that I am not prepared to accept this failure.... During all the time I have been in India there is nothing I have been more anxious to secure than unity. And unity matters far more to India than is perhaps always realised. Unity, too, means that Indians, whatever their community or whatever their party allegiance, and whether they dwell in British India or in the Indian States, must work together in a common scheme. It is worth a great deal to try to bring that about. I may have been unsuccessful so far. But I will try again. And when I try again I would ask India to remember my difficulties and give me credit for an earnest goodwill and an earnest desire to assist.'

A potential embarrassment at this time was the presence in India of Sir Stafford Cripps on a self-appointed mission to explore the possibility of a constituent assembly and in fact to give encouragement to Nehru. Even Birla regretted the visit and he told the Viceroy that he feared a worsening of the situation as a result. He made excuses for Nehru who, he said, lost his head when he was on a platform. To this Linlithgow replied that he found it increasingly difficult to guard the interests entrusted to him and at the same time to act as a First Aid Post to the Congress Working Committee, especially now that casualties were becoming very frequent. Birla said Gandhi was the only hope as Nehru was becoming more and more difficult to hold down.

But the Viceroy made it clear that Gandhi and Congress must be prepared to help the Muslims somewhere or no one would get anywhere.

By the middle of November all the Congress Ministries had resigned; it was known that most of them did so with real regret. India had now to be governed by decree. Linlithgow had done his best to avoid such a necessity but he faced it with calm resolution in the conviction that it must be temporary. In fact the situation was to be more peaceful for the next few months than it had been for a long time and the Services were relieved of much strain. They had served the provincial Ministries with absolute loyalty although this did not prevent Nehru from delivering a disgraceful attack upon their integrity and efficiency in a speech at Agra in December.

On 14th December there was a debate on India in the House of Lords. Zetland made a strong appeal for agreement between the communities and stressed the very real problem of the minorities. Nehru attacked the Secretary of State's speech and then suggested that the communal question should be referred to independent arbitration such as the League of Nations or the International Court at the Hague – a strange line of thought from one who had hitherto denied the existence of the question.

At the end of the month Linlithgow saw Cripps who had been in India for some weeks. Cripps had seen Zetland before leaving England and let him know his ideas for a constituent assembly. Cripps first explained his proposals in conversation. Zetland was impressed at this stage but found the proposals less attractive when written down. The snag to the plan was that it rested simply upon a majority decision by the constituent assembly (it was in fact insistence upon this point by the Labour Party that had hardened Jinnah's suspicions so much). Cripps, however, hedged against rejection of his scheme by proposing that the Government should say that they were willing to accept any other plan agreed between the two communities subject to the rights of minorities being guaranteed for fifteen years, at the end of which period all British obligations would cease.

A few days before seeing Linlithgow, Cripps had a talk with Laithwaite (Private Secretary to the Viceroy). At this meeting he accepted the essential importance of the minority question but showed no sign of regarding it as weighing against the claim for majority decision. They discussed India's impressions of the Viceroy. Laithwaite pointed out how friendly were the Viceroy's contacts with Indian leaders and how widely accepted throughout the country were his sincerity and sympathy, his longing for Indian unity and his genuine anxiety to achieve a settlement on a reasonable basis. Cripps replied that he had been greatly impressed by the unanimity of opinion on this point from communists upwards.

Cripps spent two days with Linlithgow. He told the Viceroy that having seen Jinnah he had reached the conclusion that it was hopeless to get Congress and Muslims together. But he urged the Viceroy to 'go in at the right moment, try to get both sides together, and make them write down in so many words precisely what they wanted and in what terms they were prepared to reach an agreement' – which was in essence what the Viceroy had been trying his hardest to accomplish for the past four years.

Linlithgow found Cripps friendly, an admirable exponent of his point of view, very quick and ready to take a point. He was much impressed by the quantity of material which his visitor had picked up during so short a time in India, by his capacity for sifting it and by the range of the contacts he had made. Cripps was not blind to the weakness in the Congress make-up or to the complexity of the Indian situation:

'I regretted the more, that being so, he should not have been a little easier to move, for I think he has gone away as wedded to his original proposition as he was when he came here.'

*

Zetland was now worried by a change in the trend of opinion at home about relations with India. He reported to Linlithgow an increasing feeling, especially now in the Conservative Party, about the need to reach agreement before very long. The feeling was even stronger, said the Secretary of State, among the neutrals, particularly the United States. There was, of course, nothing surprising in this last point, but the news of the Conservative Party's restlessness was more disturbing.

Churchill had said, in Cabinet, that all would be well if only firmness were shown and the beneficent effects of British rule made clear to the Indian masses. But the answer, if there was one, did not lie in that direction and the Viceroy knew it. He knew that the facts of the situation must be faced resolutely. At the same time he meant to lose no chance of pressing the Indian leaders to come together for the good of their country.

With these convictions in his mind Linlithgow made three conciliatory speeches on his winter tour. The last of the series was made in Bombay which he visited early in January, 1940. The visit had an auspicious beginning. As the Viceroy drove through the city shortly after his arrival he noticed the friendly warmth of his reception by the crowds. There was a happy example of this when an Indian at a street corner, dressed from head to foot in *khaddar* (homespun symbol of defiance of the raj), shouted out 'Cheerioh Linlithgow!'

The Bombay tour was extremely strenuous and the Viceroy reported that prohibition of alcohol (brought in by the Congress Ministry) was 'something of a trial at public functions where a little anaesthetic is at times so very welcome.' He noted that the European population was allowed a reasonable amount of liquor and had no great grievance, unlike the Parsees and well-to-do Indians, many of whom were strongly opposed to prohibition.

The Bombay Speech was made at the Orient Club on 10th January. In it the Viceroy repeated, as he so often had, that Dominion Status was the goal of British policy in India. But now he went further. He said that this meant Dominion Status under the Statute of Westminster. He added, as he was bound to, that the Indian States and the minorities would not be ignored and that Government was determined to see justice done.

Rajendra Prasad at once retorted that the Congress goal was 'independence, pure and simple.' But the Working Committee

L

was not so precipitate on this occasion and agreed with Gandhi
that he should seek an interview with the Viceroy. The Mahatma
published an article in which he wrote these words:

'I am not spoiling for a fight: I am trying to avoid it. I like the
latest pronouncement of Lord Linlithgow. I believe in his sincerity.
There are undoubted snags in that speech. Many i's have to be dotted,
many t's have to be crossed. But it seems to contain the germ of a
settlement honourable to both nations.'

Nehru made it clear that he himself regarded a settlement as
impossible. His negative response was exceptional amid the
generally favourable reaction to the Viceroy's speech. Linlithgow's information (which he believed accurate) was that Nehru
attributed the tone of the speech to a concealed deterioration in
the war situation. The British were apprehensive of facing the
spring without a settlement. If they were prepared to be so
forthcoming when this deterioration was not obvious the wise
course would be to stand fast now until the situation worsened
openly in the hope that the British would throw in their hand and
accept the full terms of Congress.

Gandhi now prevaricated and told the Viceroy that certain
conversations which he (the Viceroy) had had with Congress
leaders in Bombay since the speech suggested to him that there
was no change in the British attitude and that a meeting between
them would be fruitless, as if it was to take place at all it must do
so with a view to a final settlement.

In the end the Mahatma switched back to his original intention
and saw the Viceroy on 5th February. He merely reiterated the
old argument. India must choose her own status, she was not like
the other dominions and her roots did not lie in England. He
attacked the British concern for the minorities, including the
European minority. These, including the Muslims and the
Scheduled Castes, were India's business. As for the Princes, they
should be regarded, not as a minority, but as a British problem
created by the British. He would be content with a referendum of
States' peoples on the form of government which they might
want.

The Viceroy stuck to the point that Dominion Status for a unified India at the earliest possible moment was Britain's goal. Meanwhile his offer of an expanded Council still held good but he was convinced that any attempt to develop this into Cabinet Government at the centre with responsibility to the Legislature would fail. He told Gandhi that he had in mind the giving of four seats on his Council to the political parties and that he wanted to push on with Federation as the most practical means of achieving early unity. The Federal Legislature could then be used for purposes of consultation between the British Government and Indians on a revision of the constitution.

Gandhi replied that he felt there was not enough common ground to make further negotiations possible.

Once again everyone was back where he had started, but Birla wrote to the Viceroy to report Gandhi's view that there should not be disappointment at the breakdown of the talks. Nothing, the Mahatma had said, had been lost by the meeting. In spite of failure they had come closer to one another and there had been a clarification of the situation. He did not yet intend to declare civil disobedience. He meant what he said in ascribing sincerity to the Viceroy – 'He is doing his best to understand us and his duty to his superiors and his nation.' The British Government must not be allowed to plead the minorities as a bar to right action on its part, but at the same time Indians must not blind themselves to the existence of this question which they themselves must solve. They could dismiss from their minds 'the impossible and utterly anti-national stand' taken by Jinnah.

It was not unreasonable in the circumstances for Linlithgow to feel that for the time being they must sit tight and let the situation develop. Recruiting was going well. Anti-war propaganda was decreasing; Congress would not attack recruiting as such tactics would only increase the hold of the Muslims over the army.

The Viceroy held to the objective of self-government for India at the earliest possible moment but he was becoming increasingly pessimistic as to the chances of Britain being in a position to hand over power. If Federation had been achieved, he told Zetland, everything might have gone well. But the events of the last six months had greatly changed the picture. The claims of the minorities had 'hardened beyond all belief.' If he thought it would help to summon another meeting of representative leaders he would do so but he did not feel that this was the moment as there was no chance of them responding. Zetland felt that nothing would be lost by the attempt but deferred to the Viceroy as the man on the spot. There was force in Zetland's argument but Linlithgow by now had had plenty of experience of trying to help the parties to get together and of then being totally rebuffed by them. Rightly he knew the value of pause in this familiar impasse and he was not going to run after Congress every five minutes.

On the Muslim side Jinnah himself had never been in the least constructive, but now even the Aga Khan, who had always been so helpful over Federation, was deeply apprehensive about the meaning of Dominion Status. He had assumed that there would be a ten to fifteen years' interval between Federation and Dominion Status and he did not favour a crash programme. The wise Zafrullah, too, although he thought Jinnah's idea of Pakistan demonstrably unsound with its cruel implications of mass movement of populations, understood the anxiety of his fellow Muslims.

Linlithgow, as near depression as he ever was, felt that the British need have no qualms of conscience:

'We have never at any stage adopted, or tried to adopt, Machiavellian tactics or tried to play people off against one another, and our sincerity of purpose has been recognised even by our critics.'

This was a just assessment, but the British by their very honesty of purpose found themselves in a difficult position. They had no honourable alternative to defining Dominion Status in terms of the Statute of Westminster of 1931 which meant something quite different from what it had meant in the days of the Round Table Conferences and Lord Irwin's viceroyalty. Dominion Status now meant complete independence including, of course, freedom to leave the Commonwealth. Yet the federal plan under the Act of

1935 included the retention of foreign affairs and defence in the hands of the paramount power.

Linlithgow never envisaged the retention of these powers as of permanent duration and he had made this clear to the Indian leaders. The minorities for their part were now realising the temporary nature of their safeguards with a clarity which events were putting into ever sharper focus. The nearer the moment of severance approached the less did they like the prospect. The only real hope was that the majority Hindu community would show the statesmanship to assuage the fears of the Muslims, but of this there was no sign.

The Viceroy felt reasonably enough that Congress had only itself to blame for the position in which India now found herself, but the reflection hardly lightened the burden he was carrying. It was a burden which would have weighed heavily enough in peace time. He now had to bear the added weight of holding together a divided country for the waging of war.

*

Congress returned to the attack on 1st March. The Working Committee adopted a resolution which was passed on 20th March at the annual session of Congress at Ramgarh. The resolution reiterated the refusal of Congress to participate in a war undertaken for imperialist ends and for the strengthening of the Empire which was based on the exploitation of India and other Asiatic and African countries. It strongly disapproved of Indian troops being made to fight for Britain,[1] wholly rejected Dominion Status or any other status within the imperial structure; repeated the demand for a constituent assembly based on adult suffrage. Withdrawal of the Congress Ministries must 'naturally' be followed by civil disobedience to which Congress would resort as soon as it was ready or as soon as circumstances precipitated it. The responsibility for launching it was explicitly left to Gandhi.

The reaction to this performance by Congress was inevitable. The Muslim League hardened its attitude still further and now

[1] In fact they were all volunteers.

threatened to cause serious trouble if the Congress Ministries returned to office without some satisfaction of Muslim claims. The Viceroy called the Ramgarh resolution 'complete political folly.' He had had further hopes of reviving the federal scheme but Congress, he said, had now made this impossible by their claims.

A senior correspondent of *The Hindu*, Shiva Rao, saw the Viceroy after the Ramgarh session and begged him to try again to negotiate. He admitted that the Viceroy had been hardly used by Congress but assured him that he had behind him the mass of moderate opinion. He suggested a conference of Chief Ministers or ex-Chief Ministers. Linlithgow replied that Gandhi had turned that down. A meeting without Gandhi and Jinnah would be like Hamlet without the prince. Get the Congress Ministries back into office, said Rao. Linlithgow reminded him of the recent Muslim League statement. Shiva Rao then gave the Viceroy an interesting account of the origins of present Hindu-Muslim tension. These lay in an agreement reached in the United Provinces in 1936-7 between Congress and the Muslim League. The agreement was that, in the event of a Congress victory in the elections, representation would be found for the Muslim League in the provincial Cabinet. The agreement had not been honoured. Shiva Rao had challenged Nehru over this breach of faith and its fatal consequences. Nehru admitted breach of faith. His excuse for it was twofold, first that Congress had been taken aback by the very large majority which it had won, secondly that Congress had felt it would be in office for such a short time that it was not worth while bringing in the Muslims. Shiva Rao thought that this decision had been a fatal mistake and that Congress had erred grievously everywhere in failing to recognise the importance of devoting their first few months in office to modifying the acerbities of communal strife.

The Muslim League met at Lahore on 24th March. It was the first occasion on which the League staged a gathering at all comparable with the annual gathering of Congress. Its effect was greatly to enhance both the importance of the League as repre-

senting Muslim India and the prestige of Jinnah, who emerged as
the unchallenged leader. Moreover for the first time a resolution
was passed unanimously advocating the partition of India. The
Governor of the Punjab (Craik) believed as a result that only an
exceptionally courageous Muslim leader would now openly
oppose or criticise this decision. If Sikandar were to make the
attempt it would mean a split in the League and possibly serious
dissension among his own supporters in the Punjab. He was
unlikely to take the risk.

The Governor saw the League's resolution as a very effective
riposte to Congress as it torpedoed the Congress claim to speak
for India. He doubted, however, whether the responsible Muslim
leaders meant it as a seriously constructive proposal. He knew
that Sikandar had tried to secure that the resolution should
provide for at least some form of central Government. The
Governor added, with accurate foresight, that although he
thought the Muslims would accept something less than partition
at present, support for partition would grow as the interval
lengthened without a concrete alternative being put forward.

With the Muslim League resolution fresh in his mind the
Viceroy saw Birla at the latter's request. Birla said that Congress
found it impossible to understand why, if the British Government was ready to force Federation on unwilling minorities and
the Princes, they should not show equal readiness to force
Dominion Status upon them. The Government's attitude seemed
to indicate lack of good faith.

Birla's apparently awkward question gave Linlithgow the
chance to explain the situation in the clearest terms which he had
yet employed. To start with, he reminded Birla, the Muslims
and the Princes had joined in the conferences and preparations for
the 1935 Act and had accepted it because it gave to both of them
the promise of mutual support at the Centre as a counter-weight
to Congress and reserved defence for a considerable time to come
to the Governor-General. Dominion Status did neither of these
things. Moreover it would prevent the Governor-General and
Provincial Governors from being in any position to protect the

rights of the minorities or the Princes. Given the attitude of Congress could it be wondered at, asked the Viceroy, that both groups had bolted?

So far the Viceroy's answer was unassailable but he was on less sure ground when he gave Birla a warning that there was a profound difference in the mind of the Conservative Party between Dominion Status and Independence, for this was to ignore the Statute of Westminster. Even if the Conservative die-hards chose to differentiate, the Government did not, nor did the Viceroy himself. But he was back in position when he added that he could not exaggerate the folly which Congress had shown in their handling of the whole affair. He was also on the mark when he said, a little later, that Congress had done more in six months to destroy the unity of India than he would have believed possible in so short a time.

He received a moving message at this time of stress from the Governor of the Central Provinces (Wylie). It was a question whether there should be a pronouncement threatening action against civil disobedience should it break out. The Governor thought that if one was to be made (he was against it) it should be made by the Viceroy himself: 'I do not know why it is but London pronouncements since war broke out have tended to irritate even moderate Indian opinion, while every shade of opinion in India at the present time looks up to and trusts Your Excellency.' It was true. The truth made it all the sadder that the Congress leaders so adamantly refused to move an inch towards co-operating politically with the Viceroy, whom personally they trusted and admired.

Zetland, who only a month before had wanted Linlithgow to convene another conference of party leaders, now agreed that the Muslim League's attitude had destroyed the point of making any further proposals and told the War Cabinet so on 12th April. Linlithgow had told him that he did not want to seem rigid or to close his mind to constructive suggestions. He would change his view if he saw the least likelihood of an advantage but he could not do so on present evidence.

Jinnah and the Muslim League had in fact reached a position of strength which the Viceroy could not ignore even if he had not entirely foreseen it. He must now give the League what support he properly could so that Congress would realise that they could no longer treat the Muslim position with the disdain which they were only too ready to show.

Meanwhile the Viceroy ordered that plans must be ready by 15th May to deal firmly and quickly with any outbreak of civil disobedience; he knew that Gandhi had taken steps, immediately after the Congress session at Ramgarh, to organise a body pledged to it. The Mahatma wrote a characteristic article, in *Harijan* of 27th April, in which he stated that it must be clearly shown that civil disobedience was not intended to do their opponents any harm:

'I protest with all the strength at my command that so far as I am concerned I have no desire to embarrass the British especially at a time when it is a question of life and death with them. All I want Congress to do through civil disobedience is to deny the British Government the moral influence which Congress co-operation would give.'

By the middle of May, Linlithgow, seeing no sign of a move by Congress or the Muslim League, considered sending for Gandhi and Jinnah to see whether even now there was a chance of them finding a common basis or producing any practical suggestion for ending the present position of stalemate. As before he was not inclined to take the risk of another rebuff unless he saw the glimmer of a chance. Superficial criticism has accused him of too much concern for viceregal prestige but it is a baseless charge. He was certainly without any vanity as far as his personal prestige was concerned. What he was rightly anxious to guard was the prestige of the Paramount Power, which was bound to suffer if he made continual advances to Congress only to be snubbed in the event. In fact he received a letter from Gandhi dated 9th May, 1940, which was completely inflexible and increased his doubts as to the wisdom of sending for the two leaders.

15

It was at this moment that Winston Churchill succeeded Chamberlain as Prime Minister. Zetland resigned as Secretary of State for India. He wrote Linlithgow a letter in which he said that Churchill's approach to the Indian problem was so different from his own that his inclusion in the Government was scarcely possible. His words of farewell were eloquent of the strain and disappointment through which they had been together:

'My warmest gratitude, my dear Hopie, for four years of the most delightful collaboration in a fascinating task. I only wish that between us we might have been able to make a greater contribution towards the solution of the problem with which we have been grappling, but the dice have been heavily loaded against us and I am bound to say that I do not envy Amery the task which he is now about to take up.'

L. S. Amery, the new Secretary of State, was no stranger to the Viceroy as he had been First Lord of the Admiralty when Linlithgow was appointed as Civil Lord in 1924. They were to get on well together and Linlithgow thought more of Amery than he had of Zetland, much as he had liked Zetland.

The position of the Allies in Europe was now becoming critical. Amery wrote on 20th May that with the threat of a German invasion of Britain the Cabinet was very anxious not to be wholly deprived of regular troops at home and urgently requested that the Viceroy agree to send back eight regular battalions in exchange for the same number of territorial battalions. Linlithgow agreed promptly and met with Churchill's warm appreciation for doing so and accepting an awkward hiatus before these replacing troops could reach him. In fact the imminent catastrophe in Europe was to prevent the change from being carried out.

Amery also warned that events might go against Britain, and

that Italy might enter the war and cut communications through
the Mediterranean. In that case India, Australia and South Africa
would have to rely on their own efforts. He asked about the
possibilities of further developing India's output of munitions by
the building of new factories. The Government were also considering the possibilities of aircraft production in India. With
these inquiries he was touching upon a subject which had already
been much in the Viceroy's mind. Linlithgow had been asking
the home Government for months for directions as to how India
could best help the allied war effort and had already foreseen the
possibility of India becoming a great arsenal east of Suez.

Amery made his first statement on India as Secretary of State
on 23rd May in the House of Commons. He restated the objective
of the Government as the attainment by India of free and equal
partnership in the British Commonwealth. It was for Indians
themselves to play a vital part in devising the form of constitution
best adapted to India's conditions and outlook – Zetland had said
the same in the House of Lords in April, having been made by the
Cabinet to substitute 'vital' for 'predominant.' The promise
already given that the Act of 1935 and its context would be open
to re-examination at the end of the war necessarily implied
discussion and negotiation and not dictation. The Government
had no desire to delay any of the steps that might lead to an
agreed settlement which would take account of the legitimate
claims of all communities and interests: the difficulty lay in the
acute cleavage of opinion in India: he refused to regard that
cleavage as unbridgeable. Even if no final agreement on the
major issue was in sight he could not think that it was beyond the
resources of Indian statesmanship to find at any rate a provisional
accommodation which would admit of a resumption of office by
Ministers in the Provinces and the appointment to the Governor-
General's Executive Council of representative public men on the
basis already offered. Such a solution, he believed, would be
eagerly welcomed by the overwhelming body of Indian public
opinion. India had from the outset of the war made manifest her
sympathy and support for the allied cause: let the leaders of the

great political parties in India come together in agreement in support of the common effort.

Congress immediately showed its resentment of any mention of the communal problem. Its President said that the speech made no difference to the Congress attitude as proclaimed in the Ramgarh resolution. Nehru condemned it as being out of touch with facts in India and Europe. He said that the British Government must give up its conception of being the patronising overlord of India and must recognise India's complete independence to do what it liked regarding its own future constitution and the problems arising from the war. He declared that it was against the dignity and honour of India to take advantage of Britain's difficulties, but she was out to gain freedom and could not give up the fight just because of those difficulties.

Sikandar rallied to the support of the statement in the Punjab. He said it should allay the misgivings of those who still doubted Great Britain's good faith. The political leaders should now come together and hammer out an agreement. He hoped that Gandhi and Jinnah would join in reconsidering the Viceroy's suggestion that the provincial Ministries should be reconstituted and the Executive Council enlarged: this would pave the way for agreement on the larger issues: it could also lead to the formation of a small, representative body to discuss and formulate plans for the future constitutional structure of India. As a safeguard for the minorities it could be laid down that over vital differences no decision would be binding unless carried by a three-quarters majority of the community concerned on religious and cultural matters. The extreme gravity of the war situation demanded an immediate lead from Jinnah and Gandhi. It was no time now for political manoeuvring. If internal differences could not be settled at once, at least let a truce be called and let them join to offer a united front in the common cause of justice and of the freedom and integrity of their country: internal problems had waited long and could wait longer: Nazi aggression would not wait.

It is a tragedy that Sikandar's statesmanship at this critical moment was not echoed by any other leader. He was alone among them and Jinnah was determined that he should remain so. A few days after making his gesture of support Sikandar asked the Viceroy what would happen in India if Britain were overrun by the Germans. Linlithgow replied unequivocally: he would hold the fort and fight on.

On 26th May the Viceroy broadcast a call to India to rally. Stressing the gravity of the position in France he paid tribute to those detachments of the Indian army serving with the British Expeditionary Force in that hour of supreme trial. Before them all lay many long months of struggle and suffering; let Indians now sink their differences and unite. The Viceroy closed his appeal with moving words:

'I have been amongst you now for many moons, both in good times and in heavy. No difficulties or disappointments have diminished my faith in the future of this great country and that faith is as firm today as at any time. What India most needs now is selfless service for the people as a whole, without regard to class or creed. I will not spare myself in that cause. That will be easy for me, for I shall be labouring to the best of my capacity for those who have long commanded my respect and who now hold my affection. I know I shall not call in vain upon you for the best and truest service of which each one is capable. Remember that, until I speak to you again, the watchwords are Unity, Courage, Faith!'

*

Amery asked the Viceroy whether he could see any constructive alternative to the 1935 Act. He agreed with Linlithgow's strong reluctance to be gratuitously rebuffed by Gandhi and Congress but he nevertheless felt that they must try to rekindle some sort of initiative. He suggested 'a serious dispassionate study by men with brains and goodwill' with a view to the framing of possible alternatives. He was thinking, not of a meeting of elected leaders – which he believed would be futile – but of a small, detached group which could prepare something for a political body to accept or reject. Sir Maurice Gwyer, the Chief Justice, might be the man to run it. Amery's purpose was to show Indians that although there could not be constitutional change during the war period, the time could nevertheless be a fruitful one for study.

Linlithgow thought over this suggestion carefully. He felt it might be useful later on but, after taking soundings, advised against it at present. It would simply be criticised as another delaying device. In fact he knew that Nehru had stated to a colleague that Gandhi was sticking completely to his demand for a recognition of Indian independence and a full-blooded constituent assembly. Only on this basis would he talk, but on it he would talk to anyone.

The Viceroy told Amery that he was anxious, too, not to stir up Muslim apprehensions more than he could help. The Muslims alone were working the constitution in the Provinces and their support was essential both from the military standpoint (they were providing sixty per cent of the Army) and also because of possible reactions in other Muslim countries. The Muslim factor in the war context undoubtedly increased Linlithgow's difficulties *vis-à-vis* the Congress position but to ignore it would have been a flagrant dereliction of his duty to India at war. Moreover he was confident that Congress, whatever it might do, could not now stop the war effort which was limited only by the availability of arms and equipment and training facilities. Men and money were coming in fast. He was preparing to set up an organisation of Civic Guards on a provincial basis; he was examining the possibilities of an increase in steel output; he asked Amery for the inclusion of India in the Empire air training scheme which would have great political value and he registered his disappointment that he had received no help yet from Lord Beaverbrook (Minister of Aircraft Production) over the setting up of aircraft factories – the sacrifice of some technicians from Britain would be well repaid.

*

Now came the moment of truth. France fell. Amery at once warned Linlithgow that the Mediterranean might have to be abandoned and Egypt and Palestine evacuated, and that he might have to face German and Italian air forces operating from Iraq, Arabia and Iran. That was why, wrote the Secretary of State, he

THE VICEROY AT BAY

had been so anxious to get some sort of constitutional agreement, if at all possible, before they appeared to act from a position of despair. If no settlement could be found, he continued, Indian leaders might think the British Empire finished and strike out for themselves. If that happened, then they might see Pakistan declaring itself, Congress India doing the same, and the country disintegrating:

'All this may sound very wild on my part, but think how wild anyone would have thought it six weeks ago if one had said that Belgium, Holland and France were to be in German occupation and that the invasion of this island was on the programme for the next few weeks.'

Such was the measure of the disaster which had struck in Europe. A few days earlier (13th June) Linlithgow had written to the King:

'We are well, though my wife has been feeling severely the strain of having both our sons on active service. We heard some days ago that John has got back safely from Norway, which has given his mother a temporary respite from half her anxieties.'

Now he received news that Charlie was missing in France.

In mid-June Gandhi wrote an article in *Harijan* which seemed to show a determination to make no terms with the Muslim League. His theme was that Congress spoke for India and wanted unadulterated independence; others did not and there could be no agreement with them. There were only two parties – Congress and their sympathisers, and the rest; one or the other must surrender its purpose before a rapprochement was possible, therefore there was stalemate.

The Mahatma may have been as inflexible as ever, but at least on the question of non-violence many members of Congress were becoming seriously disturbed. On 21st June the Working Committee passed a long resolution which in effect discarded Gandhi's leadership and doctrine in the sphere of self-defence. Nehru and others made a series of absurd statements trying to reconcile this with Ramgarh and explain that it did not mean they would co-operate with the Government. Gandhi was not deceived and felt deeply wounded, observing that the Committee had made a tremendous sacrifice in breaking with him.

Amery urged Linlithgow to see the party leaders again. He was prepared to seek Cabinet approval to a further declaration. This would stress that the Government wanted to see a united India attain as soon as practicable its rightful position as a full member of the Commonwealth on the same footing of independence as Great Britain and the dominions: that the Government recognised the right of India herself to frame the permanent structure of her constitution under which she would regulate her own affairs: that some form of constituent assembly would be necessary for the purpose and that the Government was prepared to see such a body set up immediately after the war if agreed on by the various elements in India: that the Government was prepared to accept the constitutional provisions which might be adopted by the assembly, subject for a stated period of years to such adjustments as would be needed for Britain to fulfil the obligations imposed upon her by her long connection with India, such as defence, debts, public services, commercial safeguards, and the States. The Viceroy could suggest that the parties should set up a study group to plan the exercise.

With regard to the States two alternative courses were suggested. Either British India could frame its constitution and the States then negotiate an instrument of agreement or the States would take an effective part from the outset in the construction of a constitution for both – British India and the States. Amery much preferred the latter course. If the States should refuse to co-operate he thought that British India should go ahead without them.

The Viceroy was not convinced that these proposals would do the trick but he agreed to see Gandhi and Jinnah and probe the position yet again. At the same time he wired to Amery that he was worried by the continued failure to supply him with anti-aircraft guns, of which there were now eight in India.

Linlithgow decided to see the two leaders separately. Amery

wrote that this might encourage each of them to put his own case at its highest, whereas if they were seen together they might be more moderate. Linlithgow commented in the margin of Amery's letter:

'When I got them together I was told on every hand [in India] that I did so in order to play off each against the other. In each other's presence they refused to say one word that mattered, contenting themselves with a few sharp digs at t'other side!'

The Viceroy saw Jinnah first on 28th June. The Muslim leader seemed anxious above all to get into the administration and urged that the November offer be put into operation even if Congress refused to join. He was indifferent to whatever declaration the Government might make as long as it did not compromise his Pakistan scheme. He would do nothing, he said, to risk the severance of the British connection; he was not prepared to consider any sort of constituent assembly. He accepted the need of the Executive Council for unity and for full co-operation in the war.

A few days later Jinnah followed up with a memorandum to the Viceroy in which he raised his terms. He made two new demands: first there should be a half-share for the Muslims in the central Government and in the War Council if Congress came in – they should be in the majority if Congress stayed out: secondly all Muslim representatives in these two bodies should be nominated by the Muslim League. He was naturally told that each demand was unacceptable.

The Viceroy saw Gandhi on 29th June. They talked for three hours and Gandhi was completely immovable. The Viceroy put to him the idea of a further declaration and made clear that he was speaking personally and quite tentatively. Gandhi was wholly opposed to any sort of exploratory process which he thought would merely bring out the differences between the two sides and embitter the situation still further. It would be regarded as a golden opportunity for staking out claims without the risk of awkward consequences; (Linlithgow agreed about this). The Viceroy pleaded with him to recognise that there must be a

M

transitional period before independence and that wartime was not the occasion for constitution-making. He said that the Government might be prepared to take a chance and announce that they would try their best to bring about Dominion Status within one year of the end of the war, or even more quickly if that should prove possible.

Gandhi was completely impervious to the Viceroy's advances. He said he spoke as between friends and on an entirely personal basis. The suggested declaration would not satisfy Congress, whose view had crystallised over the last few months; he begged Linlithgow not to make it and – rather curiously – he also begged him not to hurry. If any declaration was to be made it should be one of complete independence now. But the Mahatma commented pessimistically that he doubted the ability of British statesmen to do the right thing; they had a national tendency to make bungling into a virtue.

Linlithgow thought Gandhi's obstinacy in the face of his radical approach significant. He did not doubt that the Mahatma's influence with Congress was as great as ever.

A few days after his interview Gandhi issued an appeal 'to every Briton, wherever he might be' to accept the method of non-violence instead of war. Britain should fight Nazism without arms and let Germany and Italy take what they wanted of her possessions and even occupy Britain if they wished. At Gandhi's request the Viceroy forwarded the appeal to the British Government together with the Mahatma's offer of his own services in the matter. The answer came quickly, politely declining. The appeal fell flat in India.

Gandhi had, with the Viceroy's permission, told Congress the details of their last talk. The Working Committee passed a resolution on 7th July, the same day upon which Gandhi's appeal went out. It reiterated the demand for independence as before. As an interim step it demanded the setting up of a provisional National Government at the Centre, acceptable to the Provinces. This, it said, would enable Congress to throw its full weight into the effective organisation of the defence of the country.

The resolution had been drafted by Rajagopalachari and opposed by Gandhi. Nehru declared that it heralded the rapid liquidation of British imperialism and that the administration suggested was 'all the more necessary when Empires are tottering and an old age is passing away.' But there was a row inside the Congress leadership about the meaning of 'organisation of defence.' Both the Congress President (Maulana Kalam Azad) and Rajagopalachari said it meant participation in the war. Rajendra Prasad agreed. Nehru, however, denied this to Azad and pointed out that the original draft had contained the words 'war efforts' which he then got changed to 'defence of the country.'

Rajagopalachari provided an interesting example of inconsistency in this context. Although he had drafted this resolution in such urgent terms he had spoken to the Governor of Madras (Sir Arthur Hope) in a very different key only a month before. Proposing that the solution to the Muslim problem should be sought in granting much more power to the Provinces and less to the Centre so that Muslim Provinces could not be bullied by a Hindu-dominated Centre, he affirmed that the aim was complete independence. But he wanted to work Dominion Status as an interim step and said that independence might take a hundred years or more.

Linlithgow had shown patience for a very long time in the face of Indian intransigence. This was because he never lost sight of the ultimate object of British policy, which was to hand over power to a united India. He knew that a final breakdown of relations between Hindus and Muslims would destroy the chances of achievement; his policy and his tactics had been concentrated on keeping the way open. But he felt that a point had been reached in the course of the war at which it was no longer sound, and would become increasingly difficult in view of public opinion, to continue at the Centre with an entirely bureaucratic government. He was prepared to expand his Council up to the number of twelve if necessary and to appoint a War Advisory Committee which would include representatives of the Princes. He felt that the time had come when he must now go forward with or without the support of Gandhi or Jinnah.

Linlithgow also wanted to announce that the British Government would aim at Dominion Status within a year of the war's end.

Both Viceroy and Secretary of State were thinking along the same lines and Amery also thought Linlithgow's timing was right. Together they worked upon a new declaration.

While they were doing so the Viceroy had to handle an unpleasant affair brought on by the *Statesman*. The paper had carried a leading article claiming that there were men in the British Government who were to be profoundly mistrusted; they would be capable of Pétain's conduct in comparable circumstances and they had their British counterparts in India. 'We do not speak' said the writer, 'entirely without knowledge.'

The Viceroy telegraphed Amery that this gross and damaging libel came as a climax to a long series of damaging indiscretions. He had little doubt that the article was written by Moore, whose removal alone could correct the situation. But Moore did not go until 1942, by which time he had done more damage.

*

Amery put the new proposals to the Cabinet. Churchill reacted with a vehemence which surprised the Secretary of State and he mustered strong support from outside the War Cabinet. Amery was disappointed by the weakness of his own support in the Cabinet – which he attributed mainly to the accidental absence from the meeting of Halifax, who was to back him up.

The Prime Minister sent a strong telegram to the Viceroy:

'Secretary of State has shown me the telegrams which have been passed on secret and personal file and for the first time I realise what has been going on. I must ask in the public interest and in justice to you to show these telegrams to the War Cabinet and two or three other colleagues who have great Indian experience and whom I have consulted. It does not seem to me possible to withhold the facts from my colleagues. The Cabinet, on Thursday July 25th, considered your new draft statement. We did not reach any conclusion going beyond the declaration made by the Secretary of State in the House of Commons on May 23rd which defined the policy of the new Government in broad accordance with the views expressed by the late administration in the full knowledge of your views and wishes on the subject. The Cabinet has left it to me to draft for your consideration an alternative statement in harmony with the only policies to which we are at present committed. I will send this to you as soon as I have completed it for your perfectly free consideration and suggestions.

'You must remember that we are here facing the constant threat of invasion with many strange and novel features, and this is only held off and can only be mastered literally from day to day by the prowess of our airmen at heavy odds and by the vigilance of the Royal Navy. In these circumstances immense constitutional departures cannot be effectively discussed in Parliament and only by the Cabinet to the detriment of matters touching the final life and safety of the State. I am sure that I can count upon you to help us to the utmost of your power.'

The Viceroy was thus aware that Amery had sprung the new plan upon the Prime Minister and the Cabinet as a surprise. It had naturally not occurred to him that such risky tactics would be chosen by the Secretary of State; on the contrary he took it for granted that the Cabinet knew what was in the wind. He had been put in an embarrassing position which was none of his making. Churchill knew this and sympathised with Linlithgow in a later telegram. No doubt this was a welcome vindication; what was not so welcome to the Viceroy was the prospect now of sporadic intervention by the Prime Minister in the relationship between him and his Secretary of State, although this was sometimes to prove helpful.

Churchill took the impending declaration in hand. He refused to agree (and the Cabinet backed him) to any date for Dominion Status and otherwise hedged the draft round with more verbiage and equivocation than Amery or Linlithgow had wished.

In the event the declaration might have been much worse from Linlithgow's point of view. It announced the intention to expand the Executive Council while waiving the condition

precedent of agreement in the Provinces. A War Advisory
Council would be set up including 'representatives of the Indian
States and other interests in the national life of India as a whole.'
For the reassurance of the minorities it was repeated that no part
of the 1935 Act would be excluded from re-examination. The
Government would not transfer their responsibilities for peace
and the welfare of India 'to any system of Government whose
authority was directly denied by large and powerful elements in
India's national life; nor could they be parties to the coercion of
such elements into submission to such a system.'

On the future of the constitution the declaration watered down
the Viceroy's suggested time-limit for the establishment of
Dominion Status with these words:

'It is clear that a moment when the Commonwealth is engaged in a
struggle for existence is not one in which fundamental constitutional
issues can be decisively resolved. But His Majesty's Government
authorise me to declare that they will most readily assent to the setting
up after the conclusion of the war with the least possible delay of a
body representative of the principal elements in India's national life in
order to devise the framework of the new constitution. . . .'

This was a longwinded substitute for the much crisper statement
which Linlithgow had preferred containing the words

'Nothing would give greater pleasure to His Majesty's Government
than that the work should be so expedited and the necessary agreement
reached as to make India's achievement of her full stature possible
within a year of the conclusion of the war.'

Amery felt that in spite of the less attractive form in which
Churchill had produced the statement it contained in substance
what he and the Viceroy wanted. He wrote to Linlithgow:

'. . . the whole terrific fuss which he made, culminating in my showing
him every telegram that passed between us, was really irrelevant and
unnecessary. The trouble is that he reacts intsinctively and passionately
against the whole idea of any government of India other than that
which he knew forty years ago, but when after much eloquent out-
pouring at the Cabinet he was actually faced with the task of drafting

something himself, even with Simon's help, he realised that there was no alternative line other than that which we had suggested. . . .'

Amery still felt, however, that the original form of declaration would have appealed more to the moderates in Congress and to public opinion, although it would have made no difference with the leadership.

The Viceroy's statement was debated in Parliament on 14th September. Amery made it clear in his speech that if the Indian leaders would not co-operate the Viceroy would try to go ahead with others who would. Most speakers in the debate recognised that India had been offered a great opportunity of constitutional advance far beyond the provisions of the 1935 Act.

Attlee, on behalf of the Labour Party, supported this view. To Krishna Menon[1] he had criticised Congress, who were, he said, losing an opportunity by their behaviour. He was not deterred by Krishna Menon's warning of imminent and grave civil disobedience and was satisfied with the Government's policy and with its capacity to handle eventualities. Both Gandhi and Nehru were known to be annoyed by the comparative steadiness of the Labour leadership in contrast with some of its rank and file who found no difficulty in swallowing the propaganda of Congress.

Congress immediately rejected the August offer (as it came to be called). Gandhi said he had intended to be silent, having withdrawn from Congress, but felt compelled to speak out after pressure from friends in England as well as from fellow-workers in India. He denounced the offer as widening the gap between the two countries. Maulana Kalam Azad, the Congress President (a Muslim), refused an invitation from the Viceroy to discuss it. Congress then capped its predictable reaction by childishly declaring that the British Government had rejected its offer to co-operate in the war – as though there had been one. Nehru was heard to express satisfaction that the day of action was drawing closer.

The Working Committee of the Muslim League met at

[1] Nehru's right-hand man in England.

Bombay on 31st August. The Chief Ministers of the Punjab (Sikandar) and Bengal (Huq) were present. Each of them wanted co-operation with the Viceroy and Sikandar in particular was active in supporting the offer completely. In private he urged Gandhi and the other Congress leaders to accept it and he told the Governor of the Punjab (Craik) that he and others would withdraw from the League if Jinnah persisted in his obstinacy.

Jinnah did persist but Sikandar did not withdraw. Jinnah persuaded a reluctant Committee not to accept the offer outright and they passed resolutions accordingly and obediently. These recognised that the Viceroy's declaration had made a move towards the League's point of view, claiming optimistically that it met their demand that no future constitution should be adopted without their consent, but they found many detailed faults with the Viceroy's attitude as expressed to Jinnah in a letter following an interview on 14th August.

Jinnah's tactics were to take his time with the Viceroy's invitation and progressively to stiffen his terms. For instance he showed himself in no hurry to supply names for the Viceroy's consideration of Muslim candidates for the Executive Council and the War Advisory Council. Instead he carried on, in arrogant tone, a correspondence with the Viceroy which crystallised in a demand that

'in the event of any other party deciding later on to be associated with your Executive Council to assist in the prosecution of the war, it should be allowed to do so on terms that may be approved of and consented to by the Muslim League party.'

The Viceroy had no doubt that Jinnah wished to find himself the only man who mattered in the Council and so in effect in the position of Prime Minister. He had no intention whatever of allowing that.

Linlithgow saw Jinnah on 24th September. He made it clear, as he had so often done, that he could not abdicate his responsibility to suit the Muslim leader. After the interview Jinnah wrote him a bad letter reminding him that he [the Viceroy] had appreciated and recognised that the Muslim League's terms were vital to them, as if that obliged the Viceroy to accept the terms. Linlithgow described the letter as characteristically ungenerous and said that as usual it tried to twist the facts. Amery saw Jinnah as eaten up with vanity and prepared to co-operate only as the shadow behind the throne 'and a very definite and visible shadow at that.'

On 29th September the League resolved to refuse their participation in the scheme of the August offer on the ground that their conditions had not been complied with. But they empowered Sikandar to keep in touch with the Viceroy.

The Viceroy saw Gandhi on 27th September; they talked for three and a half hours. Gandhi opened with a speech of a whole hour's duration, attacking the whole course of British policy over the past hundred years and throwing the familiar accusations on the communal issue and the minorities. At the end of what the Viceroy described as a long and confused harangue the Mahatma asked that Congress might be permitted to deliver non-violent propaganda against the war effort. He said that India was divided between the Viceroy at the head of a war army and Gandhi leading a peace army. Linlithgow, feeling the metaphysical aspects of the conversation passing beyond his comprehension, suggested taking the argument from the abstract to the concrete. He asked Gandhi whether he would be satisfied with the liberty allowed to conscientious objectors in Great Britain. Gandhi replied that this was not enough: nationalists should be allowed to object to India's whole part in the war. He must have known that this was impossible.

After the interview the Viceroy telegraphed to Amery the conclusion which he drew from it:

'I must tell you that, knowing him as well as I do, I have now little doubt that he is bent on mischief and that relations may break down at the next talk. You may count on me to continue up to the last moment to do my best to avoid a conflict, but I think the moment has come when you will wish to warn the Prime Minister and the War Cabinet that the conflict which I have laboured for so long to avoid may now, despite our best endeavours, be imminent.'

Three days later the Viceroy saw Gandhi again. Again no progress was made, the old charge of 'divide and rule' being trotted out as before. But now a tone of menace came into Gandhi's attitude. He warned that speeches might now be made which would lead to prosecutions, which in their turn would lead to anarchy: he himself had only his life to offer and it might be necessary for him to fast to death. Here was the threat of black-mail by fasting. Linlithgow was not going to be intimidated by this ugly phenomenon although it was clear that it might prove extremely embarrassing. On the personal side the two men were still friends and Gandhi stressed it at the time.

The Viceroy understood Gandhi's dilemma. If the Mahatma persuaded Congress to do nothing he would fade into the back-ground. If he caused real trouble for the Government he risked arrest and a departure from the scene in that way. Nevertheless Linlithgow felt

'there is not a shadow of doubt that he is the one real figure which appeals to the popular imagination in the great Hindu community and that the Working Committee . . . ignoring his lead would find them-selves with very little delay on the thinnest of ice.'

Linlithgow confessed, as he rarely did, to a feeling of depres-sion, not so much because no immediate advance seemed possible as because of the damaging impression made by the Indian leaders in terms of potential responsibility for governing India. He saw at this point, he wrote to Amery,

'not the slightest prospect of agreement between the parties or . . . of this country continuing to be governed save by the commanding presence of His Majesty's Government. One can but regret that so much well meant and sincere effort over so many years should now look like running out into the desert sands, but we can with sincerity claim that the fault does not rest with us.'

He was grateful for Amery's support throughout these difficult months, but under the strain of his abortive negotiations with the Indian leaders he allowed himself a light-hearted critical comment at the Secretary of State's expense. Amery had written (2nd

September) that he was moved by a letter from one of the
Princes complaining that he had been made to employ a *dewan*[1]
from outside his State. The Viceroy noted in the margin of this
letter 'I must send Amery a dozen large white handkerchiefs for
Christmas.'

On 3rd October, 1940, he received a telegram from the Prime
Minister:

'I should be most grateful if you would accept an extension of
office for twelve months from next April. A break in the continuity of
action would now be unfortunate, and it is most necessary that those
with whom you have to deal should realise the prolongation of your
authority and the support which you receive from His Majesty's
Government. I have the greatest confidence that you will hold the
position firm on the lines that we have agreed and will develop to the
utmost the expeditionary forces of India. It looks as if the war will last
and spread and we must expect a heavy campaign in 1941 in the middle
East. Large Indian forces will be needed and we shall do our utmost to
produce the necessary equipment. Every good wish to you in your
onerous duties. We are steadily feeling better here.'

Linlithgow accepted. Tired though he was there could be no
question of refusing. In his telegram of acceptance he asked for
the Prime Minister's help in authorising a supply programme to
provide a million men by March, 1943, and for help in acquiring
dollars. He urged strongly that India's contribution to the Middle
East must not be made at the expense of her capacity to defend
herself in case of trouble from Japan – he had never ceased from
anxiety in this field since his frustrated efforts in 1936 to get a road
built to Burma.

[1] Prime Minister.

16

By the middle of October the Cabinet had agreed with the Viceroy's recommendation that he should put the plan for an expanded Council into cold storage for the time being. If he could have persuaded Sikandar and Huq to ignore Jinnah's veto and to join the Council things might have gone differently. But without them there was no Muslim of comparable stature available. It was sad that Sikandar had let himself be outflanked by Jinnah, who had always intended it, but he was in a very difficult position with the Muslims in his Province, who were by no means certain to support him if it came to a showdown with Jinnah, who had skilfully based his rejection of the August offer on communal grounds certain to appeal to the Muslim electorate.

The Viceroy could see no possibility of a split in the Muslim League, nor was it the moment to hope for the break-up of the only organisation which could speak authoritatively for general Muslim opinion throughout India. In thinking on these lines Linlithgow was looking ahead. On the long view there was the post-war situation to be borne in mind; in the shorter term there was the possibility of an open struggle with Congress. There was also the question of the Muslim majority in the army in terms of morale.

Unfortunately the moderates in Indian politics, like Sapru, were of no importance when it came to the point and had never been able to stand up effectively either to the Congress machine or to that of the Muslim League.

Gandhi, now in undisputed command of Congress again, planned his campaign of individual civil disobedience. He himself was to select the exponents and he announced on 15th October that direct action was to be begun by one Vinobe Bhave, a member of Gandhi's *ashram*, a Sanskrit scholar and a devotee of spinning. He duly shouted the required anti-war slogans in public and on 21st October he was arrested.

Two pertinent comments on Gandhi's campaign were made. The Congress President (Azad) said that Congress was not a pacifist society but a political organisation struggling for a definite political objective. Sikandar's comment was that Gandhi was demanding freedom to stab Britain in the back while she was engaged in a life and death struggle. That the stabbing was, according to Gandhi, to be non-violent did not alter this position. It was a very strange way, said Sikandar, of showing sympathy for Britain.

On 24th October the Government of India prohibited the printing or publishing of any matter calculated to foment opposition to the prosecution of the war. This put Gandhi out of his stride as he was relying upon printed propaganda to stir up the popular feeling which Bhave's arrest had completely failed to excite. The Mahatma wrote to the Viceroy on 24th October and complained. The Viceroy sent a courteous reply explaining the reasons for the Government's action. Gandhi wrote again and showed signs of temper for the first time:

'Reducing your language to simple terms you tell me that I must be punished if I do not behave myself. I hardly needed to be given the warning. But I do not mind it. The language used by you shows the pains you have taken to conceal your meaning in as gentle words as the English language and your exalted office will let you. . . . The whole purpose of my letter has been missed. It was to commend to your sympathetic attention the fact that I was taking extraordinary pre-cautions to ensure non-violence, and the further fact that I was restricting the movement to the fewest possible typical individuals. I had hugged the belief that you would, as a friend, be pleased with the information, and recognising the fact you would not put yourself in the wrong by passing the wholly unnecessary gagging ordinance you have passed. . . . I ask you to believe me when I tell you that in every simple step I have taken I have thought of you and your people as your and their true friend. One day you will feel the truth of this remark if you do not today. . . . I told you about the possibility of a fast, pro-longed or unto death. I am waiting on God to find what is to be the case. I am trying hard to avoid it but I may not be able to do so. You will have another letter from me when I have come to the final conclusion.'

Gandhi explained that his second nominee for *satyagraha* would be Nehru and that he would not decide about his fast until this exercise was performed. Once again, however, the Mahatma's plans were frustrated. Nehru was arrested before he could play his allotted part. His arrest had nothing to do with his *satyagraha*, but was ordered on the grounds of seditious speeches which he had made early in October in the United Provinces. The Governor of the United Provinces (Hallett) had for some time wished for Nehru's arrest. The Viceroy had been less anxious to take a drastic line than either the Governor or his own advisers on broad policy grounds. But, after applying the brake while the matter was thoroughly discussed he backed the Governor, a man of long experience.

Nehru was convicted and sentenced to four years' imprisonment. The Viceroy regretted so severe a sentence when he thought a year or sixteen months would have sufficed. But he felt he must let the sentence stand in view of the cardinal importance of supporting the judiciary in its lawful functions, although he arranged that hints should be passed on in the right quarters with a view to future sentences. It was significant that Nehru's arrest had been followed by no serious or widespread reaction, although it is true that it was part of Gandhi's tactics that disturbances should be discouraged.

Gandhi now widened his campaign. Other Congress leaders in a steady stream joined the deliberate procession to imprisonment until in January, 1941, the President of Congress, Maulana Kalam Azad, was himself arrested and sentenced to eighteen months' imprisonment. Again there was no public excitement at the event. The Viceroy received reports that the general apathy displayed by ordinary people both in urban and rural areas was causing considerable depression and disappointment to Congress, which persuaded Gandhi to drop his threat to fast, lest the party be left leaderless.

After Gandhi had launched his campaign of defiance Linlithgow ceased to correspond with him personally. Personal friendship was all very well but there were limits. It was not pique but
policy which influenced his decision.

*

The year 1940 came to an end with India as a whole in a remarkably calm state. The politically minded members of the population may have felt troubled but there was no doubt that to the
great majority of India's millions the disappearance into gaol of so
many of the politicians was a matter of indifference, even of
relief.

The war effort had proceeded without serious hindrance. On
the administrative front the Viceroy had seen the successful fruits
of his own initiative when the Eastern Group Conference met at
New Delhi on 25th October. The Conference had been called to
promote and co-ordinate the production of war supplies amongst
British territories east of Suez. There were represented Australia,
Burma, Ceylon, East Africa, Hong Kong, India, Malaya, New
Zealand, Palestine, South Africa, Southern Rhodesia, also
Middle-East Command and the Netherland East Indies (the last
as observers). The final meeting took place on 25th November.
Its principal recommendation was to establish in India a Central
Provision Office and a Central Supply Council, each to operate
over the whole of the Eastern Group area.

Linlithgow foresaw rightly that these two organisations,
which would be fully operative within three months, would
contribute very greatly to the strength and timeliness of the war
effort in the Middle and Far East. They ought to bring definite
relief to the shipping situation through the better location of
manufacture of supplies, the rationalisation of distribution and
the fullest economy in the use of shipping space.

India had so far done what she could do in terms of her own
war production. She produced all her ammunition but was still
wholly dependent upon the United Kingdom for many weapons
including anti-tank guns and anti-aircraft guns. She had already

sent overseas a million and a half pairs of boots, the same number
of army blankets, seven hundred million sandbags, seventy-five
million yards of jute hessian, sixty million yards of other textile
materials, and large consignments of iron and steel, coal and
timber. She was producing about half of the ordnance items
needed for British and Indian forces in the Middle and Far East.

Linlithgow had tried in vain to get from the home Government
a long range production target in the first months of the war.
Now his own initiative was to fill the gap with dramatic results.
Amery wrote congratulating him on the signs of energy which
his efforts had infused into the war departments. The tempo had
certainly quickened since the Viceroy's offer to the War Office
of a division in October, 1939, received its answer in March,
1940.

On the manpower front also the story was a good one. By
August, 1940, the Indian Navy and Army were far stronger than
at the outbreak of war. Navy personnel had increased by two
hundred per cent. The first 100,000 men to be added to the
regular Indian Army were being trained and equipped as fast as
possible. Recruits were enlisting voluntarily at the rate of more
than 15,000 a month. India's territorial forces had been raised
from sixteen and a half to twenty-five and a half battalions.

It was over the Air Force that Linlithgow felt particular
anxiety. There were 18,000 applications for 350 vacancies. The
Viceroy had wanted to build sixty fighter aircraft over a period
of eighteen months, but for this purpose men, tools and plant had
to come from Britain.[1] Churchill, advised by his Minister of
Aircraft Production, Lord Beaverbrook, would not divert anyone
or anything from the United Kingdom. Linlithgow, of course,
realised that the defence of the United Kingdom in its peril must
come first but he could not accept that his demands would
infringe that priority. He feared resignations from his Council in
the event of damage from enemy bombing, since he would not
be able to disguise the facts from his colleagues.

[1] He had originally wanted prototypes sent from Britain before they were all
blown up by German bombs.

Linlithgow saw his duty clear: it was

'to see that India's war effort, which I am certain has India behind it, is
not in any way impeded, that not a single sepoy is deprived of the
arms and ammunition that he needs, whether by speeches or by more
active forms of opposition.'

During the last weeks of 1940 Linlithgow and Amery reviewed
the political situation afresh. The great Indian sage, Rabindranath
Tagore, had pleaded for yet another attempt to bring the various
elements together and was critical of Congress. Amery felt that
it would be futile to issue a further invitation only for it to be
either rejected or accepted with no intention of real response.
The snub would be worse if Amery himself came out to India, as
Tagore had suggested. Linlithgow commented in the margin of
Amery's letter containing these thoughts:

'Congress will I fear have to be beaten in the present trial of strength
before we can get forward. I dare not try again until I am morally
certain of success. No G-G can afford to be repeatedly rebuffed. I have
not the least doubt that that is what would happen if I moved too soon.'

Two further marginal comments by the Viceroy in Amery's
letter are equally to the point. Amery had asked what Gandhi
was after. Was it sheer pacifism for its own sake? Or was it based
on a genuine desire to restrain the physical force and terrorist
element in the Indian national movement? Or was it nothing
more than an astute device for getting the maximum of support
for Congress out of a peculiarly constituted public? Or was it a
constantly fluctuating blend of all three?
Linlithgow commented:

'Holding Congress together for the post-war struggle and con-
solidating discipline and his own personal ascendancy. Non-violence is
the Mystery – almost the Revelation of the Gandhian cult.'

The third comment demonstrates Linlithgow's growing
pessimism over the possibility of Indian agreement. Amery wrote
that Sapru and the moderates must get it into their heads that
there was no chance of resolving the deadlock between Congress

N

and the Muslim League unless they produced a really well thought out working plan based on a clear conclusion about those aspects of the 1935 Constitution which have made it unacceptable to the different parties.

The comment:

'They never will, and all talk of leaving Indians to put their own scheme together – while it may tickle their palates – is moonshine. But I don't want to say this just yet even to S/S.'

*

The Viceroy visited Calcutta as usual for the Christmas season. He had wanted to discontinue the state drive on his entry into the city. To his surprise he was strongly advised by the commercial community to maintain it. He stressed to them the serious risk of misunderstanding of pageantry of that type and its inappropriateness at a time when both in India and at home there was so much personal strain to be borne. The community pressed its advice so strongly that he yielded. There can be little doubt that he was right to trust local opinion on the vital question of morale, but his decision did not help him with some sections of public opinion at home and questions were asked in the House of Commons.

Gandhi called a seasonal truce to *satyagraha* but his personal contribution to Christmas was curious. On Christmas Day he sent to the Viceroy for transmission a long letter which he had written to Hitler. The letter urged the merits of non-violence and expressed disapproval of Nazism. But behind this façade it informed Hitler that one fifth of the human race had been brought under the British heel by means that would not bear scrutiny. Again it was an odd way of showing sympathy to Britain in her struggle for survival. As Linlithgow said, the workings of the Mahatma's mind were indeed inscrutable. The letter was not transmitted and its publication was prohibited.

Privately for the Viceroy and his family this Christmas was a time for relief and thanksgiving. They had heard in midsummer that Charlie was safe as a prisoner of war. Now his wife Vivienne and infant daughter, Sarah Jane (whom he had never seen), were safe in India after a hazardous voyage round the Cape. 'Nursery painted and papered,' wrote Linlithgow to one of his daughters, 'woolly pants knitted and all the rest of it – including a huge wire netting cage to keep the monkeys off, on the lawn at Simla.'

Early in 1941 Lady Linlithgow went through a most alarming experience. The family were in camp at Kaladhungi. Late one night she was woken by her *jemadar*, who was standing beside her bed saying 'Light! Light!' She shone a torch and saw by his eyes that he was out of his mind. She jumped out of bed but he caught hold of her ankles, prostrating himself on the ground. She had the presence of mind to stoop down and remove the dagger from his belt, to which he responded by imploring her to kill him. Kicking herself free she fled from the tent. The poor *jemadar* also fled and was found next morning some miles away sitting in the roadway covered in dust. It was a tragic as well as a frightening episode for he had been a devoted personal guard to the Vicereine and the family were very fond of him.

*

On the political front the New Year opened with an attempt by Jinnah to get at the Labour Party in England through a self-appointed intermediary and so to drive a wedge between Parliament and the Viceroy. The intermediary proved to be a Major Gardiner. This officer, whose war appointment was that of Military Film Censor in the Sind Brigade Area, was a member of the Fabian Society. He had been in correspondence with members of the Labour Party, to whom he had said that stupid and unnecessary blunders by the Government of India were repeatedly coming to his notice. If the party would trust him to conduct negotiations with Jinnah the door would not only be open but wide open.

Investigations into Major Gardiner, who was relieved of his appointment, showed that he was of no consequence and somewhat eccentric. Jinnah had told him nothing new but made the completely untrue accusation that the Viceroy had not given him

sufficient material in their discussions during the previous autumn
to make possible any satisfactory result.

In fact Attlee made clear that he was not at all attracted by
the theory of Pakistan and that he thought Sikandar a more
responsible leader than Jinnah.

Early in February the Viceroy had a significant talk with the
editor of the *Hindu* of Madras (Srinavasan), who was president of
the Standing Committee of the Newspaper Editors' Conference.
The paper supported Gandhi's anti-war activities. Srinavasan
blamed the Government of India for the *satyagraha* movement;
they were taking advantage of differences between Indians and
were standing aside. Linlithgow pointed out that Congress had
asked the Government to keep out and let Indians frame their
own constitution. 'Ah,' said Srinavasan, 'but that is quite out of
the question and you know perfectly well that it is out of the
question. You and His Majesty's Government must take the full
responsibility in this matter. You cannot stand aside. It is not even
enough that you should be intermediaries. You must take the full
responsibility. The present position is most unfair. The burden
has been placed on us and the Secretary of State is taking full
advantage of the fact that it has been so placed and he knows that
we cannot hope to get together.'

Srinavasan blamed Nehru for 'the dreadful blunder' of with-
drawing the provincial Ministries from office. Pakistan, he said,
had started as a bargaining point but had now caught on to a most
dangerous degree.

*

A few days after this exasperating interview Linlithgow was laid
up for the first time in five years – a remarkable record. He had a
mild attack of dysentery and was unable to do more than formal
work.

It was at this time that Gandhi launched the second phase of his
satyagraha campaign. The first phase had stirred up little response
and had been marked by the failure of the average Congressman
to match up to Gandhi's ideal *satyagrahi*. There was, for instance,

a noticeable lack of readiness to refuse nourishment in prison. This second phase made no more of an impact than the first. There was an amusing incident when a relation of Rajagopalachari's marched fifteen hundred miles from Madras to Delhi in a month. On arrival he telephoned to Gandhi for instructions and was curtly told to return home by train.

In mid-February Gandhi wrote a letter to the *Times of India* in which he asserted that the prospect of Hitler killing every *satyagrahi* caused him neither terror nor despair: if a few *satyagrahis* died without malice in their breasts it would be a new experience for the Führer. Gandhi also took the opportunity in this letter to affirm that there could be no settlement during the war short of independence.

The third phase of *satyagraha* started in April. This time the privilege of serving was extended to the poorest members of the Congress Party, known as four-anna members, thus giving the rural masses a chance to show their faith in the Mahatma's leadership. There were few volunteers.

The press, including Indian-owned papers, was becoming restive over the farce of *satyagraha* and there were demands to call it off. At a press meeting in February it became clear that most of the press wanted to see the defeat of Nazism and Fascism and did not, therefore, support the hampering of the war effort. Gandhi's characteristic comment was that *satyagraha* had never been intended to affect the war effort but was a moral protest in the name of a free people against the conduct of the war. Whatever he meant by that, *satyagraha* had been a flop and by the end of the summer the campaign was dead. But the Mahatma remained committed to it and so, therefore, did Congress. The Viceroy discussed the point with one of India's most distinguished and respected lawyers, Sir C. P. Ramaswami Aiyyar. 'Sir C.P.,' as he was always known, analysed Gandhi's attitude by comparing his state of mind with one identified in the old writings as frequently afflicting persons devoted in a high degree to disciplines such as, for instance, *yoga*. It produced a form of arrogance based on the conviction of a close personal relationship with the Supreme

Being, which led to a stiffening of outlook and serious loss of judgment. Linlithgow thought there was something in this analysis; he thought, too, that there was a growing weariness on the part of Gandhi's supporters. But he had no doubt at all that the Mahatma's control was absolute.

On the Muslim side Jinnah's control was tightening fast. In early March he recommended Pakistan to a meeting of students at Lahore, the capital of the Punjab, and was given an ovation. This was on Sikandar's home ground. The Punjab Premier was in an immensely difficult position. The integrity of the Province depended upon his holding together the coalition of Muslims, Hindus and Sikhs. This in its turn meant that he could not accept Jinnah's Pakistan. On 11th March he made a speech of great courage in the Punjab Assembly. Neither of the major communities, he said, should seek to dominate the other. Muslims should accept the Hindu majority in seven or eight Provinces and Hindus should accept the Muslim majority in the others. Let there be full autonomy in the Provinces and a central agency to administer common subjects. If Pakistan meant Muslim *raj* in the Punjab he would have nothing to do with it; he wanted a free Punjab in which all communities would share self-government.

This brave speech marked openly the growing rupture between Sikandar and Jinnah. But it was Jinnah who was playing from strength and the ring was closing round Sikandar. Even the Sikhs, fearful of the prospect of Pakistan, were now talking of a State of their own. But Jinnah got the concept of Pakistan written into the Muslim League's policy.

*

Amery for his part was becoming increasingly worried by the situation. He had written to the Viceroy (25th January):

'Jinnah and his Pakistanis are beginning to be almost more of a menace [than Congress] and to have lost all sense of realities. . . . If there is to be a Pakistan, Kashmir will obviously have to belong to it and Hyderabad will obviously have to belong to Hindu India and the Nizam would probably have to clear out bag and baggage. The whole future of his State and dynasty, as in the complementary case of Kashmir, depends on India remaining united and on a basis of compromise between Hindu and Muslim.'

Coming events were indeed casting their shadows. Amery suggested it might be worth while emphasising to the Princes the danger to their whole order from the continuing drift towards a Hindu-Muslim clash and the obligation upon them to take an active part in the search for a constitutional solution to keep India together.

The Secretary of State thought it important that the 'absurdity' of the concept of Pakistan should be exposed as early as possible and that Jinnah should be under no misapprehension as to where the British Government stood on the matter. But the Viceroy remained convinced that they could not properly pre-empt the future in that way. Jinnah knew perfectly well that both Britain and the Viceroy were dedicated to the vision of a united India.

On 20th February Linlithgow reported a development in the Assembly to which he attached the greatest significance. A member of the Congress National Party put down a motion urging Government to establish responsible government at the Centre and in the Provinces. The Muslim League made it clear that they would table an amendment demanding the division of India into independent Muslim and Hindu States and meanwhile the association of the Muslim League and other parties willing to co-operate with Government in the war. In the absence of Congress the League's amendment would obviously have been carried so the motion was withdrawn.

Linlithgow's comment to Amery was as follows:

'I regard this incident as one of great importance, for it represents an anticipation of the position in which we shall find ourselves once the war is over. The Muslims will insist on their own terms, and there will be little if any prospect of harmonising their demands with those put forward by the Hindu majority. The Muslim attitude shows every sign of hardening . . . they are now a very substantial and well-organised whole, and they have not the least intention of permitting progress to be made on lines that Congress and the Hindu parties might be prepared to consider.'

This was an accurate forecast of events. It shows that Linlithgow must have felt in his heart that it was now too late for the vision to be realised, although he never gave up hope.

In March the moderates showed that they, too, were restive. They had issued a statement in January to the effect that the Government of India, by its unimaginative and mistrusting attitude, was losing the goodwill which it had enjoyed at the outbreak of war. One of their number, Sir Cowasjee Jehangir, complained that their lot was to subscribe to the war fund and knit stockings. Now they held a conference in Bombay under the chairmanship of Sapru. Most of those present were members of Sapru's Liberal Party but some were known to have strong Congress leanings. There were only four Muslims present and they were of no importance.

The Viceroy had information that the conference was in fact the idea of a few of Gandhi's supporters and that its object was to use moderate opinion to break the deadlock and to take off Gandhi's shoulders some of the weight of the failure of his *satyagraha* campaign.

A resolution was passed calling for Cabinet Government by a completely Indianised Cabinet, but this was to be responsible to the Crown and not the Legislature – in other words it was the Executive Council under another name. The conference was not considered a success by its organisers but it had more effect than they thought. During the discussions Sir Jagdish Prasad (who had personally organised the conference) had made the comment that those whom Government regarded as representative Indians made demands which could not be conceded because they were unreasonable; those who made reasonable demands were unrepresentative. Therefore, he said, the height of wisdom was for Government to stand fast in complete arrogance.

Press reaction to the conference reflected the anxiety of many moderate Indians lest the failure of Gandhi's leadership and the widening of the communal gulf should postpone indefinitely the achievement of self-government. There was also a debate in the House of Commons which showed uneasiness at the deadlock even among members who were not normally critical of Indian policy.

The Viceroy decided in May, with Amery's encouragement, that he must now, at last, go over the heads of the parties and accept the fact that they would not co-operate except upon impossible conditions. It was not a decision to be made lightly. It meant by-passing the Congress Party which, after all, had a constitutional majority in seven Provinces. Linlithgow never abandoned his insistence that the eclipse of democratic government must be regarded as temporary, and he was rightly reluctant to take any step which compromised that position. But compelling events now presented him with the chance for which he had been waiting. He would go ahead and expand his Executive Council by including non-official Indians who would be chosen for their individual qualities and not as representatives of particular parties. He would also set up a National Defence Council which would represent communal, functional and territorial interests throughout India.

*

For many weeks there was intense activity. First of all Churchill intervened personally with the Viceroy and questioned the need for action. Linlithgow told him that if he had felt it wise to stand firm and make no move at all he would have said so. After much questioning of details Amery was able to report to the Viceroy that after a preliminary explosion the Prime Minister 'came round completely and not only blessed the proposal in Cabinet but hoped that it would be carried through as quickly as possible.'

Then there was serious difficulty with the Punjab Government which threatened to resign unless they got what they wanted by way of Punjabi representation on the Executive Council. The Viceroy was distressed by this and said so to Sikandar, to whom he explained that he was not to be deterred by this kind of threat from any quarter.

The formation of the new Executive Council was announced in July. It was seen that for the first time there was a majority of Indians upon it – eight to five. It was also clear that the new team surpassed in experience and ability any which could have been appointed on a basis of party nomination.

The National Defence Council was formed at the same time. Its composition represented communal, functional and territorial interests throughout India. There were twenty-two seats for British India and nine for the Princes. The Council would meet about every second month when it would hear from the Commander-in-Chief a confidential account of the war situation and discuss it. Between meetings the members would assess the progress of the war effort in their Provinces or States. Thus the Viceroy had brought about what he had long desired and awaited patiently – the close association of Indians with the war effort. He had also effectively strengthened liaison between the Provinces and States and the central Government. Moreover, for the first time since the shelving of Federation, British India and the States had come together.

The House of Commons accepted the new arrangements with marked approval, all parties recognising that here was a new start with great opportunities.

Gandhi remained unmoved; Jinnah was furious – 'mad with rage' as the Viceroy reported. What angered him particularly was that the Premiers of Bengal, Assam and the Punjab (all of them members of the Muslim League) had accepted the Viceroy's invitation to join the Defence Council without consulting him. They had, of course, been invited in their capacity as Premiers; each was also a member of his own Provincial War Committee. But Jinnah was not to be assuaged by that. He seized upon two excuses to strike. The first arose from a remark of Amery's in the House of Commons that patriotic Indians had come forward to work for India's defence regardless of party leaders and in defiance of party discipline. Secondly Jinnah picked up an expression of the Viceroy's that the Muslim community must be represented by men of the highest quality. Amery's words were tactically unwise in view of Linlithgow's meticulous care to make it clear that his invitations were not issued on a party basis. Linlithgow's own observation contained nothing provoking and was merely stating the obvious. The fact is that Jinnah would have found an excuse anyhow. He was out for blood and he got it. After bitterly attacking the Viceroy for ignoring the Muslim League and Amery for criticising (as he had) the concept of Pakistan, he forced the three Premiers to resign from the Defence Council in the following September.

17

In July, 1941, Germany attacked Russia, presenting a potential threat to India through the Caucasus. A further consequence of this critical development was that all the countries between India and the battle front were Muslim.

At the beginning of the year morale in India had been high as the result of Wavell's victories in North and East Africa. Indian troops had played a gallant part in the operations and India was proud of them. But the successful German counter-attack in Cyrenaica under Rommel on 31st March and the invasion of Yugoslavia and Greece on 6th April were bound to depress public opinion. The Viceroy was impressed by the steadiness with which these shocks were sustained but the war was still far from India.

At the end of January General Auchinleck had succeeded Cassels as Commander-in-Chief. Linlithgow and Auchinleck worked happily together from the start. It was as well that they did for they were soon faced with a sharp challenge in Iraq.

The strategic possibilities of Iraq were well understood by the Axis powers, who saw it as a centre for disruption of the British position in the Middle East. At the outbreak of war, although the Regent Abdulillah was friendly, the politicians in power were all anti-British and in the pay of the Axis. They were led by Rashid Ali al Gailani. This man worked closely with Haj Amin el Husseini the ex-Mufti of Jerusalem who had fled to Baghdad after leading the 1936–9 Arab rebellion in Palestine.

The R.A.F. had, by treaty, a base inland at Habbaniya. Otherwise there were no British troops in the country. General Wavell, Commander-in-Chief, Middle East, was heavily committed by 1941 in Cyrenaica, Greece and East Africa, and naturally felt reluctant to be involved in Iraq. Backed by the advice of his Arab experts, he proposed that the situation there should be dealt with by diplomatic action.

The Viceroy and Auchinleck were disturbed by the complacency with which the position in Iraq was regarded outside India. For months there had been a plan for a force of three divisions to be trained in case of an emergency but they both believed the matter was much too critical for long term planning and they wanted to get into Iraq as soon as possible. They did not share the hope of G.H.Q. for at least three months' grace and the establishment of a friendly régime. With Amery backing them they got agreement in March, 1941, that if operations should be necessary, they would be carried out under the control of India, at any rate at first.

Throughout March the situation worsened and the pro-Axis forces in Iraq gained ground. The Regent fled the country on learning of a plot to arrest him and was given British protection in a warship. Rashid Ali set himself up as head of a Government of National Defence.

With the allied reverses in Cyrenaica, Yugoslavia and Greece, poor Wavell's hands were full and he continued to advise against military action in Iraq. But now Churchill acted. He wanted troops from India to secure Basra at the head of the Persian Gulf. Linlithgow responded at once and wired that he would divert a brigade with attached artillery and services which was already embarked at Karachi under orders for Malaya. This could be followed by two further brigade groups after twenty-one days. He was also prepared to transport four hundred British infantry with machine guns by air to Shaiba starting in three days' time.

The Viceroy's offer was accepted and preparations went ahead immediately. Wavell, informed by Auchinleck of the decision, wired back that it was a critical one. It might work, he recognised, but on the same day he urged the Chiefs of Staff once again to rely upon diplomacy which might, he suggested, be backed by air support.

Fortunately the preparations for the operation were not affected by Wavell's advice but now another, graver threat to it developed. Rashid Ali, addressing the Iraqi Senate on 10th April, declared that Iraq would honour her obligations under the Anglo-Iraqi Treaty. Sir Kinahan Cornwallis, the British Ambassador, had hitherto been in favour of force but he now changed course as a result of this speech and advised that the start of the expedition should be delayed while he explained to Rashid Ali that Britain had to move troops through the country to Palestine on a future date which would be named.

The Foreign Office wanted to accept the Ambassador's advice and signalled to New Delhi accordingly. The convoy had in fact sailed so the suggestion was that it should be stopped and ordered to anchor, perhaps at Bahrein. The Viceroy reacted strongly and decisively. He felt that if they hesitated now they would probably lose their own chance to get into Basra and increase that of the Germans to forestall us with a coup. 'I have no doubt,' he wired, 'that we must be prepared to take a strong line now.' His view was accepted.

Events were to prove the wisdom of the Viceroy's policy. Before Rashid Ali could organise against the landing, 'my brigade group,' wrote Linlithgow in a letter home, 'was bobbing about like corks outside his port.' The force made an unopposed landing and an initiative of immense value was gained against the Axis powers. All was by no means over as the Iraqis rallied and attacked the air station at Habbaniya, which held out gallantly against the besiegers. There was trouble for some further weeks until the allied position was stabilised. Oil supplies and India's communications were saved. On the night of 29th/30th May Rashid Ali, the ex-Mufti of Jerusalem and the German and Italian agents slipped over the frontier into Iran.

The vital threat to the head of the Persian Gulf had been seen in far clearer perspective by Linlithgow and Auchinleck than by others who, understandably occupied by the threat to Egypt and the Suez Canal from the west, had considered Iraq more of a nuisance than a menace. Auchinleck was deeply impressed by the Viceroy's grasp of strategy which had prevailed over the com-

placency of the Foreign Office and Middle East Command at the
moment of crisis.

This was Auchinleck's last experience of this side of his chief's
versatile mind, for he was to succeed Wavell in Middle East
Command at the end of June, Wavell taking over command in
India. Linlithgow was much concerned at losing him so soon, but
was to work just as happily and well with Wavell.

*

Political repercussions in India of the events in Iraq were tiresome
but not too serious. Iraq being a Muslim country, German
propaganda naturally stirred up what trouble it could with the
Muslims. Jinnah managed to sit on the fence to all appearances,
but privately (to the Governor of Madras) he expressed his bitter
opposition to Rashid Ali and his relief at the success of the
operation. The president of the Bihar Provincial Muslim League,
however, condemned Rashid Ali openly and was violently
criticised by Jinnah's followers.

So much for India's communications to the west. Before the
summer was out the Viceroy had concerned himself also with
her north-western frontier. He was anxious about Afghanistan.
Kabul, the capital, was the centre of considerable infiltration by
Germans and Italians whose mission was to foment trouble with
the frontier tribes. The situation demanded firm but tactful
handling. Linlithgow and his Secretary of the External Affairs
Department, Olaf Caroe, were agreed that a new man was
needed for the job. The appointment went to Sir Francis Wylie,
whom Linlithgow described as 'a shrewd, active and intelligent
Irishman' and who was at present the Viceroy's Political Adviser.
Before the end of the year all nationals of the Axis countries,
except the legation staff, were out of Afghanistan.

On the question of Wylie's successor the Viceroy's letter to
Amery was eloquent of the strain of his office:

'You have no idea even with all your own administrative experience
of the enormous burden of work which falls to the Viceroy every day,
or the extent to which he is required to enter into the various aspects of

all sorts of complex matters of the utmost importance on which his
attitude is decisive. The burden would be an intolerable one unless he
was well served. . . .'

Linlithgow was to get no respite. He had asked early in July,
1941, that his successor should be chosen as soon as possible.
That would give him time, he said, to get his new Council in
good working order before his departure in the spring. It would
also ease political tension for a few months. Men's thoughts
would be 'concentrated on the rising sun and the declining orb
might be allowed to sink quietly to rest in the peace of evening.'
But on 1st August he received a telegram from Churchill asking
to agree to yet another extension of his term of office until
April, 1943:

'I have the greatest confidence in you; the war is moving East and
approaching a period which may well be one of the most dangerous in
the history of the British trusteeship in India.'

Once again there could be no question of refusal and Linlithgow
accepted.

*

At the end of October three of the new Indian members of his
Council pressed the Viceroy for the release of Nehru and Azad.
Thus began a test of endurance which was to last a month and
bring Linlithgow up against Churchill at his most obstinate.

The councillors argued that release would be in the public
interest as the detention of the two leaders was having a bad
effect on left-centre opinion, both in Britain and in the United
States. Azad, they pointed out, was due for release in January
anyhow. Nehru's offence was grave and he had deserved imprisonment, but he could be arrested again if he offended again.
They did not want the release of terrorists.

The Viceroy gave a guarded reply as he was bound to. He saw
at once that this question was involved with the much larger one
of releasing all *satyagrahis*. The Provinces in any event would have
to be consulted. There was, however, no question of delay as a

THE VICEROY AT BAY 209

motion recommending release was put down in the Assembly for debate on 12th November. The Viceroy and his Council discussed the matter on 5th and 6th November. The Indian majority were unanimous that genuine *satyagrahis* as well as Nehru and Azad should be set free. Linlithgow said that he was ready to release *satyagrahis* and Azad but Nehru's was a more difficult case. The Viceroy, as we have seen, had thought Nehru's sentence too severe but he doubted whether the Governor of the United Provinces (Hallett) would favour his release. He would refer the question to the Secretary of State, making clear that he himself felt he should support his new Council and help it to enhance its status with moderate Indians.

Amery rightly judged that what mattered was the effect in India rather than outside. He did not think there would be any harm in the plan provided that it was clearly seen to be an act of clemency and not one of bargaining. He was impressed by the unanimity of Hindus and Muslims on the Council. As for Nehru, perhaps his sentence could be shortened.

At this point pressure arose in some quarters in India for a general inquiry into gaol conditions. The Viceroy was against it, partly because criticism was essentially political but mainly because he was aware that prisoners were satisfied with their conditions. This he knew from intercepted letters. For instance a letter from a Muslim prisoner to his wife dated 9th October described Nehru's imprisonment in detail:

'Very nice and easy sort of detention but of course it is a prison, though it looks awfully like a private little bungalow built by a clerk. . . .'

The Viceroy consulted the Governors. Hope (Madras) and his advisers all felt strongly that unconditional release would be a mistake. He wanted, as a *quid pro quo*, an assurance from Congress that civil disobedience would be ended. He did not believe that there was any sign of a change of heart by Congress. Even Rajagopalachari, who was supposed to represent the conciliatory element in the party, was, Hope reported, more bitter than ever

o

against Britain and had said in private that he hoped for a quick Russian defeat followed by an enforced armistice between Germany and Britain. Congress would then launch a mass movement of civil disobedience which would bring Britain to her knees. Hope thought that the policy proposed would only strengthen Congress and dismay our friends.

Hallett was also emphatically opposed to release. Over half of the prisoners were interned in the United Provinces and the Governor believed the services would be demoralised, likewise the Muslim League. The rest of the Governors agreed with the plan for release, Lumley feeling that it would strengthen moderate opinion to see that the Indian majority on the Council had real influence.

Now Churchill entered the fray. On 13th November he sent a telegram to the Viceroy:

'I was startled to learn how far you had gone about the release of remaining *satyagrahi* prisoners. As you know I have always felt that a man like Nehru should be treated as a political *detenu* and not as a criminal and have welcomed every mitigation of his lot. But my general impression of this wholesale release is one of surrender at the moment of success. Undoubtedly the release of these prisoners as an act of clemency will be proclaimed as a victory for Gandhi's party. Nehru and others will commit fresh offences requiring whole process of trial and conviction to be gone through again. You will get no thanks from any quarter. The objections of Hope and Hallett should not be lightly turned aside.'

The Viceroy wired back emphasising the unanimity of his Council and the anxiety of its new members, including the Muslims, to show that they could get things done. Although he himself would not have favoured release he thought his Council might be right and he was quite clear that it would not be wise to resist them. There was no surrender about it and he could be counted on to dig his toes in if he thought they were going too far.

The Cabinet considered the matter. Amery strongly supported the Viceroy but Sir John Anderson opposed him on the con-

stitutional ground that the decision to release should rest with the
Provinces. Linlithgow wired back that this was a political
problem rather than a constitutional one and arose out of conditions with which Anderson was entirely unfamiliar.

Linlithgow added a warning that a difficult situation would
arise if his considered advice to the Cabinet were to be rejected in
favour of that of an ex-Governor, however eminent. Amery
stuck to the point that the real issue was whether the Cabinet
were to override the Viceroy's Executive Council and run the
risk of breaking it up – the Viceroy and his advisers believed that
this would certainly happen if the Cabinet decided against him.

The Cabinet finally backed the Viceroy over the main issue of
release. But that was not quite the end of the affair. The Prime
Minister now tried to tell the Viceroy exactly how the announcement should be handled. He wanted this done as quietly as
possible without any public announcement. He sent a typically
provocative telegram:

'I am sure it would be a mistake to make a flag day out of this very
small unwelcome gesture of conciliation. ... The extraordinary
powers accorded to Central Government to deal with war emergencies
are now to be used to override independence of Provinces in their
responsibility for law and order. This is a sad contrariety and I wish
I had been kept better informed before you reached the position now
disclosed. If you consider a statement inevitable it would be better
couched in a modest tone. . . .'

The Viceroy replied that the issue of release was now of first-
class political importance in India and could not be disposed of
privately, or settled between the Viceroy and the Prime Minister.
The Council must be in on the final arrangements and must
approve the terms of any announcement:

'I have with very great difficulty kept them together and quiet
during these last few days, but risk of resignations if they are overruled
is too serious to be faced. Its effect here would be disastrous; and press
comment from home suggests that it would not go well there, or as
enemy propaganda either.'

Amery, sending this telegram straight over to the Prime Minister, asked him to agree to the Viceroy going ahead without a further Cabinet, but Churchill told him that the telegram must be put before the next meeting. Amery reported the outcome in a letter of 2nd December:

'Winston looked round the room and then said somewhat sorrowfully "I give in," adding *sotto voce* "when you lose India don't blame me" or something to that effect.'

As the whole matter had taken up so much of the Viceroy's precious time Amery thoughtfully encouraged him to dispatch as much business as he could without reference to the Cabinet. Linlithgow did not need the advice but none knew better how much more time would be wasted if he were to go too far in that desirable direction.

In fact the release of Nehru, Azad and the *satyagrahis* had precisely the effect which the Indian members of Council had predicted although Gandhi declared himself incapable of any sympathetic response. The new Council had made its mark. It was as well that it did so in view of what was soon to come.

*

That autumn provided a good example of the massive variety of strains upon the Viceroy. On top of the continuous political maelstrom he had to deal with a crisis in the textile industry over prices, the situation in Iran, the question of tanks for India and aircraft factories. In all these difficulties his experience, instinct and strength of character were of vital service.

Congress was worried by the widespread approval of the expansion of the Executive Council. There were signs that an important section of the party was anxious to return to office in the Provinces and, upon their own terms, to accept a proportion of seats on the Council. But Gandhi made it clear that as long as the war lasted he would not allow Congress to resume any constitutional activity.

Jinnah, continuing his vendetta against the Muslim Premiers, not only forced their resignation from the Defence Council but also ejected Fazlul Huq, Premier of Bengal, from the Muslim

League. He then threw his weight behind intrigue against Huq
with the result that his Government fell. Huq, however, got his
own back by succeeding in forming another administration in
which he substituted Hindu ministers for the Muslim League
representatives. This was a setback for Jinnah but no more than
that. He was now in indisputable command of Muslim opinion.
The Viceroy admitted that he had proved stronger than one
would have thought possible. Linlithgow's dilemma was that,
much as he disliked Jinnah's dictatorial methods, he did not want
to see the break-up of the Muslim League (Amery was not so sure
about this) and find himself with only one side organised.

*

Events in Iran were of deep concern to Linlithgow. On 2nd
September he telegraphed Amery that news that the Germans
'cornered in Persia' were not to be interned had been received
with despair in India, in both civil and military quarters. He
complained of the apparent reluctance of the Government to
consult the Government of India on issues of this nature. He felt
also, just as he had felt over Iraq, that the circumstances were too
dangerous to allow of the niceties of diplomatic politeness in
dealing with such critical matters.

Churchill himself responded. Through Amery he expressed his
regret that the Viceroy had been neither kept informed of the
situation nor consulted. He sent him a copy of a stiff telegram
which he had personally sent to Sir Reader Bullard, the British
Minister in Tehran. The Prime Minister directed that there was
to be no question of a generous policy towards the Germans to
please the Iranians or anyone else: communications would be
developed from the Persian Gulf to the Caspian to supply
Russia at all costs and it was likely that large British forces and a
powerful air force would be operating from Iran in 1942: if the
Iranian Government wished to avoid Anglo-Russian occupation
they must give all help with alacrity: it was also important that
the ex-Mufti of Jerusalem be captured dead or alive.

On 29th October the Viceroy telegraphed his anxiety over a

decision to stop an arranged shipment of tanks to India. He understood the importance of keeping Russia going but he feared German attacks upon Iran and Iraq which, he pointed out, would decide the following: Turkey's position in the war, the fate of the oil fields, Britain's position from Syria to Alexandria, control of the Eastern Mediterranean and the Red Sea, the use of the Persian Gulf by enemy submarines, the defence of India and perhaps the final attitude of Japan. He thought that the German advance through the Caucasus might be rapid. At present there was not a tank in the area capable of standing up to the German cruisers. Once the Germans had taken Baku the Russians could not be expected to worry about German inroads into Asia Minor.

The Viceroy had already warned Amery of the political consequences and damage to India's staying power if Indian troops should get roughly handled for lack of armoured support:

'Our requirements in tanks are so comparatively modest while the values we shall be protecting are so vast and so vital that I cannot resist the feeling that the decision to stop our tanks is to spoil the ship for a haporth of tar. Please let Winston know my view. I shall not complain further.'

On 25th November the Viceroy heard that the Prime Minister had been helpful and India was to get, by 30th June 1942, 639 cruisers and 235 infantry tanks – just enough to equip two armoured divisions and one tank brigade.

The supply of aircraft was still hanging fire. Amery regretted that he had been unable to persuade Lord Beaverbrook to let them start production in India on a tolerable scale. He told the Viceroy (11th December) that it was not for want of trying. Beaverbrook, he said, had been just as tiresome over allowing supervisory staff to go out to India in connection with the schemes of the Eastern Supply Council. Happily, however, his subordinates were disregarding his instructions on this point and were helping as much as they could *sub rosa*. But it was 'intolerable to have anyone so selfishly short-sighted in charge of things.'

Beaverbrook, of course, had many calls upon his priorities but he was curiously reluctant to meet India's claims.

18

On 7th December the Japanese attacked and shattered the American fleet at Pearl Harbour. From that moment the security which India had enjoyed under British protection for over a hundred and fifty years could no longer be taken for granted. To the Viceroy Amery wrote:

'Now we are really up against it . . . You, with your terribly inadequate provision against air attack, will have to manage somehow against air raids on Eastern India and perhaps on your coastal ports. You will need all your courage and power of infusing it into those working with you. I know you will be a tower of strength and inspiration to them and my one exhortation to you would be not to overwork yourself, remembering how much depends on your keeping fit and remembering also that this business is not now going to come to any speedy end. . . .'

In this same letter Amery wrote that he was very interested in the possibility of increasing the cultivation of soya beans in Assam. He remarked that the beans had drawbacks from the point of view of diet and oil content and asked for more information. Linlithgow's comment in the margin was simply 'Gosh!'.

The Viceroy also received a heartening message from Churchill. Expressing his gratitude, he assured the Prime Minister that he had no intention of committing the Cabinet to any constitutional changes without full warning. He thought that there was just a chance that, under pressure from the enemy, the Muslim League and the Princes might show themselves ready to work the 1935 Act:

'But I am sure you will keep in mind the magnitude of the war effort which I am calling upon India to perform during 1942 and after, and that you will remember that as the strain begins to tell capacity for mischief of the anti-British elements to make effective trouble will increase unless I can succeed in outmanoeuvring them.'

As usual his warning was to prove justified.

*

The account of 1941 may be rounded off with a story of Nehru. Krishna Menon, his man in England in closest touch with the Labour Party, suggested to him in December that he (Nehru) should take a positive initiative and offer unequivocal help in the defence of India and in the world struggle provided that there were no legal or constitutional changes. Nehru replied in a telegram:

'. . . Your information of developments here misleading. Extreme bitterness here against British policy in India and attitude of obscurantist reactionary officials. While fully realising implications of recent international events consider recognition of independence with real transfer of power essential pre-requisites for effective step. Undesirable your interviewing British officials.'

Obscurantism is defined by the Shorter Oxford English Dictionary as 'the practice or principles of those who strive to prevent enlightenment or the progress of knowledge.' Nehru's telegram was a fair example of it.

*

The year 1942 was the climacteric of Linlithgow's viceroyalty. Before events began to gather pace, however, there was a charming exchange of letters in February between the Viceroy and Gandhi – almost the last of its kind. Gandhi wrote: 'As I have suspended disobedience, I make bold to write this letter for humanity's cause.' He went on at length to ask for exemption from tax for the All-India Spinners Association. Then:

'You will forgive me for inflicting this on you when every moment of yours is pre-mortgaged for winning the war. Though I cannot sympathise with your enterprise, much less help in the manner you would wish, you will believe me when I say that I am as much to-day

a friend of your people as I ever have been. Hence I can understand
what a strain it must be for you and Lady Linlithgow.

When you write to Lady Anne[1] and Southby please send my love
to them . . . I hope they with the baby are faring well.'

Linlithgow replied with helpful advice about registration of
charitable trusts. He added a postscript:

'The closing paragraphs of your letter are kindly, and I understand,
even when I cannot agree.

'I will give your message to Southby and my daughter, and I know
they will value it. We often hear from her. "Richard" is the most
wonderful baby in the world and the very flower of the flock! So life
will triumph in the end, despite all our blunders!!'

Gandhi wrote back a letter of thanks and ended thus:

'Your postcript breaks the pervading gloom. I wish the general
public had the privilege of knowing that your cheerfulness never
forsakes you. May God be with you always.'

*

In March there took place what is known as the Cripps Mission
when Sir Stafford Cripps came to India on behalf of the Cabinet
with a panacea for all India's troubles. But it was not just another
political mission. It was an almost inconceivable event of the kind
in which men indulge only from desperation in the face of
danger.

The war in the east was going badly. The Japanese advance
seemed for the moment irresistible. On 15th February Singapore
fell; on 7th March Rangoon was abandoned. In India there was,
of course, deep anxiety but the country was remarkably quiet
internally and no particular difficulty faced the Viceroy and his
Council, which was growing in prestige and shaping well. It was
from outside the country that pressure for new action sprang up
and grew. Certainly a telegram from Sapru and other moderate
men had shortly before been sent to the Prime Minister demanding 'some bold stroke of courageous statesmanship' at their

[1] Lady Anne Southby was the Viceroy's eldest daughter.

Bombay conference last year, by which they meant the creation of a national government responsible to no one. But the real stimulus behind the pressure lay in the success of the Japanese.

The failure in Malaya was thought by some in Britain and by many abroad – especially in the United States – to be largely due to shortcomings in the colonial system, which had failed to rouse the peoples in threatened territories to active resistance against the invader. Let the situation in India be remedied, therefore, before it was too late. In the United States sensitivities were heightened by new awareness of the strategic importance of India. They had decided to contribute to India's defence by the provision of warlike material under lease-lend and to establish in the country a large contingent of the U.S. Air Force. To the U.S. and to those who felt as they did it seemed obvious that, if India could be granted her freedom, the allies would draw new strength from the willing co-operation of her many millions while she herself would be able to stop the Japanese and to help China. It was as simple as that. President Roosevelt naïvely commended to Churchill the example of the American federation two hundred years before.

So the pressure for action mounted. A press campaign, some of it initiated by the agents of Congress in London, helped to keep it up and Parliament, too, was affected. Sir Stafford Cripps, whose political views were on the far left of the Labour Party, was now in the War Cabinet. He had lately returned from Moscow, where he had been British ambassador for two years. He is on record as having said that, shortly after his return, he told Churchill that the Indian problem must be solved and that Churchill asked him to prepare a plan.

At the end of January the Viceroy made it clear to Amery that this was emphatically not the time for constitutional disturbance. Neither of the main communities would retreat from its position, the Hindus demanding absolute independence and the Muslims a fifty per cent share of government at the Centre and a power of veto. The most vital need at this critical moment was to do

nothing that would exacerbate communal feeling. Any major
move in the constitutional field could not fail to do so.

The answer to this plea was a telegram from Amery on 11th
February. It started with the words 'Take the strongest *peg* you
can before continuing.' It went on to say that the Prime Minister
proposed to broadcast to India four days later. He would announce the Cabinet's decision that an Indian Council of Defence
should be formed to take the place of the existing National
Defence Council. As far as British India was concerned member-
ship would be decided through election by proportional representation on a provincial basis. The Princes would be represented
in comparable ratio. This elected body would be represented at
the peace conference after the war and would also be the body to
frame the new constitution for India.

Here was a complete *volte-face* if ever there was one. It was
incredible treatment and Linlithgow said so in no uncertain
terms. Amery agreed but tried to soften the blow by explaining
'The Prime Minister did not wish to treat you inconsiderately but
you know his sudden ways.' He added that Churchill had at first
considered flying to Delhi and launching his scheme there. The
Viceroy's strong reaction had the desired effect of postponing the
broadcast, which was never made.

There now took place a sharp exchange of views between the
Viceroy and the Cabinet. Amery began by referring to the
scheme as the imaginative and bold fruit of Churchill's genius but
Linlithgow had little difficulty in exposing it as amateurish and
dangerous. If the suggested new Council were to be effective it
would cut right across his Executive Council, in other words the
Government of India, on which there was now a majority of very
able Indians who had taken great political risks in joining it. If it
were to fail there would be chaos. Either way its creation would
do exactly what the Viceroy had always been determined to
avoid, for it would bring the sharp edge of communal controversy directly into the running of the war. It was crucial that this
should be avoided or the army itself might become affected: and
the army alone stood between the Japanese and their ultimate

objective, which must be a union with the German army on the Persian Gulf.

In spite of his resentment the Viceroy was at pains to tell Amery that he well understood the spirit behind the Prime Minister's impetuous action and that he realised the importance of the anxieties of the United States and of China. This was no reason to rush into unsound action but he was quite ready to see whether he could work out some alternative move, if that would help, without throwing India into political turmoil. He also sent, through Amery, a message to Churchill expressing confidence that, whatever might befall them, their relations would continue to be softened by mutual sympathy with each other's public difficulties and warmed by private affection.

At the same time he reminded Amery of the great strain under which he was working. Singapore fell on 15th February. On the following day he telegraphed:

'I am still, for the first time in my life, really cross with you all over this business, and I do again beg of you to see to it that I should be in some measure cushioned by you . . . from the full impact of these explosions in the Prime Minister's mind. I am carrying here, almost single-handed, an immense responsibility. . . .'

To make matters worse the Viceroy was now deprived of the help of Laithwaite, who was ill and would be off duty for three months. He was also coping with a visit from Generalissimo Chiang-Kai-Shek and his wife, who had arrived practically without notice on 9th February.

On 18th February he heard from Amery that his 'very effective criticism' would probably dispose of the scheme in its original form. He was now giving deep thought to an alternative plan. This he produced on 25th February. In it he risked, he said, the loss of European support, which was vital enough to him. What he could not do was to take risks which would be decisive against the conduct of the war in the east. He emphasised, in transmitting his plan, that he would not have moved if left to himself; he was responding to the Government's sensitivity to outside opinion which he fully understood and accepted as a factor. But Indians could only be reassured by an appeal based on victory rather than on panic.

*

Against this background the Viceroy made the following proposals. At the outset His Majesty's Government would declare that they had no intention of impeding the attainment of India's freedom in order to preserve British interests. As proof of this they announce that they will not insist on provisions in the post-war constitution of India for the safeguarding of British interests: these would be the subject of diplomatic negotiation to culminate in a series of bilateral pacts.

Secondly, the Government would regard the obligations which history had laid upon them as entirely separate from British interests. The Government was obliged to see that full power was transferred to a Government in India under which the different races, communities and interests in India might have the prospect of living without fear and of developing their religious, cultural, economic and political life without despair or bloodshed.

Thirdly, this was no time to make profound changes in the existing machinery of Government. Let the leaders of the great political parties sink their differences and take a full share in the power and responsibility of Government, both at the Centre and in the Provinces. The Viceroy would renew his attempts to bring in these leaders.

Fourthly, His Majesty's Government regarded continuance of official members in the Executive Council not as a political matter but as a purely practical matter of wartime administration. The Government will therefore make no promise on this matter as a prerequisite of political truce in India. But if the political leaders would respond to the Viceroy's efforts he was prepared to discuss the question with them as a practical problem of administration. The post of Commander-in-Chief must remain unimpaired but it might be possible to associate a non-official member much more closely with co-ordination of defence.

Fifthly, consistently with their desire to see created an autonomous Government of India as soon as possible after the war, and to recognise without delay the *de facto* status of India under a National Government, His Majesty's Government declared that in the interim period the control of the India Office would be progressively lightened. India's spokesmen at meetings of the British War Cabinet and Pacific War Council would be instructed from India, and representatives at the peace conference would be nominated by and directly responsible to the Government of India.

Sixthly, His Majesty's Government stood by their pledge to afford a body representative of the parties, communities and interests of India, and brought into being in accordance with the wishes of her leaders, the fullest opportunity to devise the framework of a constitution after the war.

Seventhly, to set a time-limit after which Great Britain would impose her own form of Dominion Status would only handicap agreement in India. The basis of India's future after the war must be her complete freedom to control her own destiny. It was hoped that she would remain in the British Commonwealth.

Eighthly, His Majesty's Government undertook to do all in their power within the shortest practicable time after the end of the war, to promote the peaceful setting-up of autonomous government in India. They believed that the experience of co-operation, in attaining victory, between the parties and communities of British India and the Rulers of the Indian States, would itself go far in promoting mutual respect and esteem and allaying apprehensions.

Finally, His Majesty's Government undertook to accept in advance any constitution framed as contemplated in this declaration, representing the will and desire of India as a whole.

'I have given you all I can' the Viceroy wired to Amery on 26th February, 'and I wish the necessity had not been forced upon me. It is for the Prime Minister to decide when he sees what is involved whether he can carry it and make it possible for me to carry it also.'

*

The Viceroy's criticism succeeded in cancelling the Cabinet's original scheme as Amery had foretold. But they immediately came back at him with the news that they had set up an India Committee of the Cabinet under Attlee's chairmanship with Amery, Simon, Cripps and Grigg as the other members.

On 1st March Linlithgow was confronted with a new declaration and again treated badly. He was given effectively twenty-four hours to comment without being allowed to consult the Commander-in-Chief. The Prime Minister proposed once again to broadcast the scheme himself. This declaration, deferring to the Viceroy's argument, abandoned the idea of setting up an advisory body which would also frame the new constitution. It also accepted the Viceroy's differentiation between British obligations and interests and his suggested method of dealing with these. There were two new ingredients. The first was a statement that the future Indian Dominion could secede from the Commonwealth if it wished to. As this right was inherent in the Statute of Westminster and as India was to be the equal of the other Dominions there was no need to stress this: but, as we have noted, there was a blind spot in the Government's eye where this point was concerned and they appear to have thought that they were taking an enlightened initiative rather than stressing the obvious. The second ingredient, however, was crucial and unexpected: any Province could stay out of the new constitution if it so desired, but without sacrificing its own prospects of attaining Dominion Status.

The Viceroy, in his first comments (which he had been forced to rush), did not traverse the point of provincial option to any marked extent although he saw its risks in communal terms. In fact he admitted later that he was caught on the rebound with relief at the abandonment of proposals calculated immediately to wreck his Executive Council. But after he had heard the views of the Commander-in-Chief (whose opinion he had rightly insisted upon seeking) his own attitude developed into one of deep hostility to the proposal. The Commander-in-Chief saw that provincial option would be interpreted as acceptance of Pakistan.

Its effect would be particularly bad in the Punjab. Muslims of all ranks in the army from Provinces not likely to accede would ask how non-acceding Provinces would be governed. Would they have an army of their own and if not how would they defend themselves against the rest of India, or against their own minorities like the Sikhs? In the result minds would be deflected from the task of fighting the enemy and recruiting would be imperilled. If widespread communal disturbances developed, the task of suppressing them with Indian troops would be impossible. Nor could the ultimate possibility of communal warfare in the Indian Army be excluded. The Governor of the Punjab came up with criticism on the same lines as that of the Commander-in-Chief.

The Viceroy warned the Government on 7th March that he could not stand for a declaration containing local option in this form. He accepted that it might have to be resorted to after the war but that was an entirely different matter from declaring it in terms while they were fighting the enemy. The India Committee offered amendments which, while sticking to provincial option, offered a full blooded pledge to minorities. The Viceroy and the Commander-in-Chief thought the declaration would be no less disastrous than before and would infuriate both Hindus and Muslims.

Linlithgow's mind had for some days been leaning strongly towards resignation. On 9th March his mind was made up. He wired Amery that he would resign on the day upon which Churchill made his declaration. Next day he received an answer from the Prime Minister himself. Churchill informed him that the Cabinet had themselves decided that the declaration might fall flat. They had so decided, he said, before the Viceroy's resignation message arrived. Churchill added an injunction in harsh terms. Let not the Viceroy think of 'quitting' his post lest effective resistance to the Japanese should collapse in British India and disunity arise at home. Amery was kinder: 'So, old friend, whatever else happens, you must see this thing through.' Linlithgow did not mind Churchill's discourtesy of phrasing. He knew that he himself was not the only leader working under strain. He

knew, too, that he had won his main objective: he had stopped an
ex parte declaration.

Although they had given way on a vital point the Cabinet
were not to be prevented from going ahead with their scheme.
But they at least decided to advance it by negotiation rather than
by declaration. For this purpose they were to send a Minister to
India. They selected Sir Stafford Cripps himself. He was the man
behind the plan and it was right and natural that the success or
failure of the mission should be primarily his. He would arrive at
New Delhi on 23rd March.

*

The Viceroy had little doubt that Cripps would fail but he
approached the forthcoming visit with characteristic generosity.
H. V. Hodson, with whom he discussed it on 14th March, has
given a detailed account in his book *The Great Divide*. It is worth
quoting in full because it shows Linlithgow's experienced and
unbiased mind at its best. The Viceroy said to Hodson (who
recorded the words in his diary):

'I try not to form pictures in my mind. It's dangerous. But I'll tell
you what I think. I think Cripps is coming here out of public spirit.
No one would choose this way of becoming Viceroy if that were his
ambition. And if he wants to be Prime Minister what sensible politician
would take the immediate risks of failure over this just when his stock
is very high? No, I think he realised that India might take things from
him which they wouldn't take from anyone else, and he is coming out
here in a genuine public-spirited attempt to solve the problem. And I
think he will go off very quickly unless he is confident of succeeding.
It would be fatal to his reputation to hang around here while opinion
hardens more and more against his offer – like hawking rotten fish.
Personally, I think he'll fail with H.M.G.'s policy, don't you? . . . Of
course the Congress and the Hindus are jubilant. They think they've
scored with the British Government and that Cripps is their man . . . I
don't know how he will proceed, but I think he'll work with a pretty
free hand. On our side we must avoid at all costs any suggestion that
we are standing in his way or forcing evidence on him. And I agree
with you that it would be disastrous to assume in advance that we were

P

parties to a dispute with him or H.M.G. . . . . The danger that I see is
that if Cripps feels himself to be failing he may telegraph home to
H.M.G. asking for this and asking for that. If so, I'm sure he'll soon be
out of his depth. . . .

'There's another point of danger – the point about participation in
government now. I can't have Cripps making my Council for me. He
can clear the ground but only I can do that, and he must have gone
before I begin.'

19

Before Cripps arrived there were developments in the United States over India. Lord Halifax, now British Ambassador in Washington, reported that Chiang-Kai-Shek (who had left India) had been in touch with President Roosevelt both before and after his Indian visit. Chiang's line was that without freedom India would not resist the invader. The fear of breakdown in Indian morale was being worked to death in the U.S. press as an argument for granting independence without delay. This campaign was accompanied by wildly inaccurate statements of fact.

Then the Indian High Commissioner to the United States (Bajpai, lately a member of the Viceroy's Executive Council) reported his first interview with Roosevelt on 12th March. The President did most of the talking in their forty-five minute conversation. He said that British policy in India had moved in a groove for the last twenty to thirty years: today India needed the inspiration of new thought: Dominion Status was the right objective but details must be evolved by Indians themselves through trial and error: it took six years of confusion under confederation to make the thirteen American colonies realise the value of federal unity: India would also learn by experience how to perfect the structure of self-government but its prompt creation embracing Congress, Muslims and Princes appeared essential. With Bajpai's comment that substantial agreement among the parties mentioned seemed essential to the smooth functioning of such a structure the President agreed. He added suggestively that the United States had fixed the date for the independence of the Philippines and this had accelerated Filipino solidarity.

*

Cripps arrived in New Delhi on 23rd March with his declaration. This contained the following points:

As soon as hostilities ceased steps would be taken to set up an elected body charged with the task of framing a new constitution for India. This body would be elected by an electoral college consisting of the combined memberships of the Lower Houses of Provincial Legislatures. Election would be by proportional representation so that the new body would amount to one tenth of the electoral college. The States would be invited to appoint representatives in the same proportion to their population as in the case of British India. His Majesty's Government undertook to accept the Constitution so framed subject to two conditions, first, that of provincial option (as previously defined) and, secondly, that of the signing of a treaty between His Majesty's Government and the body making the Constitution. The treaty would cover all necessary matters arising from the transfer of responsibility from British to Indian hands; this would include provision for the protection of racial and religious minorities.

During the critical period of the war and until the new Constitution could be framed His Majesty's Government must inevitably bear the responsibility for the defence of India as part of their world war effort, but the task of organising to the full the military, moral and material resources of India must be the responsibility of the Government of India with the co-operation of her peoples (this qualification was added after a few days of negotiations when Cripps saw that responsibility for defence was becoming a knotty point).

Cripps got off to an unfortunate start, which was his own fault. Meeting the Executive Council at Viceroy's House on the afternoon of his first day he explained the decision that the British Government's plan should be presented by a Cabinet Minister rather than by immediate publication on the grounds that so much depended upon presentation. But he then asked the Council to be patient with him if he did not present them with the full statement at this stage. The meeting then broke up but the Members of Council did not leave Viceroy's House. They suspected from what he said that he intended to discuss details of the plan with outside politicians before the Council itself was told of them. If that was what was going to happen they regarded today's meeting as a waste of time. The Viceroy at once let Cripps know of this feeling and Cripps agreed to meet the Council again on the following evening.

The Viceroy began the proceedings at this second meeting by saying that Sir Stafford was very anxious to have a longer time so that he might tell the Executive Council the whole scheme before meeting party leaders. Cripps then said that he had had no instructions to disclose the plan at this stage but since he knew of the Council's anxiety he was very ready to do so (he had equally, of course, had no instructions not to do so, the tactics being left entirely to him). He then read out the full plan. This was followed by hard questioning, almost entirely by the Indian majority, during which there emerged clearly those communal sensitivities which the Viceroy had foretold would be unleashed by the announcement of the plan.

The Indian Members of Council did not forget what they regarded as the insult to which Cripps had subjected them and they asked that the Cabinet should be made aware of their feelings.

*

After two days as the guest of the Viceroy, Cripps moved to a house some distance away. He opened his conversations with Indian leaders on 25th March and on that day he saw Azad and Jinnah. Reporting to the Viceroy in the evening he said that he had asked Azad whether he could suggest any way in which His Majesty's Government could give better proof of their sincerity. Significantly Azad did not answer. The Congress President went on to say that they must have an Indian in charge of defence as the Indians must be made to feel that defence was their affair. Cripps explained that defence could not be made a purely Indian responsibility at this stage. There were British and imperial forces involved and Americans also, as well as reinforcements from all parts of the world. The Government of India, he said, were already deeply involved and would be more so still, but the Commander-in-Chief must remain as the Member of Council in charge of defence.

This demand of Azad's on defence was in fact to be the focal point upon which Congress were to insist until breaking point. There was, of course, more to it than merely the defence of India. What they were asking for was nothing less than control of the Government of India now, as Linlithgow had always warned.

Jinnah, to whom Cripps apologised for some rude things he had written in *Tribune* about the Muslims, said little except that he would consult his colleagues.

The Viceroy reminded Cripps of his (the Viceroy's) views on the necessity for his own control of his Executive Council including choice of Members. He observed that he knew the Indian politicians better than Sir Stafford did, how slight was their experience of administration and how prejudiced they were and how committed by their statements to their followers. But if Sir Stafford could 'do the big thing' and get the assent of the parties to the policy which His Majesty's Government declared, the Viceroy was prepared to take great risks in terms of his Executive Council and Sir Stafford would not find him falling short. But if only one party was prepared to come in he would not take these risks; it would not be worth the price. Cripps agreed completely. Linlithgow followed up by saying that he would forgive Sir Stafford anything except stealing his cheese to bait his own trap, in other words offering control of the Executive Council as an inducement to accept the declaration. Cripps remarked that the Viceroy's attitude was reasonable.

On 29th March Cripps released the declaration in a broadcast and held a press conference. This he handled responsibly and firmly until he made a most curious remark: 'You cannot change the constitution. All you can do is to change the conventions of the constitution. You can turn the Executive Council into a cabinet.' Cripps had no instructions to say anything of the kind.

It was a rash and irresponsible suggestion and was naturally taken
by Congress as a hint that he was holding up his sleeve the final
concession of cabinet government responsible to a central
legislature. The Viceroy's anxiety was already beginning to prove
justified. Cripps was even naïve enough to show him a suggested
list of members of a new Executive Council. Linlithgow replied
simply, 'That's my affair.'

Suspicious though he had every reason to be, the Viceroy did
not believe that Cripps would deceive him. In the event he felt
sure he had been deceived and his view is supported by evidence
which has become available since his death. The evidence is
supplied by Azad's published account of the Cripps mission
which appeared in his book *India Wins Freedom* (Orient Longmans
Private Ltd. 1959).

Azad reports that he saw Cripps on 29th March and that Cripps
handed him a prepared statement:

'When I looked at the statement, I found it was a proposal for a new
Executive Council of the Viceroy. All the existing members would
resign. The Congress and other representative organisations would
then be requested to send their nominees who together would constitute the new Executive Council. This Council would function for
the duration of the war . . . the net result of the proposal was that in
place of the majority of British Members in the existing Executive
Council [in fact the Indian Members were already in a majority] there
would be an Executive Council composed of Indians alone. The
system of Government would not, however, be changed.

I asked Sir Stafford what would be the position of the Viceroy in
this Council. Sir Stafford replied that the Viceroy would function as a
constitutional head like the King in the U.K. In order to remove any
room for doubt I asked him to confirm that this would mean that the
Viceroy, as a constitutional head, would be bound by the advice of the
Council. Sir Stafford said that this was his intention.'

There was nothing in the authorised declaration which remotely
suggested this uprooting of the Viceroy's present Executive
Council. If Azad's account is accurate Cripps must have handed
to him a document of his own as well as the declaration (he must

have shown him the declaration as this was to be made public later that day). Azad's account may be mistaken and he may be confusing the written declaration with an oral statement by Cripps of his own views made at the same interview. But whichever way it was Cripps went well beyond his brief and was manifestly baiting his trap with the Viceroy's cheese just as Linlithgow feared. The extraordinary reference to cabinet government at the press conference falls into place in the light of Azad's story: Cripps had committed himself.

*

The Working Committee of Congress discussed the declaration and Azad's conversation with Cripps for two days. As a result Azad saw Cripps again on 1st April in order to seek further clarification on the question of the powers of the Executive Council. He describes this meeting as decisive:

'I found that the position had undergone a radical change since I last met him. His answers were now quite different in temper from his replies during the first interview. . . . He would not categorically state that the Viceroy would have the final say but the purport of what he said was that the Council would not have full and unfettered freedom of decision. He tried to explain this by saying that the position now enjoyed by the Viceroy could not be changed without a change in the law. However he stressed again and again that whatever might be the position in law, in actual practice the Viceroy would behave as a constitutional head.'

Azad tries to analyse the reasons for Cripps's change of position. He sums up the search by stating that he had heard that in Moscow also Cripps had occasionally exceeded his instructions in a similar manner.

Cripps sent the following situation report to the Prime Minister on 4th April. The Muslim League were satisfied and would accept the scheme as it stood.[1] In the Congress Party there were

---

[1] It transpired that Jinnah's unacceptable price for co-operation was a majority on the Executive Council and approval of any representative from the Sikhs or the Depressed Classes.

three sections of opinion. There was the Gandhi section of non-violence which was against the scheme altogether. They were indifferent as to what happened in the war and regarded Great Britain as defeated and unimportant as far as India's future was concerned. They were definitely a minority. The rest of the party was in favour of fighting the Japanese. There were two groups of them: those who considered provincial option and the States' nomination of representatives as fatal quite apart from the defence question, and those who would reluctantly accept the scheme if they could be satisfied about defence. The latter group might be able to swing the Working Committee.

Cripps was now aiming at a break-through over defence as a sort of last fling before acknowledging the failure which he felt to be imminent. The demand for responsibility in this field came, he reported, from all sides except the Muslims and Sikhs (hardly adequate emphasis on such a vital exception). If Congress refused to accept the scheme nobody else would. If they accepted, the non-violent group would probably retire from the Working Committee for the duration of the war and leave in charge Azad, Nehru and Rajagopalachari, who would resist the Japanese with courage and determination.

Over the consequences of possible failure Cripps was pessimistic. He foretold that the war would have to be carried on in an atmosphere of neutralism at best, of hostility at worst (Linlithgow did not believe this).

*

At this stage there enters the story an American colonel named Louis Johnson. This man had recently arrived in India as President Roosevelt's personal representative at the head of a technical mission. Of the politics or personalities of India he knew nothing.

On 6th April Johnson reported to Caroe,[1] the Secretary to the External Affairs Department, a meeting he had had with Nehru

[1] Sir Olaf Caroe, K.C.S.I., K.C.I.E., Governor of the North-West Frontier Province, 1946–7.

at the latter's request. Apparently Nehru thought that he had with him a letter from Roosevelt but this was not the case. Nehru spoke of hitching India's wagon to America's star and not to Britain's. Johnson then told him that the President was determined that the American people should support Britain to the end of the war. If America was convinced that Congress was solidly supporting the war effort the sympathy which she had previously had with Congress would continue. If, on the other hand, it appeared that Congress was saving face, or hedging, or taking action to slow down the conclusion of the war, it was not too much to say that America would hate Congress. She would not help India at the Peace Conference if she thought that American blood had been spilt unnecessarily and the war prolonged by shilly-shallying.

Nehru then told Johnson that Congress would not break over the issue of provincial option but they would break if India did not get control of defence.

Poor Johnson, having stood up to Nehru with admirable realism at their talk, now allowed himself to be lured by Nehru's charm into becoming the middleman on the defence issue between Congress and the Government.

The Viceroy was quite prepared to have an Indian on his Executive Council with a portfolio for defence matters other than those which were the responsibility for the Commander-in-Chief. Of course these administrative matters, although important, could not be those which vitally affected responsibility for the war, but the appointment would directly link an Indian with the campaign in an unprecedented way. There now took place a series of attempts between the Viceroy, Cripps and Congress to find a formula which would be acceptable to Congress. This developed into an incredible situation. Colonel Johnson showed Cripps a formula which he thought Congress would accept. Cripps amended it but the final draft effectively torpedoed the absolute authority of the Commander-in-Chief. Johnson took the draft to Congress for their deliberation. It was only at this point that the Viceroy heard about it. He sent for Cripps and asked how it was that Congress had come to know of this latest formula which he himself had not seen? When Cripps told him that Johnson had shown it to them the Viceroy protested. Could not Cripps see that if he (the Viceroy) were now to differ from the formula his position would be made intolerable as he ran the risk of being held up to the United States as the obstacle to a settlement? Cripps replied lamely that matters had reached a climax in which something had to be done.

Colonel Johnson, who had also been sent for, came in at this point. The Viceroy put to both his visitors the difficult situation which might arise *vis-à-vis* America through Johnson's intervention. He listed some facts which could help to bring this about: Nehru called upon Colonel Johnson uninvited: a headline appeared 'Will America intervene in time?': a telegram went to the United States from the United Press to say that agreement had been reached and that Sir Stafford and Colonel Johnson had approved (Colonel Johnson had tried to stop the telegram without avail).

Johnson's reply to this was that Congress were going to settle on the new formula on which he had agreed with Cripps that evening. He and Cripps then left. The Viceroy called Cripps back and again protested at his behaviour. Cripps repeated his excuse about urgency and added that anyhow one of the Viceroy's staff (the Reforms Commissioner, H. V. Hodson) had seen it. The Viceroy remarked that Hodson was not the Governor-General and that the Commander-in-Chief had not seen the formula. It was unfair of Cripps to involve Hodson, who had the document in his hands only for a few minutes and committed nobody to it, as Cripps knew very well.

The Viceroy reported the Cripps-Johnson phase of events to Amery. He had told his own staff and he now told the Secretary of State that, badly as he had been treated, he would do his best to work on the formula which Cripps had given to Congress although he would back the Commander-in-Chief over amendments. But he must know where he stood, not only on this question but also on the question of his powers *vis-à-vis* his

Executive Council (which he suspected Cripps was compromising). On both questions he at once received the unqualified support of the Cabinet and Cripps was told to stick to the task upon which the Cabinet had agreed before he went out.

Cripps complained that Linlithgow had gone behind his back. Considering the treatment to which he had subjected the Viceroy it would be an understatement to call this an odd reaction.

*

On 10th April Cripps assured the Viceroy that Congress would agree to the formula, which had now been amended so that the Commander-in-Chief's authority was not to be diluted, and that they would keep in abeyance for the duration their other objections to the main declaration. On the same day he received a long letter from Azad stating that Congress had decided to reject the declaration. The letter made it clear that although they were not happy about defence, because a proposed Defence Minister would deal only with relatively unimportant matters, their main ground of rejection concerned their wish for a National Government with full power now, the Viceroy acting as a constitutional head on the advice of ministers. This they claimed could have been assured by conventions without constitutional changes. Cripps was reminded that he himself had said as much in his earlier talks.

Cripps wrote a sharp reply in which he said that Congress had in fact demanded a change in the constitution, a new demand made only on the previous evening through Azad himself. He also said that India had been offered the Home Department for an Indian as well as other portfolios. Azad wrote a further letter expressing pain and surprise at Sir Stafford's attitude. It was the end. Cripps told the Viceroy that Congress had refused a very good offer. He made a farewell broadcast of regret and immediately left for home. All the minority groups rejected the now discredited declaration within the next few days.

Amery wrote to the Viceroy on 11th April:

'What a time you have had of it! . . . It does seem to me that the longer he stayed out there, the more his keenness on a settlement drew him away from the original plan, on which we had all agreed, and in the direction of something to which we were all opposed . . . What puzzles me a little is that Cripps should have been prepared to go that far with Congress without realising that this was the very thing against which Jinnah said the Muslims would rise in revolt. . . .

What I must say we have felt here rather strongly is that neither Cripps nor yourself has given us any clear indication of how far you were either prepared to go between you, or how far Cripps went in his talks with Indian leaders in the direction of reconstituting your Executive [Linlithgow in the margin: "How could I help when I was consulted by Cripps about nothing?"].'

It was only through a casual reference, Amery went on, in Cripps's letter to Azad that the Cabinet had realised that the Home Affairs Department 'surely the most dangerous in many ways as well as the most contentious between the communities' had been offered. The Cabinet had certainly not intended a completely clean sweep of the existing Executive with only the Commander-in-Chief remaining [Linlithgow in the margin: 'Done without consultation and protested against by me the moment C. told me he had done it'].

*

Before examining possible reasons for the failure of the Cripps mission we must note on the credit side that the fiasco went far to educate American opinion as to the true facts of the Indian situation. President Roosevelt's immediate reaction to Churchill's message that Cripps was about to admit failure took the form of another desperate attempt to cast the solution of the problem in the mould of the federation of the United States. But when the dust had settled the Congress Party was no longer *persona grata* in the United States as the innocent victim of British imperialism. This was a great help.

As far as Cripps was concerned, his failure was complete. He was, as public men often are, the prisoner of his own past. Congress knew of the left wing opinions he had held and expressed both in England and on his previous visit to India before he was a member of the Government. They then came to feel that he was not running straight with them in the final negotiations. The same charge must be levelled at him over his dealings with the Viceroy. Linlithgow trusted him and was shabbily treated in return. For good measure Cripps made, at a press conference on his return (22nd April), the indefensible suggestion that there was a crisis of confidence between the Indian leaders and the Viceroy.

*

Why did Congress reject the declaration? They knew that independence must come at the end of the war and the declaration provided an obvious springboard. They must have been influenced by Gandhi's implacable refusal even to consider the declaration beyond calling it a blank cheque on a crashing bank. Perhaps they would never have made a decision contrary to the old man's will. Against this both Nehru and Rajagopalachari were strongly in favour of resistance to the Japanese and thought Gandhi's non-violent creed disastrous in this context. Rajagopalachari remained defiant but Nehru, torn as he so often was by conflicting emotions, gave in.

An interesting reason for the Mahatma's attitude was given to the Viceroy later by Sir C. P. Ramaswami Aiyyar. He had been passing through Bombay to meet Cripps on behalf of the Princes. There he met Vallabbhai Patel. Patel interpreted the Cripps mission as an organised stunt by Nehru to get himself into the forefront so that he could become Prime Minister of India. When Patel found this out he swore he would wreck the scheme. Aiyyar thought that Patel's attitude was responsible for Gandhi's obstinacy and antagonism.

On the face of it the Congress refusal resulted from the turning down of their demand for cabinet government at once. But this demand came right at the end of the negotiations and was a dramatic advance upon their previous demand for responsibility for defence. Basically it is a question whether Congress really wanted responsibility at this time. If this is right, Congress pitched their demands impossibly high, hoping to show the world that Britain was refusing to grant India the independence which she was ready to take.

Linlithgow himself was in no way elated by the failure of Cripps nor was he bitter at the way in which he had been treated. He contented himself with a note in the margin of Amery's letter of 11th April: 'Some day, when I have handed over charge I will give L.S.A. my views. Till then – least said soonest mended.' Meanwhile he had to pick up the pieces, especially where the Indian Members of the Executive Council were concerned. They were still deeply hurt and angry with Cripps.

The Viceroy had been proved right both in his forecast of events and in his questioning of the whole manner and timing of the exercise. He had felt strongly that any major move should be delayed until the Japanese drive westwards had been contained rather than that it should be launched as an apparent attempt to stave off imminent defeat. The point is that India's war programme was not being held up by the intransigence of the politicians. Recruits had been coming forward in enormous numbers and munitions increasing as fast as was technically possible. The only way in which the march of these events could be halted was the way which the British Government opened up by insisting on a plan which ran a grave risk of throwing India and the Indian Army into communal turmoil at the worst possible moment.

Linlithgow had given Churchill and the Cabinet ample warning but they felt compelled to take the risks in response to heavy pressure from the President of the United States based upon a total lack of knowledge of India.

As to the long-term constitutional possibilities following the experience of the Cripps mission the Viceroy definitely felt for the first time that self-government was incompatible with the unity of India. He never quite gave up hope but he could now find little ground for believing that the great achievement upon which imperial Britain had set her heart, and to which he had dedicated so many years of his life, could be realised. It made him deeply unhappy. But this was not the time for regret. The enemy was advancing upon India's frontiers and Linlithgow's most testing hour lay ahead.

One Too Many?
Mahatma Gandhi says that "he and the Viceroy have come nearer each other than ever before" (Shankar Cartoon, March 18 1940)

The Meeting Ground.
The consensus of opinion among the members of the Muslim League appeared to be that Mr. Jinnah should get into touch with the Viceroy (Shankar Cartoon, September 3 1940)

Lord and Lady Linlithgow at a garden party

The Viceroy riding with his granddaughter

❧ 20 ❧

Early in May, 1942, there were two air raids on Bengal and two
on Assam, Chittagong aerodrome and Imphal being the targets;
about a hundred people were killed on each occasion and nearly
as many injured. The raids on Imphal had a devastating effect on
morale as the bombs fell mainly on the bazaar and in the canton-
ment. Many recruits in the Assam Rifles fled. Civilian officials
disappeared. The warders in the local gaol also fled, while the
prisoners escaped and removed a lakh of rupees from the nearest
bank.

Meanwhile the All-India Congress Committee had met at
Allahabad on 29th April. There it severed all links with reality,
passing resolutions of unbelievable irrelevance which refused 'to
consider any schemes or proposals which retain, even in partial
measure, British control and authority in India.' Any invasion
must only be resisted by 'non-violent non-co-operation as the
British Government has prevented the organisation of national
defence by the people in any other way.' Once again Gandhi had
triumphed.

Gandhi had triumphed but all was not well in the Congress
Party. On 15th May a distinguished woman member, Rajkumari
Amrit Kaur, saw the Viceroy with Gandhi's approval. What she
had to say was frank and revealing. She said that Congress were
now in a more difficult position than they had ever been in: the
Government had reduced them to pulp and destroyed the
national spirit: the Mahatma did not know what to do: he was
under immense pressure to agree to some form of violence (she
would not be drawn on the details): he most earnestly hoped that
some assistance could be given from our side. When the Viceroy
pressed her on this she replied that the Americans should leave the
country without delay and should be immediately followed by

Q

the British. The Viceroy took her through the facts, pointing out how largely the Cripps offer met the claims of Congress. The Rajkumari refused to be comforted. We had, she replied, robbed them of everything and were breaking their hearts.

The Viceroy had enough experience by now to see what all this meant: Gandhi was up to mischief. The Mahatma was in fact preparing a determined all-out attack upon public order and the authority of Government. A police raid on the Congress offices at Allahabad on 26th May had discovered that he had drafted a resolution which would have gone much further than those which were passed. His resolution declared that the Cripps mission had shown up the nakedness of British power: Britain was incapable of defending India: there was an eternal conflict between Indian and British interests: Japan's quarrel was not with India and if India were free she would probably at once negotiate with Japan: if the British withdrew India would be able to defend herself [by passive resistance], therefore they must withdraw: the Committee desired to assure the Japanese Government and people that India bore no enmity towards Japan or any other nation. If, however, the British did not withdraw and Japan attacked India the remedy was to offer complete non-violent non-co-operation with the Japanese forces.

On 15th May Gandhi had said in a press interview that since the Cripps mission he could no longer give even moral support to Britain. But he also said in answer to some awkward questions by American journalists that Britain and the U.S. might stay by virtue of a compact with a free India. He even went so far a week later as to admit that the presence of British troops might be necessary to prevent Japanese occupation and also for China's sake. These qualifications were temporary trimmings. The Mahatma was at the same time carrying on a persistent campaign in *Harijan* for the British to get out. In the issue of 15th May, for instance, he wrote 'Leave India to God. If that is too much, then leave her to anarchy.'

This kind of extremism was doing Congress no good but Gandhi drove on regardless. He now felt sure that Japan was going to win the war[1] and he was desperately seeking re-insurance against the event. This was the same man who had been near to tears at the prospect of Westminster Abbey's destruction by bombing and who had told the Viceroy on the outbreak of war that he personally would like to give unconditional support to the Allies. Such is the versatility of human nature.

It is a tribute to Gandhi's magnetism that he maintained his authority with Congress at a moment when most of his colleagues in the party thought him so wrong. Nehru, although he yielded, was much more realistic over the Japanese threat and declared that he was prepared to oppose invasion with the sword – but only in a free India. This, however, did not stop him from delivering the most bitter attacks against Britain including a diatribe against the Indian Army as a tool of the British.

*

Happily there was still another side to the picture. The Duke of Gloucester visited India in June, bringing a message of encouragement and unity from the King Emperor. In Peshawar, capital of the North-West Frontier Province, he drove through the heart of the city, and was welcomed by thousands of its people who had come voluntarily to see him. The whole of the Municipal Committee turned out and offered him garlands. This was hardly the soured and hostile India of the Congress image. Moreover it was a very different welcome from that which had been given to the Prince of Wales in the same city twenty years before by a population in ugly mood.

The Viceroy carried on with his own work during the royal visit and flew from Delhi to Madras, Vizagapatam and Calcutta to inspect defences on the threatened east coast. Meanwhile a body created by him called the National War Front was gathering momentum. This was an organisation of volunteers which went down to village level, formed to combat defeatism and to watch for any treacherous activity.

On 2nd July the announcement was made of the second

[1] Azad confirms this in *India Wins Freedom*, p. 41.

expansion of the Viceroy's Executive Council. The effect was to increase significantly the Indian majority on the Council. The Defence Department was divided into two – a War Department under the Commander-in-Chief and a Defence Department under Sir Firoz Khan Noon, their respective responsibilities following the line which had been suggested during the Cripps Mission. Of great importance, too, was the fact that the Sikhs (Sir Jogendra Singh) and the Depressed Classes (Dr Ambedkar) were represented for the first time. Jogendra Singh, at a party given in his honour, said that it was futile to deny that the Cabinet (as he called it) was largely Indianised: it would be equally unfair to describe the Indian members as mere puppets of a Government in which they were in a majority: he felt that they now had a provisional National Government. A further result of the expansion was that every major Province was represented.

Linlithgow's new Council had an extremely good reception from the press both in India and in Britain. This was a pleasant surprise to the Viceroy, who was much more accustomed to brickbats than to bouquets. He was pleased by the general recognition that he had produced as representative and political a Council as he possibly could in circumstances in which the main political parties refused to play. It was a good moment for approbation as the war situation in Libya had taken a turn for the worse. Linlithgow noted that public opinion in India was nevertheless astonishingly steady.

*

Events on the political front were now starting to move towards the most serious crisis of Linlithgow's viceroyalty. The Working Committee of Congress met at Wardha on 6th July. After a tense discussion the main resolution was passed on 14th July. Drafted in terms which were intended to appear reasonable and conciliatory it deceived nobody and was condemned by the left-wing press in Britain as well as by the United States. It demanded that British rule must end immediately: Congress would join in the enterprise of resisting aggression and securing freedom for the nations of the world but this could only be done if India felt the glow of freedom: Congress had tried their utmost to solve the communal tangle but the task had been made impossible by the presence of the foreign Power: on the withdrawal of British rule responsible men and women would come together and form a provisional Government representative of all important sections of the people of India: Congress had no desire to embarrass the allied war effort and would therefore agree to the stationing of allied forces in India in order to resist Japanese aggression and help China: if this appeal failed and the British refused to leave India, Congress would be reluctantly compelled to utilise all the non-violent strength it possessed for the vindication of political rights and liberty: such a struggle would inevitably be under the leadership of Mahatma Gandhi.[1]

These proposals were to be referred to the All-India Congress Committee which would meet on 7th August.

The attitudes of the various Indian leaders at this point are interesting. The Government had information that Gandhi wished to begin the struggle at once, starting the movement in two or three selected places and allowing it to develop gradually. Patel supported him but he was opposed by Nehru and Azad. Nehru wanted a delay of two or three weeks in the hopes of America's helpful intervention; Azad did not think the country was ready for the fight. They gave various interpretations of the resolution. Azad, for instance, denied that it was an ultimatum. Gandhi proclaimed that there was no question of further negotiations, for it was an 'open rebellion.'

On 26th July Sir Stafford Cripps broadcast in strong terms to America. He said that India had been offered complete freedom to decide upon her own self-government after victory had been won. But victory must come first and Britain could not allow the actions of a visionary, however distinguished, to thwart the allied drive for victory in the east.

Linlithgow was ready. Soon after the passing of the resolution

---

[1] Azad quotes the resolution in his book (op cit.) but omits any reference to its last vital paragraph with its threat.

at Wardha, Gandhi had sent his disciple Mira Ben (Miss Slade) to Delhi to see the Viceroy, but the Viceroy was not prepared to grant a personal interview to an emissary of the Mahatma who had just defined his party's position as one of open rebellion, so she saw the Private Secretary instead. She made it clear that Gandhi would not withdraw the movement which he had started even if it became violent: Britain must either grant independence to India or be the cause of Gandhi's death.

Amery was greatly disturbed by the Wardha resolution. He believed that it would be sheer folly to allow such a challenge to pass just because acts of defiance had not immediately followed words. Gandhi should not be allowed to work up his campaign to its climax: the Government should get in its blow first: the Viceroy should not hesitate to act on his own responsibility before any Cabinet conclusions. Amery wrote that he had no fear of being able to hold the position in the House of Commons. 'Good for you' noted the Viceroy in the margin.

Linlithgow refused to act too soon. He pointed out that violent language was a well settled safety valve and was not always followed up. He preferred to wait until he saw what the All-India Committee decided to do on 7th August. Meanwhile he had no intention of allowing the law to be broken with impunity but he was sure it would be a mistake to be provoked at this stage. He had time enough to make the necessary preparations. He was greatly impressed by the strength of opinion of his Council. Members were unanimous in the view that action against Congress must be swift and stern. Believing that the All-India Committee would certainly ratify the resolution they insisted upon advance propaganda in India, Britain, the United States and China. This was effectively carried out. The old Council was still in office, but the new one would be at work by the time any arrest had to be made.

*

Meanwhile discussion proceeded as to what should be done with Gandhi if he had to be arrested. The Viceroy proposed that he should be a state prisoner rather than a security prisoner. State prisoners were allowed more latitude over visits, letters and so on, although it was realised that Gandhi would not be able to have these privileges for a certain time. As for the place of detention the Viceroy's first inclination had been towards deportation. But he was persuaded against it by the strong views of his Indian colleagues on the Council and he agreed with them that if Gandhi were to fast and die overseas the effect would be more serious than if he died in India. The Cabinet, which had also been originally in favour of deportation, supported him. It was decided that Gandhi would be detained in the Aga Khan's palace at Poona; other leaders would be sent to the fortress in Ahmednagar.

The All-India Congress Committee met as arranged and passed a resolution on 7th August in support of the stand of the Working Committee. This resolution was also a call to action. While paying lip service to non-violence on the basis of the struggle it specifically gave to individuals the choice of how they were to react when the moment came. Thus, with Japan almost at India's eastern gateway and with Germany threatening her western flank through Libya and the Caucasus, Congress decided to strike. In the early hours of the following morning all the Congress leaders, both national and provincial, were arrested.

The Government's action was a complete surprise in its timing as Azad in his book makes clear. Gandhi had had a suggestion put out shortly beforehand that he was about to write to the Viceroy. No letter had arrived, nor was one likely to since Gandhi had announced at a press interview on 14th July, after the Working Committee's resolution, that there was no room for withdrawal or negotiation. The Executive Council was unanimous in its decision to act immediately. What is more only one European Member was present at the crucial meeting of decision on the evening of 7th August. The Commander-in-Chief, the Home Member (Maxwell) and the Finance Member (Raisman) were all unavoidably absent.

It was a most courageous decision taken by Indians who personally risked much by taking it. They had been under heavy pressure from various quarters and they knew this was bound to continue unabated. Gandhi was later to taunt the Viceroy with having secured this unanimous support on the ground that it was easy to command such services in India – an observation sadly below the level of goodness.

The violence which followed the arrest of the Congress leaders showed by its timing and pattern that it had been planned in advance. There was no substance in the attempts by Congress apologists to pass it off as a spontaneous reaction. On the day following the arrests there were attacks upon police and public vehicles in Bombay. Elsewhere there were no outbreaks for three days: just the time needed for final instructions to be taken to their various destinations from Bombay after the end of the Congress meeting.

The attacks, which were widespread throughout the country, took the form of concerted violence and sabotage. They were directed principally against communications, particularly railways, telegraphs and telephones. Post offices were attacked as well as police stations and other Government buildings. In Delhi there was a concentrated attempt to destroy fire engines while three signal cabins on the main line were burnt in one day. About 250 railway stations were damaged or destroyed: railway lines were blown up: some 550 post offices were attacked, over fifty being destroyed and most of the others seriously damaged: more than 2,500 instances of wire-cutting were reported: seventy police stations and outposts were attacked: eighty-five other Government buildings were burnt or otherwise destroyed or damaged.

In many cases of sabotage specialised tools were used and these must have been ready beforehand.

In the course of these outrages there were several cases of murder of policemen, sometimes in the most brutal circumstances including burning alive, and two R.A.F. officers were pulled from a train and hacked to pieces.

The areas most seriously affected were the eastern districts of the United Provinces and, above all, Bihar; that is to say that the most heavily attacked sector of the country was on the direct line of communication to the front which was fighting the Japanese. So serious was the situation that for a time most of Bengal was cut off from the rest of India. The Punjab, the North-West Frontier Province, Sind, Assam and Orissa were hardly affected at all.

There were plenty of troops at the Government's disposal and there was no sign of any disaffection in the army. By 15th September, when the Home Member (Maxwell) reported on the situation to the Assembly in Delhi, it was clear that the attempt to overthrow the Government had failed. There were further isolated incidents for the next month or two but nothing to cause real anxiety as long as vigilance prevailed.

There can be no doubt that the firmness of the Viceroy and the staunchness of the Indian majority on his Council saved India from a situation which, unpleasant enough, might have taken a disastrous course if it had not been dealt with in time.

As to responsibility for the rebellion, it lay squarely with the Congress Party and therefore with Gandhi as its acknowledged leader. Gandhi's personal belief in non-violence is irrelevant in this context. He knew as well as anyone the effect which his exhortations were likely to have on emotional crowds whose intellectual standard was incapable of understanding the abstruse ways of his philosophy and he knew what explicit encouragement to open rebellion must bring in its train once it was unleashed. Moreover, he knew that most of his lieutenants did not share his philosophy even when they understood it. A Bombay Congress Bulletin (no. 132, dated 9th January, 1943) shows what they thought there of the rebellion:

'Let us admit that the Revolution has not been able to attain that pitch, that momentum, which we all expected it would . . . The gigantic and sweeping mass uprisings and mass demonstrations and mass attacks that we witnessed in the beginning of our struggle have slowed down and subsided. . . . We confess that while numerous centres of usurper administration have been attacked and, in many cases, destroyed, and the war on communications has been carried on with more or less sustained tempo, we have not been, as yet, able to paralyse the administrations completely. The factories are still working and producing war materials, and other factories which have been producing intellectual slaves are still active: the students have again lapsed into inactivity and drifted into the old rut . . .'

This was typical of the evidence available. So much for non-violence when it came to the point.

*

Gandhi now embarked upon a long correspondence with the Viceroy. He wrote the first letter on 14th August. In it he blamed the Government for everything and denied that violence had ever been contemplated. He pleaded for reconsideration of the Government's whole policy. The Viceroy replied on 22nd August that he had read what Gandhi had said with very close attention but could not accept his criticisms or his request for reconsideration.

Linlithgow had to deal with this correspondence against the background of a possible decision by the Mahatma to fast. Such an outcome was, of course, the last thing that the Viceroy wanted. Not only would it make things extremely difficult for the Hindu Members of Council, who knew that they would be accused of conniving at Gandhi's death if that should occur, but it was also bound to cause an awkward reaction in the United States.

As the correspondence developed the Viceroy explained why he had no alternative to holding the Mahatma and Congress responsible for the rebellion. If he had received from Gandhi the slightest sign of contrition or of condemnation of what had happened he would have been prepared to reconsider the situation, but to blackmail by fasting he could not and would not yield. He had no confidence that he would not soon be submitted to it.

Pressure from the United States mounted. Colonel Johnson had gone, but President Roosevelt had sent another representative, Lauchlin Currie, to India. The Viceroy saw Currie on 13th August. They talked mostly about China. Currie did not mention politics but the Viceroy found out that he had had a long, confidential talk with Shiva Rao as a result of which Rao had handed him a memorandum of some sort. Linlithgow telegraphed Amery that he feared the Americans were not 'playing straight' over India.

At the same time Chiang Kai-Shek, who had already sent a message of condolence to Gandhi, sent a telegram to President Roosevelt asking him to intervene. Roosevelt reported this to Churchill and asked what the Prime Minister thought about it. He received a crisp reply (13th August) beginning with the words 'I take it amiss Chiang-Kai-Shek should seek to make difficulties between us and should interfere in matters about which he has proved himself most ill-informed . . .'

The Viceroy was anxious. His experience of the peripatetic Americans was that their zeal in teaching the British what to do was in inverse ratio to their understanding of the problems involved. He feared – with reason as it was to turn out – that it was only a question of time before one of them asked openly to see Gandhi and Nehru. He asked that Halifax in Washington should be encouraged 'to arrest at least for a time this flow of well-meaning sentimentalists from the U.S.A. to India, so that we may mind here what is still, I suppose, our own business.'

Another of Linlithgow's American visitors during these critical months was Mrs Clare Boothe Luce, wife of the owner of *Life*, who came to interview him for an article in that magazine. Mrs Luce was suffering from a heavy cold at the time. An inflexible rule of the Viceroy's was that he must be told when an impending visitor was thus afflicted so that he could switch on a powerful electric fan on his desk which would blow towards the visitor. Unhappily Mrs Luce had not been warned of this as she should have been. She had to conduct the interview in the face of an unexpected hurricane which played considerable havoc with her attractive appearance. The ensuing article lost none of its pungency as a result.

*

While Gandhi from his palace prison pondered his next step in his campaign his colleagues settled down in their fortress to a life of reading, discussion, badminton, chess and gardening. Nehru took the lead in the garden project. They were allowed to make flower beds in the compound and plant them. Unlike their leader they would worry the Viceroy no more.

Pressure upon the Viceroy, however, was unremitting and it came in its usual variety from several different quarters. First he was faced with an insistent demand by its Hindu Members for the complete Indianisation of Council, which meant in effect the addition of the Finance and Home Departments to the portfolios already in Indian hands. The reason they gave was that only a radical step of this sort could heal the wounds left by Cripps upon the Council's reputation. The Viceroy reminded Council that its composition was constitutionally a matter within his own discretion but he allowed a full discussion upon it. The Muslim Members were against the suggestion although they favoured a lessening of control by the Secretary of State for India.

Surprisingly, *The Times* in London, no doubt with an eye on the United States, came out for complete Indianisation as the best way of breaking the existing deadlock, carrying a leader to this effect in the same issue (11th September) as a wiser article in the opposite sense by their correspondent in Delhi. This embarrassed the Viceroy, coming from such a source, as it was, of course, widely quoted in India as well as in the United States. But he was convinced that the course suggested would not only do nothing towards the winning of the war (his first priority) but would also bring his Council up against the communal difficulty in its sharpest form and resignations would be rife. He instanced the situation in which an Indian Member for the Home Department would have been placed in the context of Gandhi and the rebellion. Complete Indianisation must come eventually, as he acknowledged, but he was sure this was not the moment.

From a familiar quarter in India there was more trouble. Moore, the editor of the *Statesman*, wrote a leader (10th August) condemning the Government of India's action against the Congress leaders in terms which were demoralising and defeatist. The Viceroy's Council reacted decisively and the Indian Members

declared that if Moore was not dealt with it would be proof of
racial prejudice of the most blatant kind. To Linlithgow's great
relief the board of the *Statesman* at last decided that they, too, had
had enough, so Moore departed. The Viceroy had never doubted
his essential patriotism but its virtues were effectively clouded by
a chronic lack of balance of extraordinary proportions. Moore
was succeeded by Ian Stephens. Never afraid to criticise the
Government of India when he felt it necessary, Stephens showed
a sense of responsibility of which Moore had been incapable.

21

On top of the strain of these events the Viceroy had to fight a running battle with Churchill over the question of India's sterling balances. The balances had been in Britain's favour before the war but during the war the situation was dramatically reversed. India was drawn upon in many ways, for men, supplies and so on. She became a considerable creditor of Britain and the Allies. The Treasury became worried by the possible effect upon Britain's post-war situation of India throwing on the market several hundred million pounds of free balances which she might use to extract from us goods for which we would get no return.

The Viceroy was distressed at the prospect of India being considered to have played less than her part in war sacrifice and got the Cabinet to agree to Sir Jeremy Raisman (Finance Member) being sent over to London to discuss the situation with them. Raisman persuaded them to accept the Viceroy's view that the position must be left alone. India was a poor country and any attempt by Britain, which was a trustee nation for her, to repudiate debt in any way would be disastrous. The Treasury wanted Britain to supply everything calling for payment in sterling, India to supply all that called for payment in rupees. Against this it was agreed that an unfair burden would fall upon India, a burden which would accord neither with her capacity to pay nor with the power which she was able to exercise. Moreover there had been a strong feeling in India that despite immense sums spent by her she was relatively defenceless against invasion.

Raisman's intervention was effective and the Viceroy also wired to Amery a warning of the grave consequences that would follow if Britain's financial policy got out of focus with her constitutional policy. Sympathy in India would be lost and this would include the sympathy of the commercial and well-to-do public. The Cabinet agreed that the present system must be retained but a decision was deferred until the Prime Minister returned from the Middle East where he had been arranging for General Montgomery to succeed Auchinleck in command of the Eighth Army.

The Chancellor intended to speak to the Prime Minister privately and it was hoped that the Cabinet would then need only to give its formal decision. Events, however, did not turn out as expected. Churchill was furious when he heard what had happened. Amery wrote to the Viceroy (16th September):

'Winston harangued us at great length about the monstrous idea that we should spend millions upon millions in the defence of India, then be told to clear out, and on top of it all owe India vast sums incurred on her behalf. I tried, without much effect, to make him understand that a great deal of this expenditure was for goods supplied to the Middle East and even to this country, that anyhow it was imposible to dissociate the defence of India from the general war effort and say that everything we did in the Far East was simply done for the defence of India . . .'

The battle continued. Churchill would agree with the Cabinet only on condition that a proviso be inserted that Britain reserved the right to re-open the whole question with a view to a possible counterclaim against India. The Viceroy refused to communicate such a reservation to his Council. He also refused to accept it for himself alone. The first of these two courses would mean resignations from his Council: the second he did not think honourable. Not until the end of October did he receive news from Amery that the matter had been shelved indefinitely.

Churchill's belligerency had undoubtedly been stimulated by the circumstances of the Congress rebellion. It led him into exaggerated if understandable language in the House of Commons about Congress as a whole which undid some of the good done to the British image in the United States and elsewhere. He expounded a favourite theory that Congress really had little influence in India.

*

While all these difficulties crowded upon him Linlithgow had to face a new danger which was looming up ominously in parts of India. This was the threat of famine. The rice eating districts were bound to be hit once India was cut off from her rice supplies for which she had relied greatly on Burma. Wheat also was now becoming scarce. The situation was aggravated by bad harvests, also by the pressure of the armed forces on supplies. All through the late summer and autumn of 1942 the Viceroy was pressing the British Government for help in the way of shipments of grain. What could be done by rationing was done,[1] but control was a desperately difficult business in India compared with Britain. In India supplies depended primarily on small farmers, who farmed perhaps three to five acres, bringing their grain to market in little baskets. They grew enough for their families and cattle and kept the rest until and unless they wanted cash. The tendency to hoard in anticipation of rising prices was strong and this applied to grain merchants as well.

Sadly the hideousness of famine was to cloud the last months of Linlithgow's viceroyalty, and now his term of office was extended for a third time. Having looked forward to relief in April, 1943, he accepted a final extension until October. He telegraphed his acceptance on 10th December.

Three weeks later, on New Year's Eve, Gandhi wrote his second letter:

'. . . I have thought we were friends and should still love to think so. However what has happened since the 9th of August last makes me wonder whether you still regard me as a friend. I have perhaps not come in such close touch with any occupant of your *gadi*[2] as with you . . . I am quite capable of seeing myself as others see me. But in this case I have failed hopelessly . . .'

He distrusted, he said, the press reports of violence, although in a letter to the Secretary of the Home Department a week earlier he had said that the arrest of the Congress leaders seemed 'to have

[1] A Department of Food was set up in November.
[2] *Gadi* is equivalent to 'throne.'

The Viceroy accompanied by the Maharajah of Nepal inspecting a guard of honour

The Viceregal family and staff. Front row, left to right: Lt. Col. J. Toogood (Military Secretary), Lady Doreen Hope, Lady Hopetoun, the Viceroy and Vicereine, Mr. Gilbert Laithwaite (Private Secretary to the Viceroy), Lady Joan Hope, Lt. Col. H. Elliot (Doctor), Miss R. Hill (Secretary to the Vicereine) is standing behind Lady Linlithgow

The Viceroy on his last day of office, greeting his successor, Field Marshal Wavell

The last photograph of Lord Linlithgow, September 1951

made the people wild with rage to the point of losing self-
control.' Gandhi then came to the threat which the Viceroy had
hoped he would not make. He had given himself, he said, six
months:

'The period is drawing to a close. So is my patience. The law of
satyagraha, as I know it, prescribes a remedy in such moments of trial.
In a sentence it is, "Crucify the flesh by fasting." '

He did not wish to use this remedy if he could avoid it: there was
a way to avoid it: convince him of his error and he would make
ample amends.

On this menacing note Linlithgow entered upon the last year
of his Viceroyalty. It was a troubled moment in several other ways
as well. The tide of war was still running with the Japanese on the
eastern frontier: although in North Africa it had turned in
favour of the Allies, in Russia it had not yet done so. Inside India
the deteriorating food situation was made worse in December
when Bengal suffered fearfully from a cyclone and a tidal wave
which killed 11,000 people and 75,000 head of cattle and seriously
affected over 1½ million people over 3,000 square miles. Calcutta
was raided on Christmas Eve (the damage was not serious). The
Governor of Bengal (Sir J. Herbert) was out of his depth with a
growing constitutional crisis on his hands. Two days later the
cause of wise and experienced government was hard hit in the
Punjab: Sikandar died suddenly.[1]

Never did the Viceroy need more the relaxation he had always
found in family life. He showed great pride at this time in the
achievements of his wife, whose ceaseless work in the field of
public health was now showing impressive results, notably the
establishment of a tuberculosis centre in every Province. 'Her
reputation,' he wrote in a letter home, 'is steadily rising as people
begin to realise how much she has done for them.' The tribute
was deserved. Linlithgow also derived much happiness from the

[1] Sikandar was succeeded by Sir Khizar Hyat Khan Tiwana, who continued
the struggle to maintain the Punjab coalition against the relentless pressure of
Jinnah.

R

company of his granddaughter, Sarah Jane, whom he took out riding in a basket saddle. Much to his delight she had, by sheer coincidence (she was not yet four), taken to calling her grand-father 'Gandi-boy.'

*

On 13th January, 1943, the Viceroy replied to Gandhi's letter:

'... I was glad to have your letter for, to be as open with you as our previous relations justify, I have been profoundly depressed during recent months first by the policy that was adopted by the Congress in August, secondly, because while that policy gave rise, as it obviously must, throughout the country to violence and crime (I say nothing of the risks to India from outside aggression) no word of condemnation for that violence and crime should have come from you, or from the Working Committee... When arrangements were made that you and the Working Committee should have such newspapers as you desired I felt certain that the details those newspapers contained of what was happening would shock and distress you as much as it has us all, and that you would be anxious to make your condemnation of it categorical and widely known. But that was not the case; and it has been a real disappointment to me, all the more when I think of these murders, the burning alive of police officials, the wrecking of trains, the destruction of property, the misleading of these young students, which has done so much harm to India's good name, and to the Congress Party. You may take it from me that the newspaper accounts you mention are well founded – I only wish they were not, for the story is a bad one. I well know the immense weight of your great authority in the Congress movement and with the Party and those who follow its lead, and I wish I could feel, again speaking very frankly, that a heavy responsibility did not rest on you. (And unhappily, while the initial responsibility rests with the leaders, others have to bear the consequences, whether as law breakers ... or as the victims ...'

If Gandhi was willing to dissociate himself from the policy of last summer he had only to let the Viceroy know and he would at once consider the matter further:

'You know me well enough after these many years to believe that I shall be only too concerned to read with the same close attention as ever any message which I receive from you, to give it the fullest weight and approach it with the deepest anxiety to understand your feelings and your motives.'

Back came the next letter from Gandhi on 19th January. His letter of 31st December was, he said, a growl against the Viceroy. The Viceroy's was a counter-growl. As to a positive suggestion, this he might be able to make, but only if he was put among the members of the Working Committee:

'If I could be convinced of my error or worse, of which you are evidently aware, I should need to consult nobody, so far as my own action is concerned, to make a full and open confession and make ample amends. But I have not any conviction of error . . .'

With regard to the press reports of violence:

'You are bound *prima facie* to accept the accuracy of reports that may be placed before you by your departmental heads. But you will not expect me to do so. Such reports have, before now, often proved fallible . . . You will perhaps appreciate my fundamental difficulty in making the statement you have expected me to make.

'This, however, I can say from the housetop, that I am as confirmed a believer in non-violence as I have ever been. You may now know that any violence on the part of Congress workers, I have condemned openly and unequivocally . . .

'You will forgive me expressing an opinion challenging yours. I am certain that nothing but good would have resulted if you had stayed your hand and granted me the interview which I had announced, on the night of 8th August I was to seek. But that was not to be . . .'

The Viceroy answered on 25th January:

'. . . I note what you say about non-violence. I am very glad to read your unequivocal condemnation of violence and I am well aware of the importance which you have given to that article of your creed in the past. But the events of these last months, and even the events that are happening today, show that it has not met with the full support of certain at any rate of your followers, and the mere fact that they may have fallen short of an ideal which you have advocated is no answer to the relations of those who have lost their lives . . . or suffered severe injury as a result of violent activities on the part of Congress and its supporters. And I cannot I fear accept as an answer your suggestion that "the whole blame" has been laid by you yourself at the door of the Government of India. We are dealing with facts in this matter, and they have to be faced. And while, as I made clear in my last letter, I am very anxious to have from you anything that you may have to say or any specific proposition that you may have to make, the position remains that it is not the Government of India, but Congress and yourself that are on their justification in this matter.

'If therefore you are anxious to inform me that you repudiate or dissociate yourself from the resolution of the 9th August and the policy which that resolution represents, and if you can give me appropriate assurances as regards the future, I shall, I need not say, be very ready to consider the matter further. It is of course very necessary to be clear on that point, and you will not, I know, take it amiss that I should make that clear in the plainest possible words . . .'

Gandhi came back at the Viceroy immediately (29th January). A peevishness of tone was beginning to show itself:

'I must thank you warmly for your prompt reply to my letter of 19th instant. I wish I could agree that your letter is clear. I am sure you do not wish to imply by clearness simply that you hold a particular opinion strongly. I have pleaded and would continue to plead till the last breath that you should at least make an attempt to convince me of the validity of the opinion you hold, that the August resolution of the Congress is responsible for the popular violence that broke out on the 9th August last and after, even though it broke out after the wholesale arrest of the principal Congress workers. Was not the drastic and unwarranted action of the Government responsible for the reported violence? . . .

'But you throw in my face the facts of murders by persons reputed to be Congressmen. I see the fact of murders as clearly, I hope, as you do. My answer is that the Government goaded the people to the point of madness. They started leonine violence in the shape of the arrests already referred to. That violence is not any the less so, because it is organised on a scale so gigantic that it displaces the Mosaic law of tooth for tooth by that of ten thousand for one – not to mention the corollary of the Mosaic law, i.e. of non-resistance as enunciated by Jesus Christ. I cannot interpret in any other manner the repressive measures of the all-powerful Government of India . . .

'If then I cannot get soothing balm for my pain, I must resort to the law prescribed for *satyagrahis*, namely, a fast according to capacity. I must commence after the early morning breakfast of the 9th February, a fast for twenty-one days ending on the morning of the 2nd March. Usually, during my fasts, I take water with the addition of salts. But nowadays, my system refuses water. This time therefore I propose to add juices of citrus fruits to make water drinkable. For, my wish is not to fast until death but to survive the ordeal, if God so wills. This fast can be ended sooner by the Government giving the needed relief . . .'

The Viceroy replied on 5th February:

'Many thanks for your letter of 29th January which I have just received. I have read it, as always, with great care and with every anxiety to follow your mind and to do full justice to your argument. But I fear that my view of the responsibility of Congress and of yourself personally for the lamentable disorders of last autumn remains unchanged . . .

'You have reiterated your request that I should attempt to convince you that my opinion is correct. I would readily have responded earlier to that request were it not that your letters gave no indication, such as I should have been entitled to expect, that you sought the information with an open mind. In each of them you have expressed profound distrust of the published reports of the recent happenings, although in your last letter, on the basis of the same information, you have not hesitated to lay the whole blame for them on the Government of India. In the same letter you have stated that I cannot expect you to accept the accuracy of the official reports on which I rely. It is not therefore clear to me how you expect or even desire me to convince you of anything. . . . If . . . you yourself, by any action such as you now appear to be contemplating, attempt to find an easy way out, the judgment will go against you by default.'

The Viceroy restated the case against Congress, then:

'My Government and I are open indeed to the charge that we should have taken drastic action at an earlier stage. . . . But my anxiety and that of my Government has throughout been to give you, and to give the Congress organization, every possible opportunity to withdraw from the position which you have decided to take up. Your statements of last June and July, the original resolution of the Working Committee of the 14th July, and your declaration on the same day that there was no room left for negotiations, and that after all it was an open rebellion, are all of them grave and significant, even without your final exhortation to "do or die." But with a patience that was perhaps misplaced, it was decided to wait until the resolution of the All-India Congress Committee made it clear that there could be no further toleration of the Congress attitude if Government was to discharge its responsibility to the people of India.

'Let me in conclusion say how greatly I regret, having regard to your health and your age, the decision that you tell me that you now have it in mind to take. I hope and pray that wiser counsels may yet prevail with you. But the decision whether or not to undertake a fast with its attendant risks is clearly one that must be taken by you alone and the responsibility for which and for its consequences must rest on you alone. I trust sincerely that in the light of what I have said you may think better of your resolution and I would welcome a decision on your part to think better of it, not only because of my own natural reluctance to see you wilfully risk your life, but because I regard the use of a fast for political purposes as a form of political blackmail (*himsa*) for which there can be no moral justification, and understood from your own previous writings that this was also your view . . .'

Gandhi answered on 7th February:

'. . . Your letter, from a *satyagrahi*'s point of view, is an invitation to fast. No doubt the responsibility for the step and its consequences will be solely mine. You have allowed an expression to slip from your pen for which I was unprepared . . . You describe the step as an attempt "to find an easy way out." That you, as a friend, can impute such a base and cowardly motive to me passes comprehension. You have also described it as "a form of political blackmail," and you quote my previous writings on the subject against me. I abide by my writings. I hold that there is nothing inconsistent in them with the contemplated step. I wonder whether you have yourself read those writings.

I do claim that I approached you with an open mind when I asked you to convince me of my error. A "profound distrust" of the published reports is in no way inconsistent with my having an open mind . . .'

The letter asked that the evidence for the complicity of Congress be published: so far there had only been the opening speech for the prosecution. As for the lawfulness of civil disobedience Gandhi claimed that the principle had been recognised[1] by the Government of Lord Irwin in 1931. Then:

'You have left me no loophole for escaping the ordeal I have set before myself. I begin it on 9th instant with the clearest possible conscience. Despite your description of it as "a form of political blackmail," it is on my part meant to be an appeal to the Highest Tribunal for justice which I have failed to secure from you. If I do not survive the ordeal I shall go to the judgment seat with the fullest possible faith in my innocence. Posterity will judge between you as representative of an all-powerful Government and me as a humble man who has tried to serve his country and humanity through it.'

*

Gandhi had headed each of his letters 'Detention Camp' and Linlithgow thought of reciprocating with 'Detention Camp, New Delhi.' He had been through a most difficult time. His own inclination at the outset had been to let Gandhi go ahead with the fast if he wished to and take the consequences. But the Governors were evenly divided in their views. Lumley, on whose experience and reliability the Viceroy set great store, felt strongly that the greatest harm would be done if Gandhi were to die as a prisoner. Council felt much the same. The Viceroy therefore accepted the proposal that he should be released as soon as his life was in danger. The Cabinet felt this would get the worst of both worlds. One of the Indian Members of Council then suddenly suggested that apparent surrender could be turned into deflation of the Mahatma by offering to release him for the duration of the fast. This ingenious solution at once appealed to the Viceroy, who recommended it to the Cabinet. There was more trouble from that quarter until the Viceroy sharply claimed a right to their

[1] This was not so. Irwin told the Legislative Assembly on 9th July, 1930, that mass action, even if intended by its promoters to be non-violent, was nothing but the application of force under another form, and when it had as its avowed object the making of government impossible, a Government was bound either to resist or to abdicate.

confidence over a matter of which, he pointed out, he had more
knowledge than any of them. Amery had assured him of his own
support in Cabinet, up to breaking point if necessary, if he
decided to stand firm. He did so, and received a telegram from
Amery: 'To Nelson from Hyde Parker: congratulations.'

Gandhi was told of the new offer. As the Viceroy expected, he
turned it down. He said that if temporary release was offered for
his convenience he did not need it: if it was for the convenience of
the Government he was sorry he was unable to suit them much
as he would like to do so. But to enable the Government to
consider his reply he would suspend his fast for twenty-four
hours, until 10th February.

The fast duly began. On the same day the Government of
India issued a statement explaining the circumstances: it was clear
that only his unconditional release would stop Mr Gandhi from
fasting: this the Government was not prepared to concede:
therefore if he fasted while in detention he did so solely at his
own risk: he was free to have his own medical attendants and
to receive visits from friends with the permission of Government.

The Viceroy was hopeful at this stage that there would be no
resignations from his Council by his Hindu colleagues although
he warned Amery that the strain upon some of them might
prove too great, especially if Gandhi's condition became critical.
As soon as the fast began he saw them all and told them that if
they felt any doubts they ought to go now rather than wait.
Either the policy was right or it was wrong: if they disagreed
with it they must say so now: the fact of Gandhi's physical
condition was irrelevant: if they approved of the policy they
ought to stand by it whether he lived or died.

The Muslim community stood apart from the fast, either
criticising it or ridiculing it. The Hindu press showed deep
concern and there was clear evidence of strong pressure upon the
Indian Members of Council to secure Gandhi's unconditional
release, including the announcement of a large gathering of
different leaders to be held shortly with the same object in mind.

There were adjournment motions in both Houses of the Legislature on 15th February, but these were talked out. Generally the country was quiet.

Then came the strain. On 17th February two of the Hindu Members of Council, Aney and Sarkar, and the Parsee, Sir Homi Mody, resigned. They did so in the most friendly way possible, expressing publicly their warm appreciation of the Viceroy's consideration and courtesy.

On the same day the Viceroy received a telegram from the Governor of Bombay. Lumley was, of course, in the closest touch with the daily situation as Poona came within his jurisdiction. He reported that the Surgeon-General of Bombay (Candy), supported by two other Government doctors, thought that Gandhi would probably not last beyond 21st February and they could not exclude the possibility of a sudden collapse. Lumley was confident that his Government could cope with any situation arising from Gandhi's death but he felt nevertheless that his death in detention would do permanent damage to Indian sentiment and would provide a serious obstacle to eventual settlement. He thought he could safely say that it was the general view of the European officers of the I.C.S. and the police in the Province of Bombay that irreparable damage would be done to British-Indian relations. Lumley asked, as he was entitled to, that his view should be placed before the Secretary of State. This the Viceroy did, with the comment that he would find great difficulty in supporting Lumley's view. After consultation with the other Governors the agreed policy remained unimpaired.

*

The conference of 'leaders' took place on 19th and 20th February under the predictable chairmanship of Sapru. All sorts of people claimed to be represented, Hindus, Sikhs, Indian Christians, communists, trade unionists, landlords, merchants and even British missionaries. They passed a resolution demanding Gandhi's immediate and unconditional release.

Since 18th February the Mahatma's condition had been

deteriorating. All preparations for his death were complete including the code name 'Rubicon.' The place for the cremation of his body had been selected by the Governor of Bombay and arrangements made for a plane to fetch his son from Delhi. The Viceroy ordered that the statement to be made by the Government 'must contain no unction, no excuse for, or explanation of Government's part in Gandhi's end; no word of recrimination against the man himself, while on the other hand any eulogy would equally jar.' It should be something on the lines of 'The Government of India regret to announce that Mr Gandhi died while in detention at Poona at . . . hours on . . . from collapse/ heart failure following a self-imposed fast.'

Gandhi was now attended by six doctors, three Indian and three British, including the Surgeon-General, whose presence Gandhi welcomed as an old friend who had previously treated him for illness. The six signed a daily bulletin.

On 21st February Gandhi's condition was critical and his death was thought to be very near. From that day forward he suddenly began to improve. By the 25th he was considered out of danger. It was an amazing recovery. Many believed it to be an act of God. Others attributed it to glucose, among them the Surgeon-General, who thought that the Mahatma was probably given a stimulant by an attendant whose devotion to him proved stronger than obedience to the rules of fasting which forbade such synthetic support. Whatever the truth of the matter there was a curious circumstance concerning Gandhi's weight. When he began his fast on 10th February he weighed 109 lbs. By the 16th he was down to 97½ lbs. On the 24th, when he was well enough to be weighed again, his weight was 90 lbs. But on 2nd March, the last day of the fast, it had gone up to 91 lbs. It had been a most strange sequence of events. From an Indian source the Viceroy heard that the crisis in Gandhi's condition was engineered, while the 'leaders' conference was taking place, between Birla House and the Mahatma's entourage: as soon as it was clear that the Government of India were not going to move a message was sent authorising the application of stimulants. The whole truth will probably never be known. It may well be that Gandhi himself was unaware of what was done to resuscitate him.

*

The effect of these events was of great importance. The Viceroy was under no illusions as to their impact on all those who worshipped the Mahatma. Their faith in him would be strengthened. But to thinking and articulate India it appeared that Gandhi's bluff had been called by the courage of the Viceroy and his Council with its Indian majority. At the same time a telling blow had been struck at the insidious technique of political blackmail by fasting. With the war against Japan still in a critical phase it was no bad moment for the Government of India to have asserted its authority so impressively.

It had not been easy. In addition to the strains in his Council Linlithgow had had to cope with a renewed burst of pressure from the United States. At the end of 1942 a new American representative had arrived in India. He was William Phillips, a former ambassador to Italy. Linlithgow took to him and found him attractive and discreet. But at once a difficulty arose. Phillips told the Viceroy that both Amery and Anderson had told him in London that anything he could do to bring the Indian parties together would be welcomed. Phillips seemed to assume that this amounted almost to an invitation to share responsibility with the Viceroy. A strong telegram from Linlithgow to Amery received the expected reply and Phillips realised he had exaggerated the position.

Phillips returned from a tour of the Punjab and saw the Viceroy on 8th February. He reported that he had been asked on all sides when he was going to see Gandhi. Could he therefore see him? The Viceroy told him politely but firmly that he could not. He then informed him of Gandhi's imminent fast and Phillips at once said that he would not think of trying to see the Mahatma during his fast even if he were released. Then on 18th February Phillips asked for another interview with the Viceroy. He handed him a telegram signed 'Hull'[1]:

'President Roosevelt and I suggest that you seek an informal interview with the Viceroy and convey to him an expression of our deep concern over the political crisis in India. Please express to His Excellency our hope that a means may be discovered to avoid the deterioration of the situation which would be almost certain to occur if Gandhi dies.'

The Viceroy wired to Amery suggesting that the situation ought now to be dealt with on the level of the Prime Minister and President Roosevelt. These matters, he emphasised, should have been handled through the proper diplomatic channels of Washington/London: he would never have agreed with the appointment of Phillips if he had thought that this would have meant these channels being by-passed: he did not blame Phillips, who had to obey his instructions: but he himself was dealing with a most difficult problem and he could not tolerate interference of this sort. On policy he had explained to Phillips that he was a war Viceroy, that every step he took was measured by the test of whether it would help towards the victory of the Allies: he and his Government had firmly decided that to rehabilitate Gandhi at the expense of Government at this stage would be disastrous. The Viceroy had then underlined the intransigence of the communal situation.

Phillips asked what would happen if Gandhi died. The Viceroy replied that there would be six months of unpleasantness steadily declining in volume. After it was over – as it would be before India was wanted for a major operation of war eastwards – India would be far more reliable as a base for operations. Moreover the prospect of a settlement would be greatly enhanced by the disappearance of Gandhi, who had for years torpedoed every attempt to reach one.

Next day (19th February) Amery sent the Viceroy an answer to his telegram:

[1] Cordell Hull, U.S. Secretary of State.

'*Cherchez la femme* remains ever up to date! I may be wrong, but comparing the dates of Cordell Hull's talk with Halifax, when he warmly endorsed Halifax's view that it would be a mistake for America to intervene in any way in the Indian situation, and Phillips' receipt of a telegram as a result of which, obviously at the President's direction, Phillips intervenes to ask you to release Gandhi unconditionally, I am irresistibly drawn to the conclusion that Madame Chiang Kai-Shek [then staying at the White House] and Mrs Roosevelt between them have got at the President . . .'

Something of this sort may well have happened. Certainly Halifax had previously reported Hull (16th February) as agreeing both with the Government's decision not to release Gandhi and with the wish that Phillips should not intervene in the situation in any way.

The difficulties were ironed out but poor Phillips remained under pressure from American press sources (possibly with presidential backing) to continue his efforts to see Gandhi. The Viceroy had him to stay for a few days while on holiday at Dehra Dun and was impressed by his improved grasp of the complexities of Indian affairs. But he was not sorry when Phillips was recalled early in the summer.

A further worry was now added to Linlithgow's American anxieties. He believed that the increasing strength of the American mission in India was out of all proportion to the work it had to do and he suspected that they were making ground where they could with a view to strengthening America's post-war position in India's markets at Britain's expense. He was never anti-American and he admired their great qualities. He was not so naïve as to suppose that alliance in war would eliminate anti-British feeling but this was going too far.

22

The summer of 1943 was heralded in by the great allied victory in Tunisia early in May. The Viceroy, returning from a visit to troops on the eastern frontier, broadcast a message that 21st May would be a public holiday in celebration of the event which had removed a grave threat to India's western approaches, but he warned his listeners that the war was not won until the Japanese had been defeated. On this front the failure of the Arakan campaign had naturally been depressing but the likelihood of a Japanese invasion had now receded. Two million men, all volunteers, were under arms. The Viceroy was confident: 'I reckon I can hold them now whenever they come' he had written in a private letter home. He also felt greatly encouraged by events in Russia: 'Joe Stalin is a bloody-handed old scoundrel,' he commented, 'but by God he can fight!'

But if India's safety from outside attack now seemed relatively secure Linlithgow's last six months were clouded by the tragedy of famine in Bengal and a series of administrative crises in that Province. Before discussing this we may take note of a final tussle with Gandhi.

There had been two attempts made by Rajagopalachari to see Gandhi. In November, 1942, he had asked if he might see the Mahatma in the belief that something constructive might come out of the visit. Permission was refused. Rajagopalachari, distinguished as he was, now represented nobody but himself and the Viceroy was not prepared to give Gandhi, who knew perfectly well the terms upon which his position could be reconsidered, a chance for further gratuitous mischief. Rajagopalachari did not give up trying. In February he suggested, in a talk with Laithwaite, that an emissary should be sent to Gandhi with evidence of the complicity of Congress in the rebellion, which he thought might appeal to Gandhi's legal mind. In any case he thought Gandhi should be unconditionally released and he gave an interesting reason: there was no hope of getting Nehru (who alone mattered on the Working Committee) in the position of future leadership except with Gandhi's help and guidance, while only the Mahatma could keep his excessive vanity in order. In March there was a final effort made to see the prisoner, this time by means of a deputation of so-called non-party leaders including Rajagopalachari. This attempt also failed.

Jinnah now came into the picture dramatically. At the Muslim League's annual session at Delhi in April he issued an invitation to Gandhi to write to him if he wanted a settlement with the League. The Government, he said, was a Government which freely allowed criticism of itself and it would not dare to hold up such a letter. Gandhi responded. He wrote a letter which he asked the Government to forward to Jinnah. In it he welcomed Jinnah's approach and expressed the wish that they should meet and talk together.

The Viceroy wanted to transmit the letter. He felt it would be extremely damaging if the Government were to refuse to do so, considering that they had always shown themselves anxious to encourage any action which might break the political deadlock. Moreover he would be prepared to let Jinnah see Gandhi in view of Jinnah's special position which put him in quite a different category from that of the others who had wanted access. Amery and the Cabinet, however, ruled against him and the Viceroy accepted the decision.

The letter was not delivered to Jinnah but on 26th May the Government published an announcement that they had received it. They explained the reasons why Gandhi could not be given facilities for political correspondence: it rested with him to satisfy the Government of India that he could safely be allowed once more to participate in public affairs: until he did so the disabilities from which he suffered were his own choice.

The nationalist press attacked the Government's decision as proof of British insincerity. Rajagopalachari described it as 'palpably inconsistent with all the statements made from time to time that the British Government was ever willing to give effect to the agreed resolutions of nationalist leaders in India.' Some Muslim papers were also critical, but on 28th May Jinnah himself resolved the issue. Far from criticising the Government's action he described Gandhi's letter as a move to embroil the Muslim League in a clash with the British Government solely to secure his release. He explained his invitation to Gandhi to communicate with him by saying that he had made it in response to pressure by certain Hindu leaders who had said that Gandhi realised his mistake and was prepared to retrace his steps: Gandhi had, however, shown no signs of change of policy or of any readiness to settle with the League on the basis of Pakistan. Jinnah refused to accept the letter.

The Viceroy recognised that Jinnah's move had put the Government in a stronger position than they would have been in had he been allowed to forward the letter as he had wished. But it seems in retrospect to have been a fortunate coincidence which averted what could have been a most awkward situation.

*

The administrative crisis in Bengal came to a head with the fall of Fazlul Huq's Ministry on 14th March. On the day following his resignation Huq accused the Governor (Sir John Herbert) of forcing him to resign. Herbert had not done so but he had unwisely drafted for Huq, who had lost the confidence of the Legislature, a suitable letter of resignation. Of this circumstance the Premier, always an unreliable customer, could be counted upon to take advantage. Herbert had to invoke Section 93 of the India Act and governed by decree for three weeks until a new Ministry was formed under another premier, Sir Nazimuddin.

In August the Viceroy received complaints about the weakness of the municipal administration of Calcutta and the apparent lack of any governmental pressure to keep it up to the mark. He knew, too, of criticism of the record of the Bengal Government in the financial field and of their handling of the grave food position. The Viceroy's inquiries received a routine departmental reply to the effect that the situation did not present any startling difficulty. But Herbert now tried to induce the necessary realism into his Government. This was not without effect but it was very late. The Viceroy did not alter the view to which he had been coming for many months that Herbert was not able to cope with such a difficult and volatile Province as Bengal.

Before a definite but imminent decision to replace Herbert was reached the Governor fell very seriously ill with acute appendicitis and duodenal complications. Sadly this was to prove the first stage of a fatal illness. Linlithgow, realising what Herbert must have been going through for some time, was deeply distressed at the news. But facts had to be faced and an acting Governor appointed. This was Sir Thomas Rutherford, at the time Governor of Bihar. Linlithgow wanted, as a permanent replacement, a thoroughly good man from home: 'it needed an Anderson to clear up the mess left by Stanley Jackson's administration. We are not much better off now,' he told Amery, '. . . I would most earnestly beg that we should not again go too trustingly to the Whips' Room or put in a man who is not going to be able to carry what will unquestionably be a very heavy burden.'[1]

*

Finally there was the problem of the famine in Bengal. The Viceroy, as we have seen, had warned the Secretary of State for many months that a disaster lay ahead unless shipping could be provided to bring in food grains in time. Amery, as late as 5th September, saw little hope of a favourable outcome. Linlithgow was doing his best at the Centre to deal with a problem for which responsibility lay primarily with the Provinces concerned, and it must be remembered that all the Provinces were now self-

[1] Sir Richard Casey, Minister of State resident in the Middle East (later Lord Casey, Governor-General of Australia 1965–9) was appointed Governor in 1944.

governing. He was trying to persuade those like the Punjab, which had a surplus of grain, to be generous and reasonable about disposal. But, for reasons which have been described earlier, the task was immensely difficult.

In Calcutta Indian Ministers had failed in their duty and Linlithgow was aware that the Centre would be made the whipping-boy; nor of course could it escape involvement.

Rutherford, as soon as he had had time to assess the position, gave a list of the reasons, as he saw them, for what had happened. These included greed of traders and hoarding: lack of detailed statistics (which were impossible to obtain in a complex network based on village production all over India): bad communications made worse by the requisitioning of boats by the army to prevent them from falling into the hands of the Japanese: pressure on railways for military traffic: difficulty of switching people from one diet to another, for instance rice-eaters would not eat wheat: suspicion throughout India of the bona fides and efficiency of the Bengal Government: the failure of the Bengal Government to organise its Supplies Department on a proper scale. All these powerful factors have to be placed against a background of the denial to India of her natural rice supplies from Burma, followed by bad harvests, cyclone and floods.

Whatever the reasons, the remedy lay in imports and for these shipping could not be spared by Britain or by the Allies.

There was no criticism of Linlithgow personally for the tragedy of Bengal but he was widely criticised for not visiting the stricken Province. Here it is easy to feel that his judgment was at fault. Yet it was by no means an easy decision. Apart from the fact that there was little he personally could now do to help he knew that a false step at this eleventh hour could make things immeasurably more difficult for his successor, Wavell. Bengal was self-governing and the problem, grave and terrible as it was, was constitutionally a provincial problem. He was not prepared to put Wavell at risk by a visit which might have been seized upon by the politicians as unwarranted interference and as proof of the hollowness of self-government granted by the British. He was well aware of the personal credit that would be his if he made the gesture of a visit but his obsessive contempt for personal publicity prevailed. He felt the whole tragedy deeply and brooded over it but he would not change his mind even though his wife herself begged him to go. He may have been wrong. He was certainly tired out.

*

The day of departure approached and with it the strain of farewell. Addressing both Houses of the Legislature he said, as he was entitled to say, that the federal scheme, for all the imperfections it may have contained, would have solved the bulk of India's problems had it been possible to bring it into being: no scheme will satisfy everyone: every scheme admits of improvement by experience: parties, interests, individuals, all had to be prepared to make sacrifices when it came to matters such as this. To the Princes he said that the Crown's obligations to protect carried with them equally binding obligations to ensure, if need be, that what was protected continued to be worthy of protection.

At a private dinner given by the Viceroy to the Members of his Council, Sir R. Maxwell spoke movingly of his leadership through the unpredictable years and of the qualities they had always found in him – patience, courage, faith and vision and also a kindly tolerance towards *homo sapiens* even when he became *homo irritans*. No tribute was ever more sincerely paid.

The Viceroy's old adversary, the *Statesman*, while remembering the occasions on which it had criticised him, expressed in a generous leader its gratitude for his courageous services to India.

Gandhi wrote him a final letter on 27th September:
'Dear Lord Linlithgow,
On the eve of your departure from India I would like to send you a word.
Of all the high functionaries I have had the honour of knowing,

none has been the cause of such deep sorrow to me as you have been. It has cut me to the quick to have to think of you as having countenanced untruth, and that regarding one whom, at one time, you considered as your friend. I hope and pray that God will some day put it into your heart to realise that you, a representative of a great nation, had been led into a grievous error.

> With good wishes,
> I still remain your friend,
> M. K. Gandhi.'

He replied:

'Dear Mr Gandhi,

I have received your letter of 27th September. I am indeed sorry that your feelings about any deeds or words of mine should be as you describe. But I must be allowed, as gently as I may, to make plain to you that I am quite unable to accept your interpretation of the events in question.

As for the corrective virtues of time and reflection, evidently these are ubiquitous in their operation, and wisely to be rejected by no man.

> Yours sincerely,
> Linlithgow.'

It was a worthy end to his relationship with the Mahatma, whose greatness he acknowledged but whose judgment he never ceased – in the interests of India – to deplore. He was bound to hold Gandhi and Congress primarily responsible for the eventual partition of India which he regretted so deeply.

*

On 20th October Linlithgow handed over to Wavell. As they shook hands he said with a smile that he had never been more glad to welcome anybody. He and his family then drove to the airport. Before boarding their plane they said goodbye to the members of his personal staff who had all served so faithfully and well. It was an emotional moment and Lady Linlithgow was in tears.

During a brief halt at Cairo on the way home Sir Richard

Casey gave a lunch party in their honour. The ex-Viceroy started to go into the dining-room first, as protocol had demanded for the last seven years. The ex-Vicereine gently but firmly pulled him back: 'No!' she said. 'You've done that for the last time.'

*

So this devoted servant of India came home. He was only fifty-five but he did not enter public life again although Churchill offered him the Scottish Office in the Caretaker Government of 1945. If the general election of that year had been won by the Conservatives it might have been otherwise.

He referred little to Indian affairs after his return, but he noticed the news of the arrival (in his successor's time) of the first relief ship with its load of grain and reflected how much it would have helped India if he could have had the same assistance. He also wondered sometimes whether he could have pressed the Princes harder in the federal negotiations before the war but did not see how he could have done more with his hands tied as they were by the home Government.

He spoke once in the House of Lords before the independence of India, when he stressed the need for Britain to remain impartial as between the two great communities. In this context he was to regret Mountbatten's acceptance of the Governor-Generalship of the new India in default of being invited by Jinnah to serve Pakistan in the same capacity. But he thought Mountbatten unfairly criticised over the communal slaughter which had disfigured India during his viceroyalty since by then the raj had lost the power to carry out its responsibility.

As for the Indians, he foretold Gandhi's assassination, and Nehru greatly impressed him as he grew to the authority of his position.

Honours came to him in full measure but he had not long to live to enjoy them. He was sixty-four when he died suddenly while out shooting at Hopetoun on 5th January, 1952. In his wallet, which he always carried in his pocket, was found a folded piece of notepaper. On it he had written a prayer for God's help in his task in India which included these words:

'I promise that when several obligations seem to conflict I will prefer the public duty above the private. And to this promise I will hold so long as my strength may last.'

He had kept to himself this final token of his valiant heart.

Index

279